THE GENDER BIAS
PREVENTION BOOK

gender
in crisis

series editor, montana katz, ph.d.

W e
are fitfully and certainly
moving away from a world in
which women are defined as less than
men, where masculinity and femininity
are separate realms of experience. It is clear
that gender will no longer be as determining
a factor to an individual's personal identity,
choices, and aspirations as it once was. This
cultural shift will affect every aspect of life,
from subtle daily details to broad social
principles. The Gender in Crisis Series
explores the future meaning, construction, and impact of gender on
all of our lives.

g
c

THE GENDER BIAS PREVENTION BOOK:

HELPING GIRLS AND WOMEN TO HAVE SATISFYING LIVES AND CAREERS

Montana Katz

JASON ARONSON INC.
Northvale, New Jersey
London

Director of Editorial Production: Robert D. Hack

This book was set in 11 pt. Bodoni BE Regular by Alpha Graphics of Pittsfield, New Hampshire and printed and bound by Book-mart Press of North Bergen, New Jersey.

Library of Congress Cataloging-in-Publication Data

Katz, Montana.
    The gender bias prevention book : helping girls and women to have
satisfying lives and careers / by Montana Katz.
        p.   cm.
    Includes bibliographical references and index.
    ISBN 1-56821-843-5 (sc)
    1. Sex discrimination against women—United States—Prevention.
    2. Sex discrimination in employment—United States—Prevention.
    3. Women in the professions—United States.   4. Women—United
States—Social conditions.   5. Girls—United States—Social
conditions.   I. Title.
HQ1237.5.U6K37   1996
305.42—dc20   96-13815

Manufactured in the United States of America. Jason Aronson Inc. offers books and cassettes. For information and catalog write to Jason Aronson Inc., 230 Livingston Street, Northvale, New Jersey 07647.

CONTENTS

Acknowledgments   ix

PART I: *GASLIGHT*
1   Past and Present   5

PART II: *THE NUTCRACKER SUITE*
2   Early Childhood: The Family Dynamic   29
3   Preschool: Entering the Social Realm   39
4   Elementary School: Normative Gender Roles Gel   55
5   Junior High: Years of Transition   68
6   High School: Conforming Sexuality   79
7   College: The Co-ed's Status   89

PART III: *THE RED SHOES*
8   The Second Shift: Before Children   117
9   The Second Shift: After Children   135

PART IV: *FATHER KNOWS BEST*
10 Admission and Funding in Advanced
    Degree Programs   151
11 Course Work and Qualifying Exams   159
12 Theses and Dissertations   174
13 Degrees, Dossiers, and Interviews   185

PART V: *THE TWILIGHT ZONE*
14 Male Mentors   195
15 Female Mentors   225

PART VI: *SILENCE OF THE LAMBS*
16   Professional Ambiance   239
17   First Jobs   260
18   Advancement   288

PART VII: *DISCLOSURE*
19   Women at the Top   305

PART VIII: *VERTIGO*
20   The Future   321

Summary of Gender Framework, Themes, Trends,
     Rituals, Actions, and Exercises   328

References   337
Suggested Reading   339
Index   343

ACKNOWLEDGMENTS

Many people over the years have contributed their time, their ears, their experience and knowledge, and I would like to begin to thank them here. First is Janusz Ordover, without whose dedication this book would not have been possible. Catherine Monk, my editor, has been an invaluable asset whose enthusiasm for the project never flagged. Nicole Phillips, my assistant, took on more work for this project than she probably should have between her college work, graduation with every kind of honor and award imaginable, and new career. Bob Hack enhanced the manuscript with his editorial skills. Natalie Becker, my mother, has not only provided encouragement and stimulation, but has exhibited a model of what a woman, a mother, and a professional can be, in the best sense possible. Regina Barecca, Anna Becker, Derrick Bell, Mariam Chamberlain, the late Diane Cleaver, Frances Conley, Shawn Dulaney, Pamela Katz, Paul Moore, Bernice Sandler, Catharine Stimpson, Veronica Vieland, and George Winslow all graciously gave me their time, thoughts, and comments. Most of all, I would like to thank the many women, girls, men, and boys who sat with me and my tape recorder for endless hours and spoke about their lives and experiences. This book is for them and the many young professional women in this country who deserve to pursue their careers unfettered by the bonds of sexism at work.

PART I
GASLIGHT

In the movie classic, *Gaslight*, the principal character, Paula, undergoes a transformation in a short period of time that is representative of the current enculturation process for girls and women. Paula moves from a young, confident singer-in-training to a faltering, self-doubting woman who is married to a manipulative, deceptive, and domineering husband. She is driven into such deep confusion as to question her basic bodily sensations, such as whether it is her eyesight failing or merely the gaslight jets diminishing. It is a slow and, in this case, deliberate process by which her husband strives to break Paula of her fundamental human integrity. In real life, it is a process which spans the course of a lifetime.

Contemporary women continuously experience what I call the *Gaslight effect*. This is the disconcerting feeling that one's own perceptions of aspects of life, one's observations of facts and events, even simple ones, are subject to doubt and are probably false. It is the feeling that public discourse and attitudes *prove* one wrong. The current collective understanding runs at right angles to an individual woman's own private conclusions, and slowly but surely, she will determine that it is she who is mistaken. Thus, women in this situation experience an erosion of self-confidence and a concomitant rise in self-doubt. In fact, because the Gaslight effect is a course consisting of subtle, time-released components that unfold throughout a woman's lifetime, it thus also increases in strength as it goes along. At some point, usually in young to middle adulthood, a woman will begin to recognize a key symptom of the Gaslight effect. This is a vague feeling of dissonance within oneself as if one were not properly synchronized with the rest of the world. The result is a certain uncanny feeling, often experienced as a form of mild insanity.

This book is about professional women. It is about how the course of their careers and their performance on the job are affected by gender, gender stereotypes, and bias. *The Gender Bias Prevention Book* describes the underpinnings, ramifications, and consequences of the Gaslight effect on professional women as a result of the many aspects of our culture's definition of gender.

One of the most damaging aspects of the Gaslight effect, and the one that makes it work, is that it remains unacknowledged, improperly observed. It operates sub rosa and contributes to a culture that produces women who continue to own and internalize this culture's derogatory views of women. And thus, the cycle of women's complicity in maintaining an environment that is biased against them in so many ways is ever renewed and continues to reach out to the next generation. Women working in the professions not only are not immune from the Gaslight effect, but they also may be more subject to it than other women. This is because women training or working in a professional career will run up against, and be measured according to, more gender stereotypes than the woman who has followed paths generally more accepted by our culture for women.

An overarching result of the Gaslight effect that will be examined in all of its details throughout the book is the constant process of demoralization for women, the continuous chipping away at women's personal integrity and sense of self. The sheer amount of energy consumed by every woman in implicitly emotionally fending off or keeping at bay the impact of this lifetime of deprivation of the self is enormous. There are many other unnecessary drains on women's energy and spirit, but this one in and of itself is vast. Our culture gives the appearance of being afraid to unleash women's energy stores for outward use. And there is evidence of a correlative fear of having women make conscious, deliberate decisions themselves, and for themselves, about the allocation of that energy. The final part of the book, in fact, provides a look at our culture's collective potential were women's energies, minds, and bodies thus set loose toward constructive and fulfilling locomotion, freed from the shackles and frustrations of bias.

Part I charts where we stand now as a culture with respect to gender bias in the professions. In this section, there are also descriptions of the format of the book, its contents, and the methodology used throughout and in the collecting of research for *The Gender Bias Prevention Book.*

1   PAST AND PRESENT

My female patients are definitely crippled by society by the way they were brought up. I would say in many cases much worse than for my generation. In terms of their identity, in terms of their aspirations, in terms of everything about them, they are warped by society's view of women, and they feel it. Some of them haven't articulated it, but as we go into their lives it becomes very clear that many of their conflicts and many of their problems were caused by the way their parents saw women's lives. I see it all the time; there's no doubt about it in my mind. Three-quarters of the therapy is about that.

Women who have made careers in the professional realm appear to be among the most privileged working women. They seem protected from the problems of gender bias that are so pervasive in the rest of the working world. With relatively high salaries, rewarding work, and greater flexibility, these women appear to have surmounted the sexist pitfalls of our culture and fashioned fulfilling lives in spite of them. To an extent, this picture is true. As a result, however, women working in professional occupations are passed over in much of the public discussion about sexual harassment and sex discrimination, substantially more so than women working in different arenas.

Yet, at the same time, women who work in the professional realm are exposed to a greater degree and range of gender bias than other women. Because they must attain a higher level of education than the general population, they spend years in professional degree programs in which there is great potential for harassment, discrimination, and exploitation. Because they must seek advancement in professions that remain top heavy with men, they must travel a long path upward that requires unflagging commitment, outstanding solid work, and fraternal bonding. Many women go to great contortions to fit in.

There is often more at stake financially in professional occupations, and because of this women working in the professions face an increased number and larger roadblocks along the way than women in the non-professional working world. Because the achievement of a certain status in our society goes along with professional advancement, the doors to professional success continue to be jealously guarded by those in control. Bias does not only originate from above in the professional hierarchy, but also from below. Women who achieve the highest rank within their fields confront a unique form of biased behavior from their employees, assistants, and trainees. Thus, the woman with a professional career will typically encounter *more* gender bias, *more* sexual harassment, *more* sex discrimination, and *more* exploitation of her work than her non-professional sisters. In all, the trajectory that most women follow from college graduation to advancement within a profession is bumpy, long , and difficult in ways that men do not fathom and that women in other occupations do not need to confront.

The genesis of *The Gender Bias Prevention Book* is itself a lesson in the standing of professional women today. I had set out to write a book profiling four highly successful professional women, highlighting their successes along with the hurdles they confronted as a result of gender issues. I had secured agreements from women in each of the fields of law, medicine, business, and the humanities. Each woman was in the top one percent of her field. One week after the Senate hearings for the confirmation of Supreme Court Justice Clarence Thomas, my telephone began to ring. As a result of the handling of the testimony from law professor Anita Hill, each of the four women withdrew from the project. Having witnessed the devastation wrought on Professor Hill, each feared for her own security should she speak out on her own experiences publicly.

I was flabbergasted. If these women, who had achieved more than ninety-nine percent of the people in their fields, male or female, were intimidated, then what of the women in the lower and middle ranges of the professions? I realized in that week that, contrary to public opinion that holds that professional women enjoy high status and security, there is a great need for open discourse that unveils the truth concerning women working in professional occupations. I thus set out to interview women at all levels in order to clarify the actual situation in the professions.

What most women face are the so-called low-level patterns of gender bias and sexual harassment. This basic amount of bias that every female may face, in every town or city in this country, every day of the year, every year of her life, is subtle and yet pervasive. It is not the stuff of overt job discrimination or gang rape. Because of its nature, this kind of gender bias is much more difficult to discern than the cruder varieties. What characterizes the low-level bias is that each instance of it, in and of itself, may be insignificant. However, all of the instances taken together to create a portrait of subtle bias, across segments of an individual's life show that the cumulative impact can exact a staggering emotional and professional toll. The constant wearing away, bit by bit, of one's self-confidence and integrity can be, and often is, debilitating.

Because the more subtle forms of gender bias are so much more difficult to pinpoint, they can also be more damaging. The cruder, more obvious forms, such as overt sexual harassment on the job consisting of quid pro quo requests of trading sex for advancement, or overt sex discrimination consisting of the effective barring of women from certain fields of study, for example, surely take a great toll. Nevertheless, they are generally clearer cut and can therefore incite immediate anger, resentment, or action. In contrast, low-level gender bias is usually viewed as part of the ordinary course of daily events and is not delineated as part of a larger pattern of sex discrimination.

Consequently, three crucial but hidden themes in girls' and women's lives emerge as a result of low-level bias: *internalization, personalization,* and *invisibility.* These themes play like a Greek chorus throughout their lives and are examined in the text below. All three involve the depoliticization, the de-socialization of the cultural patterns of gender bias. Each theme picks out an aspect of how each girl and woman learns to make the implicit messages of gender bias her own—to own them and to believe them to be included in the set of one's own idiosyncrasies.

By cranking up the basic level of bias a notch or two, one can readily understand why females are less confident than males, tend to be less assertive, have lower aspirations, drop out of college and professional programs in higher proportions, and leave the professions they have trained for seemingly more readily. The fact is that by the time women enter the professional workforce, they are already, to some extent, cowed. During their entire past experience they have learned and incorporated the lessons of our gender-biased culture. Even the very notion, which young women are fed at least as early as high school, that there are no more problems for women in this country becomes a piece of the pattern of bias. For incorporating this blatantly false concept into one's beliefs most often results in the individual looking inward for the source of her educational and professional shortcomings and failures. This is not always the most appropriate place to look when one is a woman trying to break into a profession that has been earmarked for men.

In spite of the attention paid to the subject of sexual harassment since Professor Anita Hill's testimony during the confirmation hearings of Supreme Court Justice Clarence Thomas, the prevailing wind of opinion has continued to be that the problems of gender bias, of sexual harassment, of sex discrimination, and of the general exploitation of women's work have largely been eradicated from American society. Women and girls seem to hold this belief almost as much as men and boys do. How did we, collectively, arrive at this absurd, Kafkaesque position in which, as a culture, we hold fast to a self-image which is patently false to the experience of at least half of our population?

This belief is, in fact, *crucial* to the operation of our culture today. It serves an important function in the history of the development of American civil rights for women. Commencing at the end of World War II, women were foisted from greater employment with relatively higher pay and status in the 1930s and '40s, into the budding American dream of suburbia, with a Baby Boom for the ladies and an economic expansion of great opportunities for the gents. Thus, women increasingly were isolated from each other and from culture at large in the 1950s and '60s. The women's movement of the 1970s began to break women out of their predicament, offering both analyses and new options. The belief that gender issues had been resolved began, unsurprisingly, to take root in the boom years of the 1980s. This was a response to the activism in the 1970s, both as a backlash movement and because of the greater funds that were temporarily available in many professions that allowed women to pass through many more occupational thresholds than previously. The consensus of the '80s was that women's equal rights had been achieved. Anyone who still felt she needed to sport her feminist credentials was looked at askance as bitter and congenitally angry. The word "feminist" became a mark to be ashamed of and to disavow. This is a sentiment that lingers into the present and is evident amongst young women in college today.

Thus, a new and ingenious way of recreating and instilling girls' and women's isolation was found. As with the best of methods, it was, in part, grounded in reality. Women's civil rights *had* expanded to a point that women were obtaining advanced degrees, jobs, and salaries in greater numbers and proportions in the 1980s than ever before. The glass ceiling was a relatively little-known phenomenon, and the young women who had heard about it did not believe that it would apply to themselves. It was something that, it was thought, if it was true at all, had applied to their mother's generation along with a grab bag of other, purportedly poorly articulated grievances of the working women of yesteryear.

It was true that, in the 1980s, in terms of entrance to advanced degree programs, entry-level professional employment, and even, in many cases, entry-level salaries, the blockades were virtually down. The amount and degree of the problems for women were substantially decreased not *everywhere*, but in several of the crucial and high-income professional arenas hitherto barred to women outright. Little remained barred *outright*, in the open. Much of the bias and discrimination, at that point, went underground and became subtler. It did not need to go far, and it is important to note that many fields, such as engineering, the natural and physical sciences, mathematics, architecture, philosophy, and computer science, to name only a few, stayed virtually the same with blockades intact.

Yet, the professional world *appeared* to be open or at least more open. Law school student bodies were approaching the forty percent mark for female students, and medical schools were reaching the thirty percent mark. In terms of obtaining first jobs, the numbers were not as good from the perspective of equality, but from the vantage point of a generation or two earlier *who did not expect to obtain jobs within their professional training at all*, the situation appeared much improved, and it was.

Advancement is another story. *That* didn't look good from anybody's point of view. Nor did the amount of work that women in the degree programs or first jobs had to perform relative to their male colleagues to obtain the same credit, acknowledgment, and standing. The cliché that a woman has to work twice as hard as a male colleague to hold her position three paces behind him in salary, title, and respect level is only partly true. Another piece of the picture is that that double amount of work is the work that is counted *as hers*. A woman must also perform a few more units of work that other people—men, that is, her superiors—then take credit for. And a third portion of the story is the sheer amount of a woman's energy that is consumed fending off, whether explicitly or, more likely, implicitly and within her own psyche, generally annoying instances of gender bias, male advances in the workplace of a sexual and inappropriate nature, direct discrimination, and exploitation.

Nevertheless, as a culture, we were able to convince ourselves that gender equity had been achieved, and achieved tout court. As a result, a generation of young women, aspiring to hold professional careers, hadn't a clue about the real obstacles that they would face on the job. They also hadn't much of an inkling concerning the obstacles that they were in fact facing everyday in college, and even in high school. But because these girls and young women purportedly *knew* that gender bias was no longer a live issue, any difficult situations, any self-doubt, any being left back or out, any *rape* even was of one's own creation. Any such problem must, in fact, it was too often felt, be one's own doing. It was personal and, probably appropriately, meted-out justice.

Thus, à la 1950s with a professional twist, women began once again to internalize and personalize the messages of gender bias, harassment, discrimination, and exploitation in record numbers. Internalization was, and remains today, an epidemic among females. There are several consequences of internalization and personalization. One, which fits very conveniently with the belief in the existence of equity, is a false sense of control. The reasoning behind this conclusion proceeds along the following lines. If an instance of harassment is *my* doing, if it is the result of my own incompetence, a mistake, a false signal I gave to the perpetrator (my clothing, perhaps?, a certain pause in between sentences?, a smile I smiled out of learned politeness and deference?), if it was caused by some aspect of my behavior, then it is *my* fault. It is thereby also within my control. For, if I just don't do it again (whatever it was that I did that incited the behavior, breathing maybe), then it won't happen again—he (the perpetrator) won't be led (by me) down the garden path to harassing behavior.

In fact, these kinds of considerations are a distraction from a more accurate assessment of problematic situations involving gender bias and thus from obtaining some actual control and true self-determination. The continuous process by which girls and women consume and incorporate external events and attitudes that are harmful to them is part and parcel of the gender-biased mechanism in place in our culture.

Another consequence of internalization and personalization is women's isolation from each other. If the prevailing explanation is that it's just a woman herself causing the trouble for herself, then she's probably going to be fairly humiliated by her own behavior. She's also therefore not going to be likely to find her experiences in this regard to be noteworthy since they are entirely idiosyncratic and, not to mention, under this interpretation, hardly anything of which to be proud. So, the woman has now found a new reason to separate herself from other women, a commonplace old reason being the general cultural disdain and undervaluing of women as a class, a group with which no one in her right mind would willingly identify. Sadly, at this stage, women are the very people, in point of fact, who are most potentially valuable to other women. Yet, women tend to stay away from other women and keep their experiences to themselves. Thus, a neat and tidy system is born for effectively keeping gender bias, sexual harassment, sex discrimination, and exploitation in the closet.

Internalization and personalization are not the only methods by which the real issues are kept away from the public eye. Another contribution comes directly and almost solely from men's quarters. This is the strategy of exaggerating the consequences of raising the issue of gender bias. Just as "crying rape" loomed large in the early days of rape awareness, "crying harassment," although not a term yet coined, is the new banner issue. It is what has become important about sexual harassment—that men can be falsely accused. In fact, a much acclaimed play and its movie version were devoted to this issue: David Mamet's two versions of *Oleanna*. The question that has been looming over our heads for several years is, what about false accusation? Underlying this query is fear, and this fear serves the function of distracting us from the true issues that cry out for clarity.

The male fear of unjust accusation runs deep in our culture and has several consequences. Above all, it shifts the focus of the discussion in a manner that inverts and obscures the true balance of control of harassing behavior. The fear obliterates the fact that a claim of sexual harassment is not about female dominance over the accused man, but rather the reverse. In this way, the responsibility of the accused, or even of the potentially accused man who fantasizes about this fear, evaporates. Sexual harassment is transformed from a certain kind of male behavior toward women to an instance of female dominance over men. And, thus, we encounter the false sense of control theme here, and, it is the woman who appears to be the guilty party.

The fear also serves to raise the stakes of a complaint of sexual harassment and thereby casts doubt on the possible contents of an accusation. Thus, at the same time, it makes it psychologically more difficult to bring such a claim. Not only are the real consequences for the perpetrator of harassing behavior minuscule and fleeting but also most women who have experienced sexual harassment never bring a claim at all. They never bring a claim even to their friends, since the isolation theme surfaces with great force here, and even to themselves in the privacy of their own minds. Most often, the woman will feel confused and seek an explanation based upon her own behavior, in accordance with the patterns of internalization and personalization.

Although there are reasons for a lack of professional recognition other than gender bias, when one looks at the numbers and overwhelming proportions of men who achieve professional success relative to women, one is compelled to conclude that something deep and pervasive is going on that effectively bars all but a small set of women from persevering. It is clearly not the case that the responsibility for gender bias in our culture can be attributed solely to the male population. Nevertheless, nor can the opposite be true. Yet, there is a constant trend in our culture to absolve the male of his accountability for his own actions. The father who commits incest against his daughter claims innocence: it was his child who seduced him by her sexually provocative behavior. The same goes for the acquaintance and stranger rapist: it was the woman's clothing or behavior that compelled him to commit the crime. Even the defense in brutal gang rapes has tried to pin the fault on the promiscuity of the victim. Similar explanations have been used time and again in cases of sexual harassment. Even clear-cut job discrimination is not the fault of the employer; the comparably or better qualified female candidate just isn't right, she won't fit in, she isn't congenial enough. This is all longhand for the recognition that she just isn't male.

Taking gender bias, sexual harassment, sex discrimination, and exploitation seriously is hard to do. One of the first steps to move beyond the existing media coverage is to recognize these problems as the patterns of behavior that they are, enmeshed with others, and interwoven in the fabric of our society. That is, they are political trends, and deeply entrenched ones at that. One of the aspects of this fact that is most difficult for us to swallow is that as actions they are not directed at specific women *personally*. The beauty of internalization and personalization is that, although a woman may not feel great about herself while engaging in these patterns of thought, at least as a consequence of this reasoning, she is a person. For, if what's happening is her fault or responsibility and she can do something to change it in the future, then she must be a real, live person. In some strange, backhand manner, her existence is being affirmed.

But if, on the other hand, what is closer to the truth is that, in fact, most of these incidents are not personal, then the recipient of the biased behavior is not even being responded to as a person. She is not being accorded enough dignity to be an individual in her own right. *That* is hard to swallow. No wonder women resist acknowledging the variety of biased behavior doing so renders them largely invisible.

In fact, virtually every woman that I called to interview for this book commented that she would be delighted to discuss sexual harassment with me, but that she herself had not had any personal experience of it, nor of sex discrimination or even of gender bias generally. But, in every case, not more than a minute passed into the interview before the woman began to spill out experience after experience with sexual harassment, and feeling after feeling after feeling—her own experiences and her own feelings. In one case, it had been raining that day, and wearing a raincoat, I had barely entered the interviewee's office, let alone taken off my coat or loaded and turned on my tape recorder when the woman had already started to speak volumes. She was well underway before I was set up and ready.

The women I contacted were not being coy about their experience. Rather, the women's initial assertions are another measure of the depth to which gender bias is so deeply ingrained as to be commonplace. All the women wanted to speak with me and share their ideas and ultimately to record their own, often extremely painful and professionally costly experience confronting the realities of the professional women of our day: that they will be thwarted and demoralized at almost every possible turn, that there in fact is a battle of dominance raging in the professional suites that has hardly played itself out yet.

There are many fears that come along with this battle. Women in the top one percent of their fields were afraid to speak with me, even under the agreement of anonymity, as if each had a fear of being unmasked *as a woman.* There is a real fear of being labeled a feminist, as if that would be the death knell for one's career. But I also witnessed another, more subtle fear: the fear of voicing daily reality. Several interviewees, even when safely ensconced in a location far from earshot of their employers and colleagues, would speak in a barely audible whisper while recounting particularly sensitive events. In fact, this happened frequently enough that tape transcription became a large headache, literally. Everything about an interviewee's comportment and demeanor would alter while she was relating an incident or pattern that was particularly taxing or troubling. The modulation of voice, facial expressions, and body language were enough to tell the stories of acute demoralization.

It should come as no surprise, although it in fact did surprise me, to find that women have well-formulated and thought-out fantasies of living professional lives as men. Virtually every woman whom I interviewed had a very clear idea of what her work life would be like had she been born male. They all saw themselves as more assertive, decisive, and successful than they currently are now. And many saw themselves in different fields altogether. They recognized the ways in which the sex they were born with, and the gender they were raised into, determined their career selection and their professional style. Some felt it necessary to hold themselves back, consciously, because they are women; others felt that the powers that be in their fields held limits over their heads.

Perhaps even more alarming is the fact that the young women whom I interviewed, girls still in high school, had clearly articulated visions of what their lives would be like were they male: they would be allowed to play sports in the way and amount they would like, they would be taught math and computers from which they feel they are being held back, they would have greater freedom of expression, they would be bolder, teachers would pay attention to them, and their parents would love them more. Clearly, if girls in the 1990s are witnessing such vast discrepancies in the attention paid to children divided according to sex, then our equal opportunity programs have not yet begun to do nearly enough, and we need to look deeper into the actual mechanics of gender bias. As a society, we are fairly well informed about the basics, the cruder forms, of what men do to promote and perpetuate gender bias. Now, we need to refine our thinking by turning our attention to three areas, all discussed in the text below. The first is the deeper, subtler level of male gender-biased behavior. The second area is the dynamic between female and male in gender-biased situations. And the third is the set of factors involved in women's collusion with a gender-biased culture.

This book provides a view of the daily experience of professional women. Much of the text recounts the minute *details* of daily life. At first when I was compiling the excerpts from the interviews I conducted for this book, I was immersed in such details from woman after woman after woman. I began to find the particulars of their stories enervating, perhaps in a much diluted form of the women's experiences who had lived them. Looking, however, at the larger picture simultaneously with the smaller steps involved in each woman's experiences, I realized that it is from the smaller details that we can profit and learn to restructure ourselves and the professional workplace. Although the results for each woman of the general trends are largely the same story of exclusion, self-image deficits, energy drains, and stumbling blocks to advancement, it is in the gritty details of everyday life for professional women that we can grasp what they have to go through and their internal responses to the situations they confront. It is the step-by-step accounting that many women provided me with of the hurdles professional women must learn to conquer that became the foreground of this book.

Thus, in order to convey the wealth of information available to me, I created a composite character to represent and walk through the lives of American professional women. I named this woman Emily, and this book will tell her story, from birth through advancement to the top of her profession, with all of its twists and turns, setbacks, difficulties, and accomplishments. Dotted through the terrain of Emily's trek through professional advancement are the voices of the actual girls and women interviewed for this book; they are printed in italics throughout. In this way, variations on Emily's path will unfold, providing greater depth to the picture painted.

Each chapter follows a different phase in Emily's life, broken down chronologically insofar as possible, and is divided into four main parts: The Basics, Gender Lessons, Gender Compounds, and Gender Action.

In *The Basics* segments, Emily lives through the lowest common denominator of female experience with regard to gender bias. That is, she experiences the *minimum* amount of bias possible in our culture. For clarity, Emily is constructed to virtually avoid other forms of bias. Thus, her family is middle class, she is white and is not a member of an ethnic or religious minority in her community, she grows up to become comfortably heterosexual, and she is not physically challenged in any way. A look at how Emily's personality and choices evolve over the years, getting by with the least amount of gender bias, will demonstrate starkly that the minimum is quite enough.

In the *Gender Lessons* portions of each chapter, the themes and trends found in *The Basics* segments are highlighted and examined, along with Emily's response to the bias described in those segments.

In the *Gender Compounds* portions, the impact of multiple forms of bias from gender plus race, class, ethnicity, sexual preference, age, as well as other dimensions along which one can experience bias from the larger community, is explored in detail. In addition, forms of increased gender bias over and above the minimum level described in *The Basics* are examined.

In the *Gender Action* portions of each chapter, the remedial action appropriate for the bias described in the chapter is explained and discussed. Actions included consist not only of interpersonal activities such as complaint procedures and bringing biased behaviors to the attention of persons in authority but also intrapersonal activity as well. The more a person can raise her own awareness of behaviors and the underlying issues, the more her own attitudes and actions will change and her confidence in herself increase. Thus, personal exercises and projects are an integral part of the *Gender Action* segments of each chapter.

I would like to be able to say that one particular subject, among those I cover in the book, is the crucial one for women in the professions. And, at various points in the writing of this book, I have felt that one chapter or section over the others is it. In fact, however, I have concluded that each stage of professional development holds its own pivotal moments and choices, and sadly, no aspect of professional women's private lives is considered to be private and irrelevant to their employment and performance on the job. Whether it be sexual preference, marital status, life choices of her partners, children, divorce, attire in and out of the office, and even often choice of hobbies, all of these factors and more are included in the evaluation and experience of the professional woman by her employers and colleagues. Thus, I structured the book, as much as was possible, chronologically according to career development.

STRUCTURE OF *THE GENDER BIAS PREVENTION BOOK*

Part II contains six chapters beginning with Emily's birth taking her through college graduation. The purpose of this part is to examine the state of mind and level of readiness with which women enter professional training. The impact of early experiences with gender bias, sexual harassment, and sex discrimination on how a woman views herself and her capabilities and thereby how she enters career development is discussed in this part. It covers the social, institutional, and family factors that contribute to the future planning and projections of college graduates.

Before proceeding on to professional training and employment, Part III pauses to examine the second shift required of women in addition to their paid, professional work. The impact that the additional tasks have on the potential productivity of women on the job is canvassed. The decision of where to place this section in the book was difficult, but it was put here because so many of the components of the second shift are already expected of women fresh off campus walk.

Part IV takes Emily through professional training, largely in the form of advanced degree programs. It covers admissions to the programs through job interviews at the other end. In between are chapters concerning the details of getting through the programs themselves, their courses, exams, and the production of theses and dissertations.

Part V also posed a placement issue. This part consists of two chapters about the very important mentor–mentee relationship. Mentors are acquired at different points and in different ways according to the specific profession under consideration and according to the individuals involved. One key factor that gives rise to a host of issues that remain virtually constant across all dimensions is the mentee being female. Similarly, two distinct sets of considerations apply according to whether the potential mentor is female or male. And thus the chapters are split according to the sex of the mentor.

Part VI concerns three different strands in women's professional life and is divided into chapters accordingly. One chapter describes the components of the atmosphere on the job in the professions with regard to gender. Another describes the specific experience of women in their first jobs just out of professional training programs, and the last chapter discusses the factors involved in professional advancement.

Part VII concerns the specific situation and experience of the relatively few women who have advanced to the top level of their chosen profession.

The eighth and final part discusses projections for the future. It projects current trends into the future and describes what true gender equity in the professions would look like, examines the benefits derived from it, and assesses the factors that are stopping us from achieving it. A picture is drawn of professional life in which gender bias is not operative. The state of mind of the women involved, as well as a description of their energy level and productivity on the job, are provided within this model. This part also describes what it would take to hasten the process and ensure the result of equity.

TERMINOLOGY USED IN *THE GENDER BIAS PREVENTION BOOK*

The use of the term "professional" is loose and fluid as it is in practice in this culture, and I follow the Bureau of Labor Statistics definition, which includes the requirement of substantial post-secondary education or equivalent in preparation for the work.

Throughout the book, I maintain a distinction between sex and gender. Put simply, sex is what one is born *with*, and gender is what one is born *into*. That is, sex concerns little more than the shape of one's genitals and the reproductive capacity that it entails, and gender concerns the social meaning that is attached to that shape and correlative physical ability. This is a now common distinction that proves to be constantly useful throughout this book.

My use of the terms "gender bias," "sexual harassment," and "sex discrimination" all require explanation. My use of both "sexual harassment" and "sex discrimination" follow the current legal characterizations, as are spelled out in Title VII of the Civil Rights Act of 1964, Title IX of the Education Amendments of 1972, The Civil Rights Restoration Act of 1991, and in key court determinations. Title VII defines sexual harassment as follows:

> Unwelcome sexual advances, requests for sexual favors, and other verbal or physical conduct of a sexual nature constitute sexual harassment when
>
> 1) submission to such conduct is made either explicitly or implicitly a term or condition of an individual's employment;
>
> 2) submission to or rejection of such conduct by an individual is used as the basis for employment decisions affecting such individual; or
>
> 3) such conduct has the purpose or effect of unreasonably interfering with an individual's work performance or creating an intimidating, hostile, or offensive working environment.

Title IX states, "No person shall, on the basis of sex, be excluded from the participation in, be denied benefits of, or be subjected to discrimination under any education program or activity receiving federal financial assistance."

For the purposes of this book, I am more interested in the more general term "gender bias." Both the meaning of sexual harassment and sex discrimination are subsumed under this broader term, as are all of the pervasive but subtle forms of belittlement due to gender stereotyping and biases that make up the fabric of females' life experiences in this culture at this time. The discussions in *The Gender Bias Prevention Book* try to capture and characterize gender bias at its most subtle and constant level in order to analyze the fundamental experience of women who attempt to achieve standing in professions that have not been traditionally and remain not fully open to them.

CONCLUSION

Our culture is caught in a Catch-22 situation. Persistent gender bias results in authority and autonomy being wrested from the female, but men also claim no role in the process at any level. Thus we are stuck in a relatively static condition. Although some advances in the status of women have been achieved, many of them are thin when held up to the light of daily life. Although I assume that the majority of readers of this book will be female, an important conclusion found in this book is that change cannot be achieved if gender equity in the professions is yet another task for women only to take on. By the end of the book it will be clear how eradicating gender bias from the professions can benefit everyone, that it must be part of the program for change, that it comes about as a mutual process between women and men, that, in other words, the process itself must become an integral part of the end result.

The Gender Gias Prevention Book is dedicated to the idea that my daughters' generation will not need books about gender bias in the professions (we do have *some* time; as of this writing, Liana is 7 years old and Miranda is 2).

What is both sad and encouraging at the same time is that there are small, simple steps that would go a long way toward undermining the two-class society that has been erected. As is brought out in every part of this book, there are relatively easily implementable actions that would forever change the nature of gender divisions in our culture. They do not involve great sums of money, nor do they necessitate tinkering directly with vast, complex institutional webs such as our legal system. Rather, they require awareness and thoughtful interaction between adults and children, teachers and students at all levels, employers and employees, and among peers.

By participating in these changes, however small, each of us, one by one, can take a pane out of the professional woman's walk down the garden path to the glass ceiling, until finally the sky will be the limit.

PART II
THE NUTCRACKER SUITE

The story underlying the ballet, *The Nutcracker Suite*, is an encapsulation of a large portion of the upbringing of girls in Western culture, and much of which remains true to the contemporary picture. In the party scene, the girls, dressed in petticoats and dresses and ribbons, are given dolls. They rock and cradle and baby the dolls while the boys are given swords and wooden horses. The boys swagger about with their paraphernalia, torturing and bullying the girls. The principal female character, Marie, is given the nutcracker doll by her uncle, Mr. Drosselmeyer; she rocks and cradles the doll and eventually sleeps with it on the living room couch. Passing over, for the moment, the continuous allusion to incest between Uncle Drosselmeyer and Marie, *The Nutcracker* is a coming-of-age story for girls. The nutcracker doll transforms into a prince who saves Marie from the mice. While the prince is fighting off the mice, sword in hand, Marie frets and looks on passively. In fact, however, although it is Marie who swings one of the decisive blows to the mice, it is the prince who is celebrated as the conqueror. Victory accomplished, Marie is swished off the prince's castle to be entertained by his dancers. In the end, it is the uncle who orchestrates the conclusion of the romance between the girl/woman Marie and the nutcracker doll/prince.

Although the tale is about Marie qua generic girl and her process of sexual awakening, the true principal characters are the uncle and the nutcracker prince. The beginning and end of the ballet focus on the uncle, and the middle segments are about the transformation of the doll to prince and then the prince's exploits with the mice. The girl and her own transformation are secondary and auxiliary. The crucial points of her part of the story are that she receives the proper training at the outset and that she then serves as a vehicle and support system for the male characters.

What I call the *Nutcracker virus* continues to infect the lives of girls. It is endemic to our culture, the various waves of feminism notwithstanding. This part of the book examines the virus in its current form. It provides an overview of the prevailing conditions and trends that lead up to professional life for females. It is divided into six chapters according to developmental and educational levels from birth through college graduation. It is here that the beginning of the evolution of the composite character Emily is marked. She is followed as she travels through each of the life phases that lead to entering the professional realm. Thus, the frame of mind of women as they enter professional training and the workforce is put in perspective.

The fact remains that until issues of gender are dealt with at the first appropriate moment, problems will ramify throughout girls' and women's lives and more work will need to be done at later points in women's lives to overcome them. While supplying girls with physical competence in grade school would be relatively simple, for example, undoing the manifold effects of cutting girls out of competitive sports in women's later lives is much more complex. In this case, it is not merely an issue of starting girls young in creating healthy, strong bodies. In addition, through sports they learn team building and cooperation skills. And the accomplishment of mastery of sports and physical competence breeds self-confidence in other arenas. Sports are an important vehicle to the creation of an integrated self and self-knowledge, not to mention that they are a national pastime among adults and are used to forge professional relationships and connections.

Another clear example is that maintaining girls' intellectual curiosity and appetite in the move from elementary to junior high school is relatively simple as compared with dealing with the future impact of squelching it. It will become evident in the subsequent parts of the book that professional women must expend a good deal of their energy on issues that have already arisen in their childhood and young adult years and would have been best eradicated then. That is, the problems that professional women confront are perhaps more sophisticated versions of what many of them have already experienced in childhood.

Thus, in this part care is taken to note the first place in girls' lives at which specific issues of gender bias occur. Time is also taken to specify how to avoid or undo the problems at these early moments. Trends, themes, and syndromes involving gender bias are clearly labeled for future use in the book. By the conclusion of this section, a picture emerges of what the expectations and self-concepts are of women entering the professional world. It will thereby become clear how much of the patterns of gender bias that women confront at work can remain elusive to them: much of it has come to comprise the background music with which they conduct their lives. It remains unremarkable, in fact unheard, except when it is either turned up too loud or stops altogether.

This part provides a road map for change in girls' lives so that they can walk into professions without carrying the baggage and bruises from gender bias. Subsequent sections examine where and how the same problem situations crop up in the professional realm and how to deal with them at that point.

2 EARLY CHILDHOOD: THE FAMILY DYNAMIC

THE BASICS

Emily is born into what eventually evolves into a moderately unegalitarian family. She lives with her mother and father, an older sister, and a younger brother, until she leaves home for college.

Emily's mother stays at home while her children are young and her father commutes to an office job. Emily's father often works long hours, missing the family dinner, and occasionally he goes away for a few days at a time on business trips. Her mother does the bulk of the shopping, including buying clothes for all members of the family: the cooking, except the occasional barbecue; and the cleaning. Emily's father takes out the garbage, attempts to fix things around the house, and attends to the dog and the car, including cleaning both, until his children are old enough to take over these tasks.

When Emily is born, friends and neighbors bestow gifts similar to those her parents received when their eldest was born: cute, pink baby wrap-ups with bows; soft, fuzzy, furry dolls and stuffed animals; and toys with ballet motifs. The visitors coo and remark how soft and gentle and pretty the infant Emily is. They ask her older sister if she is a good girl, acting as mommy's helper. And, they ask her dad if they are going to try again in order to have a boy.

Emily's main outward cognitive achievement of her first years of life is that she learns to speak. In so doing, Emily begins to acquire the concepts of our culture. This happens by the ways in which language breaks up the world into perceptible chunks. Emily learns English based primarily on what she hears at home and may pick up supplementary pieces from the world outside.

When her baby brother is born, it is Emily's turn to be mommy's helper. Friends bring gifts with baseball motifs and crib toys for the baby to pull and flex on. They call him things like "tough guy" and "buster." They note how he'll grow up to fill his father's shoes and be just like him. Emily's older sister, now 5, plays her part by dressing in frilly clothes and carrying around a small tray with snacks on it for visitors. It is remarked with delight what a perfect little hostess she is.

Once the fanfare of her brother's birth winds down, Emily is less pleased with the addition to the family. She feels that he is getting all the attention and that his mother holds him much more than she ever held her. Emily is in fact correct. Overall, boys generally receive more attention, physically, verbally, and emotionally, than do girls. The times and situations in which girls receive more attention are when they are being cautioned not to climb too high, not to fall, not to play too rough, not to hurt themselves. Their brother rarely, if ever, hears such remarks directed at him. Rather, he'll be coddled in infancy, talked to more, and encouraged early to grab, throw, play catch, and solve problems. This differential treatment of the siblings, determined by sex, is most often inadvertent and unacknowledged.

From infancy on, Emily and her sister's lives have been dominated by the color pink, from nightgowns, clothing, bedroom decor, and toys to even the color of their birthday cakes, whereas their brother's is dominated by blue. When her baby brother is born, a new set of infant equipment and attire, from crib bumpers to shoes, has to be bought in blue. Emily continues to get her sister's hand-me-downs. Emily and her sister have dolls, play strollers, plastic tea sets, tutus, and velvet horses. Their brother has trucks, toy swords, blocks, and boats. All three converge in the sandbox out back, but even there they have learned different games to play. Emily makes cakes and castles, whereas her brother uses the sand as a launching ground for his toy airplanes and as a battleground for his toy soldiers and dinosaurs. Her father roughhouses with all three kids until they are a certain age and then defers to chatting briefly with the girls and throwing around a football or building models with his son.

Until she goes to school, Emily spends a good deal of time with her mother. They go shopping and do other errands while her sister is at her morning nursery school program. Emily plays quietly with her toys while her mother vacuums and mops, and she often tries to help while her mother is preparing dinner. In short, Emily is being trained in the ways of home management, and even at this young age, it is not lost on her that this is the mother's province. By the same token, Emily observes that it is the part of her father, the man, to go out into the world, to have ambitions that do not solely revolve around the family and the household. And she is beginning to catch on about money, who makes it and who does not, and that it is valuable.

By the same token, at this juncture of her life, her mother may seem to be the more powerful of the two parents. It is Emily's mother who decides when and where she can go play, what and when she can eat, and when she must go to sleep. It is her mother who does everything, at this point, that Emily considers important. Her father does unknown and unseeable things that take his attention away from her. Yet, a dissonance is germinating within Emily's mind between what is of central importance to her and who seems powerful to her versus the attitudes she is beginning to perceive, if not understand, in the members of the community at large.

GENDER LESSONS

By the time Emily reaches 3 years of age, she has incorporated a large chunk of society's gender roles, not only from what she finds at home but also from those reflected from the larger community. Although her mother and older sister, at this stage of her life, may seem all powerful and her father somewhat tangential, Emily is also learning what their lives entail. Even her sister is encouraged to take on household duties and to look after, play with, and take care of Emily. Her mother may not spend inordinate amounts of time on her physical appearance and that of her daughters, but as compared with the father it is monumental. Thus, Emily is already becoming indoctrinated into the world of fashion, make-up, and normative female beauty.

To gain perspective on the gender balance in Emily's home, consider how it might be different were Emily's older sister a boy instead. The mother's role would remain the same. The older brother in this case would be likely to receive more attention as an individual and not so much as a potential caretaker for Emily. In fact, at these young ages, it would be unlikely to be expressed nor expected that the brother be mommy's helper. Emily's father, on weekends and after work, would be more likely to tumble around with his son and provide him with more verbal engagement than he does with his daughters. Now, upon coming home, he gives the girls a kiss and a hug and goes off to relax in the den. On the weekends the son would be engaged to help with dad's chores and perhaps come along to sports games and the like.

Even if Emily's mother were to work full time at this stage of her life, Emily's perspective might not be all that different. In fact, her early view of the female role might be even more stereotyped. Emily, in such a case, might be in the care of a nanny who would be female and perhaps more invested in gender norms than Emily's mother. In that case, although it would be Emily's mother who gives instructions and directions to the babysitter, the mother would be likely to be perceived as less powerful seen through Emily's young eyes than if she stayed home. If Emily attended a day care facility instead, the workers there would be likely to be all females, and a similar situation would result.

In addition, Emily would still take in the fact that it is her mother who performs the bulk of the household duties. The mother would still most likely be the one who shops, cooks, and cleans. Thus, during this tender period of concept formation and language acquisition, Emily is developing her grasp on the balance of authority between the sexes as a reflection of what she sees around her.

GENDER COMPOUNDS

Suppose that Emily's family practices a religious faith. In such a case, the church or temple would provide another glimpse into the outside world for her. Here again, the overwhelming likelihood is that gender stereotypes would be reinforced. Depending on the faith, females may even be barred from certain activities or may sit in a segregated location. Even in a seemingly more egalitarian setting, the person or people leading the service and in authority at the place of worship would almost certainly be men. Emily may hear talk about the issue of permitting women greater involvement in the hierarchy of the faith and hear females referred to as "them," clearly delineating their outsider status.

Further suppose that Emily watches some amount of television regularly. Assume that she isn't yet acquainted with the thoroughly sexist and violent cartoon programming. Rather, suppose that Emily is restricted to the more benign shows such as *Sesame Street* and *Barney*. From this exposure, her emerging world view is constantly being broadened and confirmed. On television she will find that most of the characters are male; certainly, the active ones are. The underlying assumptions and the language of these shows and others like it are sexist at the core, and she will find nothing on television to cause her to challenge her forming conception of gender. By the age of 3, these added dimensions to Emily's life serve to help guide her in forming a clear self-perception and in finding her place in the world.

To summarize, here is the gender framework Emily has already learned to some degree:

GF 1. Household labor and child care are a female province, and it remains unspoken and unpraised.

GF 2. Men spend their days out of the home, at work, and this is often discussed and highly valued.

GF 3. Females and not males attend to their physical appearance in great detail.

GF 4. Girls need to be careful, do things smaller, quieter, and be "mommy's helpers."

GF 5. The world's active population is largely male.

GENDER ACTION

There is nothing that Emily can do for herself in these young toddler and early childhood years to counteract the gender bias and imbalances around her. Yet, think of what a different world it would be if simple changes were made inside the home.

One reasonably simple change within the household would alter everyone's gendered perspective immeasurably, children and adults alike. Imagine that Emily grows up in a home in which the language spoken is gender neutral. This does not entail speaking in awkward she–he phrases and other travesties that have blossomed out of the genuine discomfort people feel in altering language. Language is, after all, the vehicle for everyone's conceptual framework. But, because language does indeed shape the way we think and view the world and even determines to some extent how we *can* view the world, it needs to be modified to be as inclusive of females in the world as it is of males.

Given the transformative nature of the impact of relatively minor language shifts on adults, the lasting impression on children as they first acquire language could be absolutely breathtaking. For example, in Emily's home, suppose that words like police*man*, fire*man*, Congress*man*, and the like were all consistently replaced by gender-neutral expressions, such as police officer, fire fighter, and Congressperson.

Further imagine that the pronouns used were not uniformly masculine, except in cases where a definite female was being referred to. When speaking in the abstract about some indefinite person or animal, feminine and masculine pronouns are used interchangeably and relatively equally in place of the traditional use of masculine generics. Moreover, imagine that all those stuffed animals, real animals of unknown sex, and other entities of undetermined gender were not all presumed to be male, but were evenly referred to by 'she's and 'he's.

Were Emily to grow up learning a language modified in these ways, she would reap both immediate and long-term gains. The effort of accomplishing small language changes in every household is minimal as compared with the lasting benefits. Emily's mental life would no longer be populated virtually solely by males and mommies. She would also be able to readily imagine *herself* in a variety of situations as an active, vocal, capable person and in the full range of jobs and careers. Chances are that as Emily gets older and begins to draw, she would draw herself and other females in non-traditional roles. That is what her modified language has enabled her to imagine, rather than ruling out such mental possibilities as the current form of English does.

A more long-term goal that can be addressed in small steps is a household system in which parents share equally in the responsibilities each has incurred by creating that household, including the children in it. Modifications toward this goal would forever change the gendered perspective of the generations to come. Once the first generation born into egalitarian households grows to maturity, vast changes in the educational and workplace structure would begin to unfold. Imagine that our culture gave up the notion that the male adult is exempt from responsibility at home, that as long as the male does his "job"—that is, goes to work at his vocation—he is done. Imagine that we give up the idea that, whether or not the woman has a full-time job as well, she is still expected to perform the bulk of the child and home care. As the director of an elementary school observed,

> *Children in my school are seeing a lot of parents working together on household issues. They're seeing a modeling of both male and female at home doing chores. And the kids' attitudes are different in these families. For example, we were studying Ethiopia and we were having a meal and we said, "For this meal we serve the males first because it's a paternalistic society." A 6-year-old girl stood and said, "Not even for make believe!"*

There are many complex and hidden flaws and misguided assumptions in the structure of the traditional American household, to be sure. It is, however, clear how it needs to change:

household chores need to be split equitably and probably rotated. Child care should be an equally shared activity, and both parents must be able to pursue satisfying outside employment. Were this to be achieved, the female and male roles would be blurred, and both girls and boys would mature with an egalitarian gender model in mind. Even if schools somehow remained as biased as they are today, the household model would remain a strong and powerful spur for the children's imagination and notions of self-potential.

Yet, a vicious cycle blocks this egalitarian home from becoming a widespread reality. Underlying this cycle and undermining potential change is the ever-present theme song that maintaining the status quo is the simplest, easiest, and somehow therefore the best way to go. Set habits perpetuate themselves in myriad forms.

The vicious cycle comes into play by virtue of the fact that men continue to earn substantially higher incomes than women, often even when performing comparable work. And, families, typically pressed for money and when child care is not a viable option, will defer the woman's job to the man's in the name of genuinely needing the larger salary more. Now strangely, though, this situation persists even when child care is in place. It is the male's job that always takes precedence. And the cycle continues not only because women are viewed as less competent and less reliable; in fact, they do generally take more personal days to care for sick children and other household concerns. Wrenches clearly need to be thrown into this cycle wherever and whenever possible until the status quo is forever transformed.

Thus, the corrective action appropriate to this stage of Emily's development has two key elements:

GA 1. *Language*: Teach children correct English that is unhampered by gender bias. Modify the use of generics to use feminine and masculine in equal proportions or the feminine solely. Change noun phrases to be gender neutral.

GA 2. *Home and child maintenance*: Create a housework schedule that is equitable. Have all adults in the household create multifaceted relationships with the children.

EXERCISE 1

In addition, adults can try the following thought experiment and share it with others.

1. Imagine yourself as a female toddler learning constantly about all the things people do when they are older than you are, the places they go, the ideas they have, and so on. You hear little about yourself and your own age group. Take your time and try to grasp what your thoughts and desires would be in this situation before proceeding to the next step.

2. Now, imagine a similar situation in which *sex* is substituted for age, so that you are a girl learning largely about what boys can do. Think through the implications of this on a young female mind.

3 PRESCHOOL: ENTERING THE SOCIAL REALM

THE BASICS

By the time Emily enters preschool at 3 years old, she is already forming conceptions of female and male along stereotypical lines. She is also beginning to see herself as falling into the female category and is trying out the role in a variety of situations. Chances are that she walks into preschool on her first day with a mixture of excitement and trepidation. Emily was feeling bold all morning, yet when her mother flung open the outer school doors for them to enter, she began to quaver, and by the time they reached the preschool classroom that by now Emily was familiar with, she faltered outright.

Emily reaches up and asks her mother to carry her. Once folded in her mother's arms, she clutches fast to her mother's sweater and leans her head against her mother's shoulder. For the first time, Emily is confronted with a group of peers, boys and girls, in which she will be left to her own devices. Emily has a heightened awareness of this fact, and it is evident to her that the world of the classroom is noisy and unpredictable.

Another child could come over and strike her or grab a toy at any moment. Some children are wailing for their mothers, and others eagerly dart from one activity to the next as if finally set loose. There is a division by sex about how children walk into the classroom at the preschool level. In the words of one seasoned preschool teacher,

By the time kids come to preschool they've already learned a lot of the biases of the culture. Parents' voices are more soothing to girls, soupier and softer. They come well ensconced with an image of themselves. To get through their day, the girls will fall back on being helpless emotionally. They're passive, and they expect the adult to fix it up. The boys, when they're anxious, will strike out. Girls are culture identified. Girls are pretty and girls dance and girls are mommies; they're the fairy tale characters. Boys check out that they're strong. It's strongly embedded at that young age.

To adult eyes, some elements of the room are all too predictable. For Emily and the other children, they appear as part of the assumed backdrop. Most of the girls have their wispy hair in clips, ribbons, or ties. They are also likely to be wearing dresses and perhaps even tights. Many of the girls are *dressed*, whereas the boys simply had clothes put on them. Right from the beginning, because this has already been set up at home, the kids' activity is separated by gender: Emily looks around the room and sees the boys building a jail out of blocks and sees a group of girls huddled at the water table, playing in the detergent-bubbled water.

Emily is not at all nonplussed on her second day at school when a 4-year-old girl, a one-year veteran of the program, approaches her and beckons, "Come on, Emily, let's make sandwiches for the guys; they're busy with the car!" The 4-year-old nods in the direction of three boys playing on the gigantic car toy. Emily understands this remark; it fits into her fledgling conceptual picture of the world. She turns her head to the indicated corner of the classroom and, in so doing, takes in a sweeping glance of the myriad activities underway. She observes boys playing with boys and the girls playing with girls. Emily sees a group of boys climbing on the jungle gym, yelling and stomping, and girls piecing puzzles together, quietly looking at the picture books in the reading loft, and painting. All of this fits too, and it tacitly confirms Emily's growing view of gender identity.

In her first few weeks in preschool, Emily quickly catches on to a coding system that the girls have devised for each other. It is a game of dominance, submission, and exclusion that persists throughout girls' and women's lives with the format modified only slightly as the years go by. The game of girls checking each other out physically starts right here in preschool, and Emily does not escape it. She learns that the girls already savvy to this game have set standards for acceptability and so-called friendship. A girl needs to look a certain way before she'll be played with by the others. It is a method of exerting control, and where this fails, it is a method of exclusion. This preschool-level game is the seed for the full-fledged method women employ to chastise themselves for being inadequate while simultaneously disassociating themselves from other women. Consider the following description of the game by a preschool teacher attuned to this pattern:

One of the ways girls exclude each other from play is if they haven't got the right costume on. They'll say, "You can't sit here, you can't come here, because you're not wearing . . . ," that is, the correct garment. They whip themselves right into line. You either have to wear tights or never wear tights. You have to wear dresses or never wear dresses.

Then it can get more fine tuned, "But your dress doesn't have ribbons on it," they'll say. "Only girls can come up here who have dresses with ribbons." The girls go crazy; they weep and

cry and gnash their teeth. The boys don't care unless they have
something that's special that they're wearing for the first time
that they want to show [the teacher].

The girls want to be validated. They ask me all the time, "Do
you think my dress is pretty?" "Am I pretty?" "Look at my hair,
my bows, my barrettes." They need three heads each to carry
all that gear on them.

By the time Emily is 4 and in her last year of preschool, she
will readily announce that she hates boys and no longer even
considers playing with them. She has also learned to sing several sexist rhyming tunes, taught to her by other friends, such
as one about boys pulling down girls' underwear. She does not
fully understand their import, but at the very least, the songs'
divisive nature is not lost on her. She has also begun to use
the word "people" to mean males more often than not, using
such phrases as "people and their wives." This is a clear signal that her imagination has already become male dominated.

The two caring and competent teachers, both female, consistently use masculine pronouns whether they are speaking
of real people, a stuffed bear, or the actually female guinea
pig in the classroom. As is demonstrated by many studies,
including the well-publicized 1992 Association of University
Women's report, *How Schools Shortchange Girls*, teachers inadvertently encourage the boys to be bold and to try new things,
and generally give them more attention. They direct the girls
most often to the more subdued or detail-oriented activities,
equally inadvertently and without even being vaguely aware
that this is in fact what they are doing. The teachers take over
tasks for the girls when they call for help and give careful,
patient instructions to the boys to show them how to do it on
their own. Most of this "teaching" in its myriad forms is unin-
tentional; it is part of the teachers' own enculturation and training. And to date, there remains virtually no discussion of gen-

der equity in schools of education that would alleviate some of this perpetuated socialization.

The books in the classroom, even for this age group, encourage gender stereotypes. When Emily flips open a book, she will almost always find that the main character is male and the female characters are passive and diminutive or evil. The pictures reinforce the same concepts, to the point of depicting the females as smaller, lower, or physically deferential in some other way. Even the songs that Emily learns to sing in school with the music teacher are gender biased. Most are in fact about boys or men or male animals. She learns "Old MacDonald," "Peter Works with One Hammer," and, "Puff the Magic Dragon." At snack time, the kids are directed to two tables and are often split up according to sex outright or by some sex-identifying characteristic.

GENDER LESSONS

In preschool, the gendered pigeonholing that began in Emily's home is expanded and embellished. Female roles from the home are carried into the school and take on new meaning. It is likely in school that Emily will come to feel that her social circle consists of girls and that her range of activities falls into a fairly clearly circumscribed selection. Notwithstanding the fact that Emily is taller than most of the boys in her nursery school group, she learns quickly to defer if challenged by a boy for a spot on the swings or a toy. She does not see it as *her* space that is being invaded, but rather that she is a place holder in the space she readily cedes to her male peer.

Emily is also now aware that there is a war raging between the sexes, though at her age it is still more or less good-natured and its import not fully understood. Nevertheless, the girls "hate" the boys, and the boys "hate" the girls. Each group calls the members of the other sex names such as "stupid" and "dumbhead." At this stage, Emily still admits to liking to play with individual boys, yet she is becoming keenly aware of the gendered two-class nature of our society. Emily tries to carry this war on at home in her family as well. She attempts to set up alliances with her sister and mother against her brother and father. Emily's sister, being older and thus better versed in this war, gives her pointers and pitches in to fill the role of ringleader.

Emily is tacitly learning that she is rewarded in a variety of ways for quiet, neat behavior and that if she behaves in the brash fashion that her classmate Jimmy employs as a matter of course, she will be reprimanded. Her view that the active, outside part of the world is populated virtually solely by males is becoming stronger and well ingrained into her thought processes. This view began to form as soon as she began to understand language and divide the world into discrete objects. In school, this perspective has been given depth and richness through story books, pictures on the wall, songs, games, activities, and the differential manner in which the teachers speak and react to the children according to sex.

GENDER COMPOUNDS

Given our national statistics on the incidence of sexual abuse, it is not out of the realm of possibility to suppose that Emily might receive inappropriate sexual attention in this phase of her childhood. If she does, how she manages in the aftermath greatly depends upon how the situation is handled, that is, if the incident in fact ever comes to light. If she was the object of inappropriate sexual attention, in addition to the ordinary, everyday gender lessons Emily would learn a powerful lesson about herself as a female in our culture. She would be likely to develop a view of the female body and her own as horrible, in need of constant attention and vigilance, and of herself as culpable for the incident.

Every woman interviewed for this book who was asked about this topic had a childhood incident of this sort to relate, which they reported as having a profound impact on their future selves. Even though some of the ages in the following excerpts are out of the range of this chapter, four are quoted here serially in order to demonstrate the pervasive nature of such events and to discern clearly patterns integral to the experiences.

I was very small standing in an ice cream line. There was a crowd rather than a line, and I remember a man pushing himself against me. And I remember being afraid to say anything. And I remember just standing in that line and not even moving out of it. And the man was constantly pushing himself against me. I wonder if it was any more than that, like taking my hand and rubbing it on him. It might have been, because I remember feeling sort of petrified, and I didn't say a thing. My parents were waiting for me not far away in a car. They'd let me off to get the ice cream and come back to the car. And I didn't say anything to anybody, ever.

I realized what set up the ground rules and what set up my attitudes happened way before college. At 6, I was in first grade and I went to a movie and this man sat next to me in the movie, an adult. And his hand kept slipping into my lap, on my crotch, and on my thigh. And I kept excusing him. I would just move my leg and think, "Oh, that's an accident. If it happens again then I'll say something."

Here I am, 6 years old, and this horrible man is sitting by me and his hand keeps falling. And I said to myself, "Okay, if it happens five more times, then I'm going to say something." Again. Again. Squeezing my thigh, his hand falling into my lap. It went on for an hour. Finally, I leaned forward to my sister, who was right next to me, who was 2 years older, she was 8, and I said, "Kathy," and I screeched, and he just got up and left. Kathy went for the manager, and he called our parents, and they came down. Nothing was said, you know. It was just, "Okay, now we have to go home."

When I was 9, some gardeners came to plant ivy. And I went out to the garage to get some milk from the refrigerator, and there was this old man drinking in the garage. He got into a conversation with me and was telling me how pretty I was. And I'm thinking, "Yeah, right." You know, I was really plain with this little boyish hairdo, and I didn't feel pretty at all. He was asking me if I had a boyfriend, and all this sort of sexual innuendo talk. And then he sort of motioned me over to the corner of the garage. He hugged me and he french kissed me and he rubbed his groin against me. I'm sitting there, completely disgusted, being polite because he's an adult and thinking, "Well, gosh, I don't want to be rude."

He was being very rude. But I was really freaked and I said to him, "I'm going to go in the house now and put on some shorts, and I'll be right back." Like, I'm going to slip into something more comfortable. Because I was savvy even then to know that this would be good; he would like that. So I went in the house, and I locked the door.

I completely freaked out. My sister helped me, and called my mother. She comes home, and a big to-do is made. You know, looking in my eyes and sobbing, "What did he do to you? What did he do to you?" And I didn't even want to say it. I said, "He just kissed me, that's all." And I tried to make it seem like nothing, no big deal. Well, he got fired.

And that had a profound effect on me and my sexuality and self-esteem. For many years I never enjoyed kissing, until I was in college. I never went through that teenage stage where it was fun to kiss. The really horrible thing about it, I thought he was going to come back and murder me.

I used to ride on a bus to go to Sunday School. I was con-firmed when I was 14, maybe I was 13. I would go to my temple for pre-confirmation classes. I remember during one period of time a man started to appear on the bus. He would sit down next to me, and he would take my hand and put it on him.

I pretended that nothing happened. I would talk to him dur-ing this, and he would be talking about anything that was not related to sex. This happened on so many occasions I don't even remember how many. And I didn't tell anybody. I was so hor-rified and maybe ashamed, and there was no way to talk about it. And I would just be happy when the bus stop came and I had to get off. But I wouldn't tell anybody about it.

One striking theme that threads through these experiences and countless like them is the girls' *silence*. Girl after girl, woman after women, *tells no one of her experience*. There are several different parts to the internal explanations of why not. One is a disbelief in the event itself, a doubt of the girl's own perception. In tandem with this is a desire to not make the event real, to keep it to oneself, to disassociate oneself from the experience, to not have to acknowledge its existence. Fear is also a large factor in the silence. In addition, generally, girls and even grown women do not perceive that they have any-one to tell. If they do not fully believe it themselves, no one else will surely, and there is, in their minds, after all nothing to be done about it anyway.

All of these reasons and more have solid bases in reality. They were learned, not created by the females who found themselves in these situations. Nevertheless, they, taken to-gether and in their implications, form a significant portion of another important and lifelong trend of girls and women that will be run up against time and time again in this book and in women's lives. This is the theme of the tacit *collusion* of women in the cultural system that is biased against them. Girls' and women's silence, their letting things happen and letting things go by unacknowledged, abetting events in certain cases, following the mode of operation that does not seek to name and correct situations, all contribute to collusive forces. Female collusion is an important buttress to the gender bias in our culture, and it creates a vicious cycle that calls out for understanding in order for it to be broken.

One factor that abets collusion is the generation of guilt. This guilt is part of an *internalization* process. If it is the girl's doing, then the perpetrator is not responsible, and the event, perceived as an affront, is less real. If the man was someone close to the girl, he can, by means of the guilt and internalization process, remain a special person in her life. If it is her own doing, even indirectly, then in this way of thinking, she can also take steps to avoid such incidents in the future. In other words, guilt is a way to maintain a semblance of control over one's own self and autonomy. It creates a false sense of security.

Internalization is a process that continues to evolve throughout most girls' and women's lives. In their young years, internalization may absorb incidents of sexual abuse, classroom issues involving the stereotyping of girls, and family issues such as the clear precedence a brother may take in the parents' minds. Internalization is a process that operates on a general or social level. Like the psychological concept of identification with the aggressor, when applied to the issue of gender bias, internalization is a process whereby a female adopts as her own the prevailing evaluation and expectations of females, of the existing hierarchical social structure, and of female–male interaction. As girls grow up, this process adapts to many situations, as is examined in the following chapters. And in adult years, it continues to be employed to fit a variety of situations.

Internalization leads to two conflicting responses that most women incorporate simultaneously and continuously: personalization and invisibility. *Personalization* operates at the individual, idiosyncratic level. It is a state of mind in which a female believes that the actually biased behavior, decisions, and evaluations of oneself are the result of her own competence, ability, actions, and behavior. She believes that the treatment she receives is deserved, that it is due to her own actions, and that she thus holds the responsibility for it. The tendency to personalize fits well into the following pattern of thought: because the problems for women have supposedly been eradicated, any and all failings, slipups, and setbacks must be individual. Whether the situation concerns not making it into an advanced course in high school, making remarks and writing papers in college courses that are received coolly at best, being dissuaded from certain career paths within a profession, or not getting that promotion one felt one deserved, each becomes construed as personal, whether it is or not.

Invisibility also operates at the individual level and is, in some respects, the flip side of personalization. As a result both of the internalization process in which a female will receive a certain amount of responses and other behavior toward her simply due to the shape of her genitals and not because of anything specific to herself, and the common female experience of one's own behavior passing largely unrecognized, females are led to feel insignificant, perhaps without real existence. That is, one not only has no responsibility in this state of mind but also virtually no dimension at all. A female may feel invisible, as invisible and malleable as the fashion in which she was treated assumes she is. Her desires and needs are overridden to the extreme, to the point where she may feel as though she does not exist or does not have the right to exist in her own right. She may, as a result, have trouble clearly delineating the boundaries between herself and others, particularly males. Because girls and women receive little attention in general, and receive affirmation for staying contained, quiet, and small in myriad ways, they often suffer the feeling of nonexistence. A symptom of this feeling of invisibility among teenagers is the struggle for self-assertion and control over one's integrity and destiny. Another key time when this state arises forcefully is when a woman enters into marriage and finds her life subsumed by her spouse's. This is such an ingrained pattern in our culture that it would probably occur if the bride were the President of the United States. Again, in the professional realm, women's work and achievements can be treated so marginally as to also create the disconcerting feeling of non-existence or invisibility.

The internalization process also leads to *ambivalence*, which is expressed on many dimensions. A female could feel ambivalent about the sort of attention that is actually sexual abuse, although she would not have that name for it. On the one hand, she is singled out and special. She is getting attention, which she may crave. But, of course, on the other hand, she also knows that this is not an appropriate or desirable form of attention. She is also likely to experience ambivalence and confusion over the question of self-determination and control. She cannot quite elect either to have or to lack this power fully. This situation is likely to lead her into an obsessive search for control in her life, resulting in a sad and paradoxical condition such as anorexia nervosa.

Ambivalence is a theme song that runs through girls' and women's lives. The ambivalence in the face of our biased culture is felt with regard to many different factors. Because women receive far less recognition than men for comparable achievements, sometimes any attention feels welcome, even sexist attention. A vulgar comment on the street can feel better than no attention to some women. A biased remark couched in the language of a joke can make the girl or woman feel accepted on some level. The reason is that the attention confirms the woman's existence; it outwardly recognizes her presence. From this also comes the ambivalence, since these are not the sorts of recognition one dreams of. Usually, a raging internal battle ensues that never reaches the public domain.

The woman must struggle, even if for the most part only tacitly, with whether to let an offending incident lie but at the cost of sacrificing part of her personal integrity, or whether to break in and protest in some fashion, thereby running the serious risk of being viewed as a humorless shrew and facing further ostracization.

Another compounding factor that becomes relevant even in preschool is socioeconomic status. Suppose that Emily and her family belong to the lower economic class, and her nursery school group is economically mixed. Emily would be likely to come to feel the differences between her and her more affluent peers. She may not have the right toys or in fact have few toys of her own. Her friend's home may have a playroom, whereas Emily's family squeezes itself into a tiny apartment. She may need to go hungry on certain days, not being able to bring a lunch to school; she just sits and watches her classmates eat during snack period. These are hardships enough in themselves, but when combined with a growing sense of being a member of the lower gender class, a whopping blow is dealt to a sense of oneself as worthy and entitled. In later years, this impact accumulates to reach greater proportions and at a more sophisticated level. In this case, the issues of internalization, ambivalence, personalization, and invisibility come to the fore.

Here are the elements of the gender framework that emerge at this stage:

GF 6.   Boys are entitled to take up space of all kinds; girls must defer.
GF 7.   Boys and girls are divided and in conflict.
GF 8.   Boys are loud and active; girls are channeled toward quiet, neat, and attentive behavior.

Added to this framework are six themes in girls' and women's lives that are prevalent enough to single out here:

Theme 1. Girls checking each other out as a method of
dominance, submission, exclusion, *and*, most
important, disassociation or disdain of other females, together with dissatisfaction with oneself

Theme 2. Tacit female collusion in the system that is biased
against them

Theme 3. Internalization

Theme 4. Personalization

Theme 5. Invisibility

Theme 6. Ambivalence

GENDER ACTION

In the preschool years it is appropriate to question what the
nursery institutions and teachers in particular can do to help
secure gender equity. Here, again, as in the home, small
changes would go a long way.

If Emily's teachers modified their use of language in the
manner outlined in the previous chapter, the influence would
be felt, not just on one family of kids but on a whole classroom full, and the same benefits would be reaped on a larger
scale. Moreover, the impact on teachers', and thus implicitly
the children's, awareness would be far reaching, as the words
of this pre-school director attest:

*We [staff] consciously work on saying "she" for doctors. . . .
What's more subtle and ingrained are statements like, "I need
someone strong, John . . ." We work instead on saying something like "Who feels they're strong?"*

As a corollary, schools can be judicious in the selection of
new books, posters, and other educational materials for the
classroom. In preschool, the books are mostly picture books

with simple story lines. They virtually all have lead male characters. Yet, other books do exist. Early childhood books with strong or leading female characters still remain few and far between, but there are now enough of them to comprise half the library of any preschool.

Similarly, the songs taught to the children can be selected with greater care. Most of the old songs could remain, as long as others are added that sing tales with female characters as well. There is also no reason that some songs such as "Old MacDonald" could not be modified. Since there is nothing intrinsic to the song that requires the farmer to be male, imagine the far-flung future consequences if teachers sang it thus, "On her farm she had a . . ." Or, what would happen if the game "Simon Says" became "Sarah Says."

Finally, teachers could subtly try to undermine the budding divisiveness along gender lines they see, and often foster, in their classrooms. They could stop splitting the group by sex for activities. Instead, they could encourage girls and boys to play together, and they could try to direct boys to the more typically girls' activities and vice versa. Teachers could also, gently and using an age-appropriate vocabulary, discuss gender when it comes up in the course of the children's play.

These changes and redirections suggested in this section are simple and do not place additional financial burdens on already pressed schools. Nevertheless, this does not mean that they will be implemented easily. Much of what is required may go against the grain of teachers' way of thinking and acting, even when, in principle, they agree with the methods and the objective. In order to institute the changes, teachers may need to undergo a period of self-consciousness and reflection. They too will benefit from this process that widens gender roles, emerging as stronger persons and thereby stronger teachers as well.

The new corrective actions from this chapter are the following:

GA 3. Select or modify classroom materials including songs and games so that they are gender balanced.

GA 4. Encourage respect and play among girls and boys in school.

EXERCISE 2

Girls and women often incorporate other people's desires into their own concept of the world. In order to address this tendency, try the following three steps:

1. For two weeks, whenever you are confronted with a choice, pause, count to five, and ask yourself, what do I want? Give yourself enough time to thoroughly consider a serious answer to this question, no matter how small the decision seems.

2. At the end of the two weeks, examine the results. Try to recognize how successful you were in choosing what you actually want rather than what someone else wants you to want or what you think you're supposed to want. Try to determine what sorts of decisions were most difficult to make independently, and continue working on making conscious deliberate choices in those areas.

3. If there is a toddler in your life, allow her the space to make as many decisions for herself as is feasible. Try to expand the realm of choices open to her. In this way, she'll develop the mental habit early of allowing herself to discover what she wants in a situation.

4 ELEMENTARY SCHOOL: NORMATIVE GENDER ROLES GEL

THE BASICS

When Emily enters elementary school at 5 years old, her conception of gender is pretty well entrenched, and she tries to emulate the stereotypically female model. She has Barbie dolls and several Polly Pockets, two marketing concepts that have captured much of the cultural conception of femininity. Emily loves to dress up with nail polish, lipstick, and her mother's high heels. She even has her own kiddy make-up kit.

Much of the same issues that were present in her preschool crop up again in Emily's elementary school years, but this time with more intensity. For example, the books take on new significance as Emily begins to read them herself, poring over the words and pictures time and time again. Almost every one of these books contains substantial gender stereotypes, and because of the repetition of reading them in the process of learning to read and write, their underlying messages become well entrenched in Emily's and her classmates' minds.

In a tacit fashion, Emily is continuing to learn that she and her girlfriends are rewarded for their neatness and orderliness and for looking cute or pretty. She is expected to be able to learn to spell and read with relative ease. She is subtly and often less subtly channelled to play at being mommy, or to do pretend or real cooking, or to engage in such activities as braiding hair and jumping rope. She is also learning that boys receive more attention and are allowed and even often encouraged to be loud, rambunctious, and tough. The boys are expected to lag behind the girls in reading, writing, and fine motor skills.

The boys spend a good deal of their outdoor time learning and playing sports, such as soccer and baseball. Somehow, even during the youngest primary school years, the girls do not get to play these games. When the girls do engage in physical activity, whether at home or at school, they are likely to hear immediate admonishments not to hurt themselves. Many of these implicit gender lessons are highlighted for Emily when her younger brother enters the same elementary school. She ingests the fact that the rough-and-tumble aggressive behavior that she would be scolded for, he is rewarded for. One girl who was interviewed recalled her puzzlement at the growing division between girls' and boys' activities:

I didn't understand why girls and boys couldn't play together and do the same things. As you grow older, things separate, or you're supposed to separate. And you're supposed to be doing one thing or the other. And I just didn't understand why people were separating. Or why, as a girl, you couldn't do these things because you'd look funny or get hurt.

It is all right for Emily's brother to chip a tooth or bruise himself; that is part of his life. But, because for Emily, a girl, her appearance is so pervasively important, she must preserve her body and not engage in the amount of physical risk taking that sports engender. And her brother is almost never asked to sit still and concentrate on a book or learning to write letters the way it was just assumed Emily can and will do.

In the upper grades, when the kids start to learn about specific subjects such as American history, literature, and science, there is at best scant mention of women as active members of any field, whether by teachers, texts, or posters on the wall. Marie Curie is one of the only exceptions to this gross omission.

Emily is also exposed to some other gender-related agendas as she moves along through her primary school years. By the time she is 7 and in second grade, she has a well-defined image of the "ideal" female body. Much of this was learned from dolls such as Barbie, television, and magazine pictures of fashion models. Some of it was learned in school and at home from friends, teachers, parents, and, perhaps most significantly, from her teenage babysitters who are all female.

Emily is in fact of average weight and is a nice-looking girl. Yet, by nine or ten years old her own image of herself is of a fat, ugly hippopotamus. She is on a diet, knows something about counting calories, and wishes her straight brown hair were strawberry blond and curly. Throughout the summer months she pours lemon juice on her hair and bakes it (along with the rest of her body) in the sun, hoping to lighten it. At night, she braids her wet hair to achieve a wavy look. If her mother would only let her, Emily would, by the age of 9, willingly sit for hours in a hair salon having her hair dyed and permed.

As it is, Emily has refused on more than one occasion to go to school without the right look. When she was younger, this right look consisted of having and wearing the appropriate kind and number of hair clips, as she advanced to second grade it became needing to wear the same sort of clothing as her girl friends, and later in elementary school Emily's fashion requirements became stylistic, such as the proper tightness to her jeans, a certain kind of school bag slung in a studied manner over her shoulder, and so on. The motivation of this readiness to conform is the terror with which Emily looks at the school day if she cannot attend properly clothed and outfitted. Putting aside issues of economic class for the moment, at the very beginning of elementary school, Emily has already incorporated a large chunk of what constitutes being female in America: that appearance is vastly more important than thoughts or actions, and that what appearance is is determined by consumer marketing, the brain child of a largely male-dominated industry based on sexist and outmoded assumptions about girls and women.

During these years, gender divisions become more and more defined. The chasm created between girls and boys invades all aspects of life and colors how young minds see and will see the world. Thus, there is a powerful normative element to the perception of gender roles that causes those who do not neatly fit the categories, even down to minute details, to question themselves, as this young girl's query shows:

I sort of feel like sometimes it's a balancing act. Feeling feminine or feeling like a woman, and also doing the things you like to do, if it's active or sports or wearing a baseball cap or whatever, and balancing those two sides. When I was really young like 6, I loved to play with Barbies and I loved to climb trees. I would go in the woods and run around and find salamanders, and things like that with my friend who was a boy. And with my friend who was a girl, I played Barbies. I loved to do both. And I remember asking my mother about it. I said, "Mom, is there something wrong with me, that I like to do both these things?"

In addition, a virtual war between the sexes begins to brew in the early years of elementary school. In Emily's classroom it started in kindergarten with the boys-push-the-girls "game." This is typically the way the seeds of war are planted. It is the beginning of what will become, by junior high, outright peer harassment. The evolution is from pushing to pushing, pull-ing, and jabbing. It may begin to be called a war of boys against the girls by second grade. The boys are likely to take sly slugs and swipes at the girls, to pull their hair, and to put dead frogs and mice and the like in girls' cubbies. Girls in turn are more likely to lodge quieter, less violent forms of attack or retribu-tion. They might write mean notes about the boys or attempt to solicit the teacher's aid in fighting the boys. The girls are generally the losers, and this fact is well known to the girls even as they are in the midst of battle. It also becomes part of the objective of the game.

By first grade, Emily and her friends already have a bud-ding awareness and curiosity about sex. This often begins by hearing older kids and peers use such words as "fuck" and "sex," without having any idea what they mean. Slowly, peers "explain" or at least define, for the time being, their mean-ings. The definitions typically include a lesson in female pas-sivity, such as that "sex is something that boys do to girls." By the end of elementary school, Emily and her peers are likely to feel the pressure to be interested romantically and sexually in members of the opposite sex. In addition, a deeper antago-nism, the seeds of which have been germinating from birth, may blossom. The war between the sexes comes into its own at about this time, ready to blow up in girls' faces at the com-mencement of junior high.

GENDER LESSONS

Much of the gender lessons of elementary school are more sophisticated versions of those Emily already learned in pre-school. Now Emily can read and write and knows a great deal about the world and its history. She thus has a more complex view of the female's role in society. Her view will at this point be defined largely by an absence, whether it be in American history, science, or literature. Emily is learning that boys and men are the heroes and girls and women are generally the helpers. This lesson may be taught in school with regard to sports, to history, for example, concerning battles and wars, or in domestic and foreign affairs and politics. Thus, Emily is already, in a significant sense, being tracked in terms of her future potential and life goals. Her imagination and self-perception are hampered. Consider this mother's story:

I was driving my 7-year-old to school, and we were talking about her sister's strong personality. When I made the offhand remark that one day she'll probably be President, I was wholly unprepared for my daughter's response. She asked, incredulous, "Mom, can women be Presidents?"

I was so taken aback by the depth of her surprise that I didn't know how to respond. I merely stuttered out an indignant, "Of course."

With the early indoctrination that girls receive at home and at school, it becomes virtually impossible for Emily to imagine without a sense of confusion a woman as a physicist, neurosurgeon, or metallurgist. It will take a sustained effort at retraining her mental imagery to change this perception. As a corollary, Emily cannot picture *herself* in any of these professions. She can, however, easily see herself excelling in any one of the traditionally female roles.

A great deal of inner conflict arises in the minds of the girls from this hidden curriculum. On the one hand, Emily may be genuinely thrilled by the chemistry experiments she performs in sixth grade or may be fascinated with the ideas of military strategy. On the other, somewhere near the surface of her thought processes, Emily knows that her involvement with such subjects are likely to be only peripheral, such as being an assistant to a chemist or perhaps secretary to a war general. This knowledge is constantly being reinforced by the very set-up that teachers create inside the school walls. Emily may indeed be assigned to take notes and read measurements while two boys from her class conduct a scientific experiment, for example. The class may act out a historical or even hypothetical event, and she may be relegated to playing the President's wife. She would not be assigned the part of the President, for example, since this just does not come naturally to the teacher nor to the students. She is evolving the concomitant view, however subconscious it is at this stage, that a great deal of her importance and stature will consist in her physical appearance and the males to which she attaches herself.

GENDER COMPOUNDS

Suppose that Emily's school has a strong computer or science program and also a sports program that figures centrally in the life of the school. All of these are likely to be programs from which Emily is, to varying degrees, effectively barred or discouraged. Such exclusion has both immediate and future consequences for girls. In the case of sports, for example, the myriad ways that girls are kept off the field or are allowed on only grudgingly deprive them of the strengthened confidence that results from mastery of a game. They are deprived of an excellent opportunity to learn and practice team activity and cooperation, and they are deprived of physical competence. All of these aspects of sports, which girls still all too rarely are able to participate in, breed confidence in oneself. Instead, girls express the following sorts of experience with the sports programs at their schools:

I went out for the soccer team, I thought that would be fun, but I was the only girl. That turned me off and I didn't go back. And that's too bad, that that stopped me from doing something.

In gym class if a boy did like a girl would, the teacher would say something like, "What are you doing?" But if a girl did it he'd say, "Oh good job, you're trying hard."

I was playing hockey with the guys and I'm scoring. I made a small mess up, and this guy says, "It had to be a girl. It had to be a girl." One little thing I did wrong. I got so mad I hit him in the face with the hockey stick [frenetic piercing laughter from the other girls in the room].

The gym teacher would make lists, with girls on one side plus the two boys who weren't athletic, and the rest of the boys on the other side of the gym playing floor hockey.

I got really upset and said, "This is ridiculous. First of all you ostracized these guys and put them with us, and you give us the bad hockey sticks and the bad side of the gym. Last year we all played together and it worked out fine." She said, "What happened was I put all the aggressive players on one side and all the nonaggressive people on the other. So that nobody would get hurt."

Then she changed it, and she tried to split us up by basketball and aerobics. It wasn't even real aerobics; it was Jane Fonda, versus a full court basketball game. One girl said, "I'm going to play basketball; I don't like aerobics." So we walked over, and the teacher said, "Okay, no more full court game; everyone just shoot baskets." Because we were there she didn't want to have a full court game. I just gave up and didn't say anything. It's so frustrating.

Assume further that Emily goes to many movies in her elementary years and is exposed to and becomes more conscious of advertising. However bad the role models in her readers in school are, movies tend to be worse. The pervasive Walt Disney movies are notorious not only for their racism but also for their horrific female roles. Yet, Emily and her friends are encouraged in a variety of ways to watch these films time and again. Even shows such as the 1995 *Big Apple Circus* contain repeated messages about female passivity, sexual and otherwise. The message of *The Nutcracker*, a classic that many American girls are exposed to holiday season after holiday season from 5 years old through puberty, is a lesson in gender identity, as discussed at the beginning of this part. Girls learn young what the cultural norms are and to subscribe to them as closely as possible. One woman saw this clearly as she reflected on her youth:

The immediate thing that comes to mind is ping-pong. That it was very bad to win at sports if you are a girl. Sometimes I would not win if I was playing with a boy because then they wouldn't like me.

Emily's conception of gender is constantly reinforced and embellished through advertising, such as when household products are clearly being pitched by and to women. Advertising goes beyond mere reinforcement at this age, however. Much of advertising, such as even for cars and sports equipment, consists of the promotion and definition of sexuality, particularly female sexuality. Because Emily is likely to be just beginning to come to grips with her sexuality by the end of elementary school, the ads and commercials that she sees may be consumed whole. The endless ads with high-fashion models, replete with parted, pouting, blood-red lips, eyes closed, choker collar neck bands, and clothing slit open from every angle, can play a highly formative role in Emily's development. The subliminal message that sexiness consists of appearing dead or passive, thin to the point of frail, bonded, tightly clothed, spike heeled, and with elongated lacquered finger and toe nails becomes incorporated into Emily's own beliefs. Conversely, the media presentation of beauty and sexuality becomes a standard against which Emily measures herself and her success. And, she will always fail in such comparisons. No matter how thin and how painted she becomes, she will never have the back-up of high-fashion advertising. At the same time, conflicts may arise in Emily's mind over the tacit recognition that much of achieving the right look is uncomfortable, inconvenient, and demeaning. Because of the peculiar sort of focus on women's appearance endemic to contemporary culture, it becomes difficult to draw the line between healthy body building, and, say, excessive exercising. This is a quandary that does not arise for boys.

The further supposition that Emily is a member of a racial minority yields another compounding factor. In such a case, she would likely receive even less attention and encouragement from her teachers. Her teachers would probably assume that she is less bright and less capable than were she white. In addition, Emily might be teased by her peers. The racism of their parents might come hurling out of their mouths, directed at Emily. Racism in conjunction with sexism provides powerful messages to Emily that she in turn will incorporate into her own self-perception. Somewhere deep inside, Emily at times feels that much of the derision is true and applies to her personally. As a female member of a racial minority, Emily will perceive an even smaller set of future options for herself than would her white counterpart.

There are three additions to the gender framework from this chapter:

GF 9.   Intellectual and public achievement are a largely male province.

GF 10. The war between the sexes is a backdrop to everyday life, and the girls are supposed to lose.

GF 11. Sports are for boys; girls need to take care of themselves and not get hurt.

The theme that emerges in the developmental phase is one that has a lasting, daily impact on most girls and women.

Theme 7. Physical appearance above all else

GENDER ACTION

The remedial actions recommended for the preschool staff can be used in elementary school as well to great and lasting effect. In later grades, the staff can include girls and boys equally in all programs. This goes for sports, science, and mathematics as much as for painting, reading, cooking, and games. Teachers can make greater efforts to teach and insist upon cooperation, particularly between the sexes. In elementary schools, teachers and administrations can begin to provide a more realistic picture of history, the sciences, and the arts with regard to women and women's contributions.

At home, parents can begin to talk with their children about gender roles and, if it becomes appropriate, about the varied forms of sexuality and the limitations of media images of it. Parents can continue to strive for an egalitarian structure in the home and to discuss the stereotypical portrayals found on television and in the movies. Parents can reinforce the inner strength and character of their daughters, and not let a surface emphasis on appearance, lowered self-esteem, or the expression of gendered limitations pass without discussion.

An important concept for parents to begin to think through is that of parent–child rituals. Every family has them, and they differ depending on the sex of the child. Parent–son rituals tend to be oriented toward future achievements, whether in sports or widening future options. Parent–daughter rituals tend to focus on appearance and so-called beauty issues. They are often lessons in preening more than anything else. Taking a look at the rituals in place within a household gives insight into the gender imbalances at play. Creating new rituals that enhance a girl's chances for self-determination and success is one of the most valuable efforts a parent can make.

For example, kindergarten has become the first step into learning and a real measure of budding independence. A ritual for girls celebrating this phase could help set up a strong and positive attitude about this entry into the world. Some sort of celebration and acknowledgement that a daughter has reached this stage, whether it be a little party, a special dessert, or a bedtime conversation, would convey the message that the girl is valuable, that she can strive for excellence, that her accomplishments in school matter, and that she is not merely a future clothes rack.

The new gender actions derived from this chapter are as follows:

GA 5. Secure equal inclusion of girls and boys in all subjects and sports.
GA 6. Include women's achievement in the actual curriculum.
GA 7. Create play time with kids that debunks gender stereotypes.
GA 8. Begin parent–child discussions of sex and sexuality, at least by the time it becomes a subject among peers.
GA 9. Begin parent–child discussions of gender roles.

Ritual 1. Celebration of entry into kindergarten

EXERCISE 3: THE TEN-SECOND BARBIE MAKEOVER

Another move that especially parents, but teachers as well, can make at this point is to take emblems of stereotypical female gender identity and turn them around. Barbie, for example. Why does she have to be considered a bimbo? Granted, her appearance does not promote a healthy attitude about oneself in girls. Yet, in many ways, for the time being, Barbie is a fact of life for many of our nation's girls. Thus, why not put her to work?

Using Barbie as a tool of change is not difficult. Create games that include Barbie playing sports and winning, for example. Build a Barbie-sized baseball diamond in the dirt and have her play hard. Play an imaginary game with Barbies in which

Barbie is a scientist or a mathematician or an expert in mining and minerals. Why not? Play games with Barbie in which she engages in assertive, self-determined behavior and words.

Do not let her frilly attire or heel-ready feet affect what she says or does: make it irrelevant. If Barbie must play bride to Ken's groom, then have her do the asking and make sure she gets an agreement with Ken about mutual respect and independence, have them split the housework, and have Barbie enjoy at least as satisfying a career as Ken's. Just because Barbie has been manufactured and marketed to fit and encourage a certain mindset doesn't mean we need to keep her stuck there for good.

5   JUNIOR HIGH:
YEARS OF TRANSITION

THE BASICS

In junior high school, Emily's budding social awareness as a girl begins to bloom. The social aspect of school comes to the fore. After eight years in school with gender-segregated play, all of a sudden girls and boys become interested in each other. Concomitant with this trend is also a rise in the hostility between the sexes and an evaporation of the few existing friendships and simple exchanges between girls and boys. As one student observed about her own evolving social role:

The boys would come over to us at lunch time and play Frisbee or something. I'd want to play Frisbee with them, and people would make fun of me because I wasn't sitting around flirting; I was actually just playing.

Another student mourned the new attitudes she confronted:

At 11, a friend and I swam together at the Y. Everyone used to tease us that we were boyfriend–girlfriend and all this. We used to tell people we were brother and sister so it was okay for us to hang out together. Then no one would make fun of us. I'd hear, 'Oh, is he your boyfriend?' I would answer, 'No, he's a friend that's a boy.' That's what I used to say when we couldn't convince people we were brother and sister anymore.

Emily herself begins to pay even more attention to her appearance and clothing, and her whole family teases her about how long it takes her to get out of the bathroom in the morning and to get dressed before school. Becoming the target of family jokes exacerbates her mounting anxiety about how she looks and her changing body. Emily's breasts have begun to grow, and she feels the need to succumb to peer pressure and wear a bra. She has hung around outside lingerie stores a couple of times, trying to muster the nerve to go in and try on bras. Emily has also, on several occasions, tried to bring up the subject with her sister, who has been wearing bras for over a year, but her mouth has fallen silent each time. Girls quickly learn during this period of change to curtail their behavior, as one student clearly observes:

They were too busy trying to look pretty. If you start playing sports you might be put in a spot where you don't look that attractive. Or you might look clumsy, or you might ruin your hair or something.

Emily and her friends use up a large portion of mental space on issues stemming from the self consciousness that has arisen from their new bodies and the public response to them. They begin to learn, if they have not done so already, to count calories and monitor their food intake even if they are not officially on diets. They are beginning to be concerned about how they sit and try to make sure to have their legs crossed because this appears to them to be the mature way to sit. When ambulatory, Emily has her mind half the time on how her hips are moving and what someone on the street might make of it. She experiments with trying to learn to walk completely straight, walking with a small sway, and attempting what she thinks is a more sophisticated wiggle. Emily also begins to wonder about how sexually provocative she might be. Her walk, her clothes, her smile, her comportment—nothing escapes scrutiny from this vantage point, as if other people's reactions to her are her own responsibility. And superimposed on this growing framework of self-consciousness is a budding sense that, because she is female, because she may be provocative, perhaps she is not safe out alone, particularly at night. Feelings of dependence on a male presence begin to surface and are supported by the tendencies of her parents, friends, and the community.

Emily is not sure why the physical changes taking place so intimidate her to the point where she cannot ask for help. Perhaps it is in part because so much is happening at once. Her pubic hair is darkening and thickening, and virtually every day Emily checks herself, thinking that she has started to menstruate. Moreover, every person to whom she could turn seems to have a demand about her budding female body. Her peers want her to emerge in full maturity as a finished package. The knowledge they seem to Emily to have is intimidatingly much as compared with what Emily feels she understands at the moment. She does not want to be caught asking "dumb" questions. Her sister is not the comforting type, and she does not appear to be forthcoming with advice. It never once occurred to Emily to turn to her mother, and in turn, her mother has not broached any of these subjects with her on her own accord.

At the same time, Emily has started to grapple seriously with questions about sex and sexuality. These are areas that are even more murky from Emily's vantage point than are her bodily transformations. Emily begins to flirt and be flirted with. Boys taunting girls is also on the rise at this time. Out on the schoolgrounds, Emily's developing breasts are grabbed and pinched a few times. She overhears the boys talking about "fast girls," and the girls gossip about the boys—whom they have crushes on and which boys just want sex. Emily's reaction to the taunting is governed by ambivalence. On the one hand, in a confused fashion, she feels that something is amiss, but on the other, she is flattered by the attention and craves more. This is not because Emily is a weak or insecure person. Rather, it is because so much in our society and her local environment act together to ensure that girls of Emily's age have a hard time sorting through and differentiating among the different kinds of attention they receive from boys.

As the 1992 report, *How Schools Shortchange Girls*, documents, junior high school can also be a pivotal educational phase for girls. This is the period in which girls' schoolwork typically begins to suffer. Their self-esteem and future aspirations begin to plummet precipitously while boys' self-confidence and aspirations soar. Emily begins to feel incompetent at math and science and loses interest in both. Emily speaks up little in her classes, even the ones she likes and does well in, and hesitates before each time she raises her hand. She second-guesses herself and is reluctant to put forth her ideas. She is interrupted often and accepts this as a mark of her lack of competence and poor mastery of the subject. She begins to focus less and less on classes and more and more on social activities planned for after three o'clock.

Hesitant patterns of speech inside the classroom and out are a hallmark of adolescent girls that can become a lifelong habit of self-deprecation. These speech patterns usually go by unnoticed as normal, but the following girl was well aware of her own behavior and that of her peers:

Girls, when they got up would talk, but, they talk the ways girls talk using reassurance words like "kinda," "I think I sorta," "maybe." But guys got up and went out attacking everybody, an immediate difference. Guys seem to really do things without looking back.

Two other girls also remarked,

When I hit sixth-seventh grade, girls started saying, "I don't know," and acting stupid. There is pressure for girls to act stupid. I know I definitely do it. Girls preface questions in class with "This might not be right but . . ." I do that. I don't see that from the boys.

When guys do something they seem to jump right into it with a lot of confidence. If they've made the decision, they'll go ahead and do it without looking back. A girl needs reassurance.

Just as in elementary school, the boys in Emily's class receive more attention and encouragement from the teachers. But now there is the added edge—that the subjects the students are being taught are treated as more serious, as precursors to high school and life beyond. So when Emily's involvement in school, particularly in the perceived hard subjects, wanes, this contributes to her feelings of inability and intellectual inferiority. And all of this is in spite of the fact that Emily's actual grades in school are good overall.

The teachers' differential treatment does not go by unnoticed by the girls, even if they are generally silent about it and end up eventually internalizing the teachers' behavior. Two students note,

This teacher would make girls smaller than they were. He'd condescend to them. He'd say, "Oh, you little . . . ," and touch her nose.

At shop class there were certain machines the teacher just never taught the girls how to use. He'd teach the guys, but never the girls. He'd say, "No, it's dangerous, and you really have to know what you're doing."

During this period, Emily may, for the first time, truly listen to the lyrics of popular music she and her friends have begun to play incessantly. Here the sexist and often misogynist messages may be taken to heart and incorporated unreflectively. Emily begins to fully recognize the structure of authority in her family, that her father earns the bulk of the money and determines how to spend it, and that he, in effect, makes most of the large decisions. In part, Emily is seeing this clearly now for the first time. Her father's presence is more evident at this juncture since he has become protective and demanding of her as she begins to go on dates with boys.

GENDER LESSONS

In junior high, Emily lets go of her entitlement to education almost entirely. In part because of the heavy emphasis on sports, science, and mathematics, from which girls remain largely excluded, girls' performance and achievements are placed far away, on the back burner in school. This trend can reach its first peak in the transition to junior high school. Junior high itself is a period of transition, from childhood to adulthood. Girls become disenfranchised from the educational process at this point and begin to learn to set lower sights of achievement for themselves.

In middle school we didn't read many female authors; we didn't read any really. My mom used to ask about it. She'd say, "Aren't there any female authors?" I think you have to go out of your way to read the books. And now in high school when we read something by a woman it's introduced as "Now we're going to read a book by a famous female author." When is a book ever introduced by, "Now we're going to read a book by a famous male author?"

Girls also begin to incorporate the lesson that they should not perform better than the boys if they also want to be attractive to them. As social roles come to the forefront, Emily learns to be deferential here too. She readily downsizes her mental capabilities and her self-determination. Junior high is one long lesson in the act of deference for Emily—in school, with friends, and at home.

GENDER COMPOUNDS

Suppose that it is as a young teenager in junior high that Emily first begins to experience street harassment: lewd or belittling comments and gestures directed at Emily from men on the street. It occasionally involves pinching, grabbing, and other touching, and it is often threatening. Emily is not scared by it so much as confused. Ambivalence concerning attention from males rears up again in this new context.

The internalization and personalization themes are also present in that Emily suspects and comes to believe that she has solicited this attention through her attire and demeanor. Maybe her sweater is too low-cut? Maybe she walked with a sway in her hips? Emily ponders such questions as she erases every trace of responsibility from the men. Eventually, when Emily begins to recognize that the attention is not personal and has nothing to do with her as such, she will also begin to feel invisible, as a merely convenient target present at the moment. Emily's already self-conscious teenage persona is amplified with the advent of this constant barrage of street attention. Emily's awareness of herself as female and the concomitant feelings of powerlessness are highlighted.

The beginning of a significant incidence of acquaintance rape occurs in junior high school. Suppose, for example, that Emily was raped by the older brother of a friend of hers when he was assigned by his parents to walk Emily home one evening. Chances are that Emily would not view it as rape and a crime so much as pressure to which she succumbed. She may even believe she brought it on herself or that she did not say no enough and did not fight him enough. Again, she takes on the burden of responsibility as she wrests it away from the male.

The aftermath of the rape, perhaps for the rest of Emily's life unless it is addressed head on, will likely be even lowered self-esteem and confidence. Emily may become more obsessive about her appearance and more self-conscious about her behavior. She will begin to second-guess herself with regularity. And in a deep sense, her views of female sexuality will become more muddled. Emily's feelings of personal integrity and entitlement will plummet further.

The additions to the gender framework, the themes, and trends found in this chapter are:

GF 12. Peer harassment, as an everyday occurrence, is a piece of the backdrop of life.

Theme 8. Masking one's intelligence to bolster boys'
Theme 9. Self-consciousness about appearance to the exclusion of all else

Trend 1. Lowered self-expectations
Trend 2. Lowered self-confidence
Trend 3. Opting out of sports, science, math, and computers

GENDER ACTION

Teachers and administrators in junior high schools can evolve strategies similar to those in elementary school. They can also pay special attention to making girls feel welcome in the classroom. This can be done by ensuring that every student has a voice in the classroom, that girls are encouraged to speak up, and that they are listened to and not interrupted. Their work and their achievements must be given equal attention to those of the boys.

Girls can be encouraged to try new things and take risks in their school work. Neatness, quietness, and deference should not be overemphasized within the school walls. Girls could be put at the helm in science labs and can be drawn into the computer room and onto the mathematics team. Girls must be allowed to play all sports and in fact encouraged to do so. Gender segregation can be dismantled, and again, cooperation put in its stead.

Parents can cultivate an atmosphere at home in which girls' academic achievement is important. They can do this in simple ways, by asking questions about their daughter's homework, encouraging her to take the subjects she's interested in a step further than what was covered in class, and by seeking out exhibits and events in the larger community that are stimulating and thought provoking. Sitting comfortably at home in the evening reading together can send a strong signal in itself.

Mothers and fathers could pay special attention at this point in time to their daughter's growing self-consciousness. They can make sure to discuss the emerging body shape that their daughter is experiencing and celebrate the transformation. One way to do this would be to create a family ritual to celebrate the onset of menstruation. It could be in the form of a family party, a special outing, or simply a set of warm comfortable exchanges between mother and daughter that affirm the joy of femininity.

At this age, Emily can begin to pull herself out of the confines of gender stereotyping. She can begin to look and listen critically at what she finds around her. She can set out on a path of self-determination that does not consist in swallowing gender norms whole. She can, for example, listen to the messages being conveyed through music, television, movies, and advertising and decide that she does not have to accept them for herself. She can decide that she may not want to be someone's "baby"; that her model of beauty can be other than gaunt, white, and blond; and that she can conceive of broader visions of adult femininity than those consisting virtually exclusively of the roles of mother, helper, and housekeeper. In short, Emily can learn the skills of taking control of her own life and ambitions, of taking the social, academic, and emotional space required to do so.

These additional actions and rituals are found in this chapter:

GA 10. Involve girls in sports as a matter of course.

GA 11. Involve girls in science, mathematics, and computers.

GA 12. Enhance the classroom environment so that girls participate freely.

GA 13. Give girls permission and encouragement to take risks.

GA 14. Assist the growth of self-confidence and self-determination through gentle encouragement of entitlement to make choices.

Ritual 2. Celebrate the onset and process of menstruation.

Ritual 3. Celebrate girls' academic achievement.

EXERCISE 4

1. Imagine yourself as encapsulated in a box that fits snugly around your body, but that can be expanded. Now, spread your arms sideway, front and back, upward, and diagonally to enlarge your imaginary box. Then push the box out in all directions with your legs. Move your body outward in any way you can in order to create the largest box possible. Stand back, and compare your initial box size with the one you ended up with.

2. For the next two weeks, take note of your "box size," and try to enlarge it comfortably. Notice your size in particular when you are seated in conversation. Find positions

that take up maximum box size. For example, shift from a legs-crossed, hands-folded position to putting your feet square on the floor, legs parallel, with your arms comfortably open.

3. Try steps (1) and (2) in tandem with a girl, and encourage each other to expand your "boxes."

6   HIGH SCHOOL:
      CONFORMING SEXUALITY

THE BASICS

High school is like a pressure cooker version of junior high, and it lasts longer. Female–male interaction looms larger than life. On the whole, girls and boys in high school strive even harder than before to conform to gender stereotypes and the prevailing sexual mores. This holds true even when an individual clearly does not fit them. Emily's previous dieting savvy is brought to the fore and intensified. At five feet, five inches tall, she strives to get her weight to under 100 pounds. In her second year of high school, she even makes a bet with her classmates that she can reach 99, from a more normal 116 pounds, by the big Halloween school dance. She leafs through magazines such as *Seventeen*, but finds them too childish. She heads straight for the more sophisticated, adult fashion magazines and tries to emulate the gaunt look of the models. Emily is fastidious about her clothing, donning brief miniskirts that she has sewn herself, tight scooped-neck leotards, lycra blouses, and the like.

Among her peers, the hostility between the sexes begins to take on a sexual nature in high school. The vocabulary of the put-downs has broadened and almost always contains an allusion to sex or sexuality. Boys scribble on walls what specific girls have done and have had done to them sexually, while girls are scribbling about which boys are cute and which are rapists. Boys now grab the girls around the waist or on the breasts. They walk up behind them and whisper lewd comments or suggestions in their ears. The prevailing ethos is that boys just want sex and that they should get it and that girls who want sex rather than a relationship are bad and whorish.

When Emily begins dating, she eats little in the presence of boys, opting to binge after a date at home in the safe and private confines of her family's kitchen. She is very much aware of which boys are interested in her, and this has an influence on whom she, in turn, is interested in. Emily does not become sexually active until the beginning of her third year in high school. She has nevertheless felt the pressure to have sex from her girlfriends dating to the end of junior high. Emily's breasts developed slower than her friends' or, at least, so it seemed to her. It also appeared that Emily's friends had more vast and intimate knowledge of sex than she did. Emily herself was not motivated to have sex; she was not yet particularly interested in her own sexuality, or in boys qua dates and objects of sexual desire. But by her junior year the peer pressure was too great, and a senior boy showered her with attention. Emily asked her friends about contraception and subsequently had the boy procure condoms. She then began having sex with him.

The two of them became an "item" at school and were treated as an established couple. From her new boyfriend, Emily learned what the inside gossip was amongst the boys about herself. She learned they had all taken her to be a lesbian because she had shown so little interest in boys. She learned that her so-called boyfriend himself had started to focus his attention on her as a result of a bet he had placed with some of the boys that he could "break" her, make her straight, and get her to have sex with him. At first, Emily was furious, but after some consideration she concluded that the two know each other, like each other, and respect each other enough to go beyond such a bad beginning.

Much of her boyfriend's ideas about sex came from his father and from his friends. He would ask or command Emily to try new things that she, very vaguely, felt were demeaning to her. These feelings were somehow tossed aside in the name of assuming, rather than experiencing, that sexual activity is fun and desirable and the acceptance that it is what people do. In addition, her newly forged sexual alliance brought many benefits in her social circle. She was much more wholeheartedly accepted and even revered now, although she had not been unpopular before. Her status had definitely been elevated.

Throughout her high-school years, Emily also had crushes on two of her teachers, one male and one female. But when it became clear that the male history teacher with whom Emily was infatuated felt for her reciprocally, her fantasy life took off. This teacher gave her extra attention in her schoolwork and spent many after-school hours with her discussing her term papers and other assignments. History was a subject Emily truly excelled at, and the extra and double-sided attention from her teacher both enhanced and muddied her talents. In a tacit fashion, the sexual dimension to the teacher's interactions with her undermined Emily's self-confidence in her ability as a history student. Nothing of an overtly sexual nature ever transpired between Emily and the history teacher, even though each of them, from different positions in the male–female and teacher–student power hierarchies, wished for it.

Some of Emily's other high-school instructors were cruder in their sexual innuendos. The physics teacher, fairly uniformly, called his female students "honey," "cookie," and "sugar." The high-school principal was known for patting the girls, but never the boys, inappropriately on the shoulder, occasionally on the buttocks, and even hugging them from time to time. Most of the inappropriate attention from male teachers was shrugged off or barely noticed explicitly by Emily.

In her junior year, Emily took the PSATs, and the reality of the future began to loom over her. She watched as her boyfriend and his senior classmates were advised about college applications, vocational schools, and jobs. She observed the school's college advisor hand her boyfriend a list of impressive colleges to apply to and noted how much self-confidence the advisor inspired in the students. She helped them prepare their applications and even went over their essays for them. She orchestrated letters of recommendation and helped the seniors navigate the morass of standardized testing necessary to apply for college admission and financial aid.

When Emily's class entered their senior year, the same advisor bestowed the same interest and encouragement on them as she had on the previous senior classes. Emily, however, left her meeting with the college advisor disheartened and disappointed. Emily's grade-point average was slightly higher than her boyfriend's had been, and her test scores had been comparable, although she tended to score better on the verbal sections and he had done better on the quantitative. Nevertheless, the list of colleges the advisor suggested for Emily did not even begin to approach the stature of those on her boyfriend's list. In fact, Emily had not previously heard of a single institution on the list given to her. The advisor had given Emily a lengthy explanation about selecting colleges for her where she would best fit in and where she would be more likely to get in.

Fortunately for Emily, she did not take that advice. Emily put together a list of seven prominent colleges to apply to, and she wrote her applications and essays without consulting with the college advisor or with anyone else from the school, for that matter. The letters of recommendation she received from three teachers were very good. Nevertheless, when the advisor put together a composite letter, based on Emily's overall school record and including the recommendations, it was tepid, lacking enthusiasm. In spite of this, Emily got into two colleges and ended up attending one of the women's colleges on the East Coast.

An overarching message that Emily received during this process is one that girls hear both at school and at home. It is, as one therapist describes it,

I haven't had a single female patient who was brought up to believe that she could do anything she wanted, and these are all well-educated women. But not a single one was brought up to believe that she is as good as her brothers.

The many ramifications of this message became evident as girls in high school responded rapidly in their interviews to the question of what would be different about their lives if they had been born male:

- *I'd be more athletic. I like sports a lot and never tried them until last year.*
- *I'd be better in math 'cause right now I'm really bad at it, and I think part of it is the myth that girls are not as good as guys. I don't think it's true, but I've adopted it over the years.*
- *I think it's easier for guys to be individuals. If I were a guy it would be easier for me to develop my individualism.*
- *I'd be a lot stronger in science and computer skills. What I learned on computer I learned myself or from my dad, not school. It was always the guys who were shown how to do stuff on the computer at school and encouraged to work on the computers. I had to go and do everything on my own.*
- *I totally think that my father would feel safer when I'm out if I were a boy. He has this idea that THINGS can happen to girls out and not to boys. Like I won't be able to defend myself. So I have to stay home a lot.*

- *I would speak out a lot more in my classes.*
- *I would go out for things more.*
- *I would be louder; a lot of times I'm embarrassed to say my opinion.*

GENDER LESSONS

In her high-school years, Emily's views of gender become stronger and sharper. Barring an unusual event, she will not be called upon to revise her beliefs. Rather, the high-school experience will serve to confirm what she has already learned.

As sex and sexuality become dominant, Emily learns that girls and women are expected to supply sex and to achieve through the use of their sexuality. School work and intellectual pursuits recede even further in importance, even though Emily continues to receive decent or good grades. She learns that her intellect is not her strong point nor would it be desirable for it to be so.

Emily begins to tacitly acknowledge the male–female power hierarchy among her peers. The lesson learned from her alliance with her boyfriend is that she can gain prestige and authority of sorts by fusing herself with a male. She also learns that conformity to the female heterosexual role gains acceptance from diverse corners. The identification with the male as the nexus of power and talent takes a strong hold on the mental lives of girls. As a result, girls' growing isolation and disassociation from each other increase in force. Girls learn to check each other out physically and to covet each other's accomplishments with boys.

GENDER COMPOUNDS

Suppose that in order to make spending money, Emily babysits throughout high school, mostly for families that she knows in her neighborhood. Generally, the father of the children she watched takes her home at the end of the evening. In several instances over the years, on some of these walks or drives home, Emily got the impression that the father was attracted to her sexually or, in one case, that he was just incredibly lecherous. Emily never paid much attention to these incidents and shrugged them off as insignificant. One father, however, could not be ignored.

One night, while he was driving Emily home, he put his hand on her knee. Another time, he put his arm around her shoulders. Emily sat stark still in both instances. A few more occasions of this nature occurred in Emily's junior year. He never looked at her while he was touching her and usually chatted about inconsequential subjects. Emily finally took to sitting as close to the door and far away from him as possible. This put a stop to the touching, and Emily relaxed again. It had never occurred to her to say anything to him or to anyone else about what was happening.

However, one night, on their drive home, the man rubbed his hand along Emily's thigh, up to her crotch and underneath her panties. He took his hand out, and flattened her skirt neatly on her legs, all in silence. Emily was mortified, but again did not move or say anything. This time, she considered telling her parents, but declined because the four adults were good friends and she did not want to spoil anything and get people upset. She wasn't confident that she would be believed anyway. From then on, when Emily babysat for that family she insisted on walking home alone, even though it was far and not entirely safe. Her parents never knew that she wasn't driven home.

A further compounding factor occurs with frequency in the high-school years. Suppose that Emily decides at some point in high school that she would like to experiment with homosexuality or she decides that she is homosexual. In either case, if this decision comes to light among even just her friends,

she is likely to be ostracized and worse. She might be the subject of even more hostility and perhaps violence. She might
get rape threats from the boys and heckling to the effect that
she is defective, horrible, and unnatural.

Again, any and all of these compounding incidents are likely
only to serve to place Emily more firmly in a position of self-
doubt and low self-esteem.

These additions to the Gender Framework, Trends, and
Themes are found in this chapter:

GF 13. The female role is subsidiary in sexual/romantic
attachments with males.

GF 14. Sexuality informs most other behavior and attitudes.

Theme 10. Disassociation from females

Trend 4. Self-restricting choices for the present and the
future

GENDER ACTION

The additional measures that can be undertaken by the school
staff for this age group are many and depend on the make-up
of the student body and the specific issues at hand. This is a
crucial age in terms of gender issues because the students are
trying out gender roles on a large scale. High school is the first
place in the educational spectrum in which some sort of intervention and awareness programs would clearly be beneficial.
The administration could institute awareness seminars for its
teachers about the sorts of gender bias that can crop up in the
classroom and about the gendered violence that can occur
among the students. The students can also be provided with
seminars or mini-courses that not only raise their awareness
about the issues but also open up a dialogue among the stu-

dents and staff that can continue well beyond the confines of the seminar.

The school should also adopt policies on gender bias, sexual harassment, and sex discrimination. Students and teachers should be informed of this policy and must have access to a bona fide grievance procedure. Grievances must result in clear determinations and in specific actions where warranted. The female students should feel free to voice their complaints with strict protection of confidentiality.

Emily herself can do a lot to preserve and build up her autonomy and self-confidence, although it will not be easy in the face of the power of the peer pressure to conform. She must continue to question what goes on around her and to question friends, teachers, and parents about their gender-biased behavior.

These are additional Gender Actions and Rituals found in this chapter:

GA 15. Create intervention and awareness programs in school for students, teachers, and staff.

GA 16. Develop school policies and procedures for gender bias.

Ritual 4. Celebrate girls' emergence into young adulthood, responsibility, self-determination, and career planning at the end of high school. Start early in their senior year; don't wait until graduation.

EXERCISE 5

Girls and women often start off questions and remarks in the classroom with disclaimers that discount their own credibility, such as "I may be way off base here, but . . ." This occurs even when they have a good knowledge of the subject being discussed. In order to combat this self-defeating tendency, try this three-part approach.

1. Make a simple chart in a small notebook that you can carry around with you easily. Mark down the number of times in a day that you speak tentatively and unsurely and in what situations this occurs. Do this for one week.
2. At the end of the week, go over your chart. Try to find out if your disclaimers are clustered in specific sorts of situations. Examine whether the patterns you've discovered are the result of really feeling shaky with the subject or situation. For the next two weeks, practice more direct ways of getting your point across.
3. After these two weeks, carry the notebook around once again and take note of when and where you are still using disclaimers. Discover if there have been any changes in your pattern, and determine how to sustain the progress.

College: The Coed's Status

THE BASICS

Emily loved college from the first day. Unlike high school, her courses are stimulating, and the work is challenging. She lives in a dormitory composed of suites and experiences a new social freedom that is exhilarating. In her first year, she takes several history courses and a wide selection of other subjects. Emily happily immerses herself in her studies and is a bit nervous that she cannot compete with the other students, who appear to her to be better prepared than herself. The world is truly opening up to Emily in a new way, as she becomes exposed to new ideas, concepts, and perspectives.

Emily has three suitemates in her first year, and although they are all from different backgrounds and parts of the country, they get along well. They hold parties together in their suite and go to campus events as a group or in pairs. They create a fulfilling, if sometimes bumpy, social life together.

The "brother" college to Emily's women's college is situated on an adjacent campus. Thus, apart from the required courses at each institution, the classes are for the most part coeducational. And, on each campus, one dormitory is set aside as the coeducational one. This sharing of resources is seen to be beneficial to both campuses since students and faculty automatically have double the facilities to draw upon. Whereas the men's college has a better gym (and the bare minimum of a women's locker room), the women's college has a more fully equipped theater. The mathematics department is stronger at the men's college, but the French department is stronger at the women's college, and so forth. Thus, there is in fact quite a bit of cross-registering for courses, and the bulk of the courses on either campus are genuinely mixed. A certain amount of taunting and rumors go back and forth about both student populations, and there is the underlying tenor that the men's college is more serious and that it purportedly maintains a more difficult curriculum.

An issue that has an unfavorable impact on women's college education and one with which institutions are only now beginning to grapple in a clumsy and sometimes counterproductive fashion is the curriculum itself. Virtually every college in the United States has some basic set of courses that all students must take in order to graduate. Emily's college is no exception. Usually the basic curriculum is a mixture of literature, history, mathematics, and science courses. And in each and every course, it is largely the legacy of Western white male thinkers that is presented.

In Emily's college, since it is a women's college, there is somewhat greater sensitivity to this fact, and some accomplishments of females, minorities, and non-Western civilizations are included, even if scantily and peripherally. Emily, like most other students, does not really notice the omissions. She does not know what she is missing, and she is not cognizant of what the official course selections are implicitly teaching her about herself and women's potential.

The women's college has sororities, and the men's college

has fraternities. Although some of the sororities are organized loosely around themes, the fraternities are very clearly demarcated by sports teams. Many of the fraternities regularly hold Saturday night beer bashes, after which the beer cans can be seen piled up on the ground outside, sometimes reaching past the window ledges of the first story. These parties are known to be wild, sometimes involving brawls and almost always including sexual activity of some sort. Throughout the year, casual rumors fly around both campuses about who was raped at which frat party. Often such talk is made the brunt of crude jokes.

Emily's suite is located in a dormitory generally relegated to first-year students. Emily and her suitemates receive many visits and much attention from the upperclassmen of the men's college. In fact, they each have more invitations to parties and dates than they can handle. Emily and her friends are flattered and pleased by the attention and accept many of the offers over the course of the year. Emily often goes to the campus movie viewings on these dates and goes to a frat party or two her first semester. She tended to feel intimidated at these parties, because there was such a high level of alcohol consumption and because of the ever-present tendency of violence among the men. There was a great deal of sexual bantering, some male flashing and mooning, and people engaging in various levels of sexual activity in every nook and cranny. Once, at a pre-midterm bash at the football fraternity, the punch was spiked so strongly with gin that Emily was more than tipsy after drinking just one small serving. She found herself being tugged into a bedroom by her date. When she groggily became aware of what was happening and cut herself loose, she made her long way home by herself in the dark autumn night.

College students relate a variety of similar experiences:

*There were times as a freshman where I'd be approached.
. . . These two guys who graduated but were coaching lacrosse*

surrounded me at a fraternity party and started saying, "Oh, well, you're cuter than your sister." And I freaked out. I just dropped my glass and I ran because I just felt this is really strange. Incidents of people poking me and grabbing me that I had never had before.

One guy who was really drunk just attacked me; he went straight for my chest. I had to literally wrestle him to the floor. He was really drunk so he didn't have too much balance or coordination. I went to quite a few formals, and the goal of these fraternity guys was to get their dates drunk and have sex. The men in the upper classes would pick out women in their first year. Their plan: get the freshmen, unknowing freshmen, and get them drunk. There was a lot of that, and as a freshman you don't really think about it as someone violating you or as kind of disgusting. You think of it more as attention, flattery, and then after a while you're like, "This is horrible, there's something wrong with this. This isn't very flattering, it's degrading."

At my boyfriend's fraternity, by this point I'm good friends with a lot of the people there. They're always nice to me, but once one of the guys just kept pinching my butt. And it scared me. I think my boyfriend had gone upstairs and I was in the basement and I went upstairs and I was like, "Don't you ever leave me alone." And that's scary that I feel like I need him there to protect me. That's how I really felt. I mean there have been times where I think I've said that to him. Like when I go into bars and sometimes they're really crowded and if he walks in ahead and goes off and then I get guys who say, "Whoa, who's this?" and making comments to me and I say, "Don't leave me alone." It's terrible. I get more upset that I feel that way. I can't let down my guard. I feel like I have to have someone there. That, I think, upsets me more than what's going on.

On Emily's campus, acquaintance rape had received scant attention, and all but one or two cases went by completely unreported and unrecognized. The prevailing sentiment on campus is the notion, which should have been outmoded, that no woman gets raped unless she wants to and that if you walk around fearing rape it means you really want it. Acquaintance rapes go down in campus history undocumented and untold, one after another, chalked up to sour grapes on the part of the woman, to the woman's getting what she asked for by wearing "sexy" clothing, to her going out on a date, to sexual teasing such as kissing, or to her saying no when she really meant yes, and other such personalized excuses to blame the woman and relieve the man of all responsibility.

Stranger rape is definitely feared on campus, although few instances were ever officially reported. The women students feel it is unsafe to walk alone on campus at night or to be alone in buildings at off-hours to attend an early morning or late evening class. Generally they lock their dormitory room doors at night before they go to sleep. Emily herself hesitates to go to evening campus events alone and either goes with a date or with some other group of friends. She feels the same trepidation in going to the library alone after dark. Sometimes, when she really needs a particular book or other reference material, she scoots in quickly after dinner in the cafeteria and tries to find someone at the library to walk back with her.

Although the campus is situated in a fairly safe area, some crime nonetheless occurs on the school grounds. It ranges from petty theft, to bias crimes such as the scrawling of racial epithets, to rapes. Such incidents are few and far between, at least as reported in the campus and local newspapers. At finals time, there have been suicides or suicide attempts. Basically, though, the campus is congenial and peaceful with a multiplicity of cultural and scholarly offerings.

Professor–student and student–student classroom interaction can include a range of biased behavior, which, for the female student, informs every aspect of her college experience because it is so pervasive. In addition to the female college student's already intact tendency to discount her thoughts in class, both her professors and her peers abet this lack of confidence by their behavior inside the classroom. Male peers are constantly ready to cut any and everyone off to make their own point, and they find it especially easy to override a female voice. They too have learned the lesson of discounting women's thoughts and authority. Professors do not usually attempt to correct this form of student behavior, nor do they, in fact, even notice it most of the time.

Professors generally make more eye contact with male students and are much more likely to listen intently to the comments of male students and to take them seriously. Professors can often be observed sorting papers, looking distractedly into space, and generally paying scant attention when a female student is speaking up in class. The same comment may be treated in an offhand manner coming from a female and in a serious and weighty fashion when it comes from a male student. And, all of this is not to mention the occasions when a male professor makes a sexist joke to spice up a lecture or goes further by using demeaning and sexually explicit materials in class, such as in the following:

The professor was talking about Rome and the lead pipes, and he would say once a month the water that flew through it was red and all bloody and it was because all the women were having their periods.

Attending a women's college gives Emily some insulation from these problems, but not enough. Some of the basic courses she takes have an all female student body, and thus she does not encounter the student–student problems. However, she still must contend with the professor–student issues of gender bias in the classroom. Just like the teachers of primary and secondary education, both female and male college professors were raised in our gender-biased culture and went through the academic process in an environment hostile, whether subliminally or not, to women's achievement. Thus, it is all too easy for a professor of either sex to unreflectively create a gender-biased classroom environment as a matter of course.

Teachers give more attention to men, listen to them more intently, achieve more eye contact with them, and generally treat them more seriously than women. Teachers direct more complex, intellectual, open-ended questions to men and encourage them more. They ask women the simpler, more factual, or subjective questions and pick them out for the female point of view. Consider this woman's college experience:

So it was definitely the experience the whole time there, being other, for a lot of different reasons. For ethnicity, and class, as well as gender. But gender was the biggest issue. And I remember very much wanting to be accepted as a person, instead of as a woman. Because there were a lot of times when you would be singled out as a woman. As a women, I got asked questions such as "As a woman what do you think about Tennyson?" "As a woman, what do you think Shakespeare means?" And I'd say, "Well, can't I answer as a person?" or "Can't I answer as a student?" Then I started to say things like "As a woman, you know, I'll have meat loaf for dinner. As a woman, I think it's cold for April. As a woman . . ." So it started to become a joke because of being treated so differently from the run-of-the-mill students.

One element of the use of biased language inside the classroom is something that only a male professor can accomplish: creating a fraternity in the classroom, leaving the women students out in the cold. It can be done through the whole range of classroom expression from body language, such as winks and nods, through overt speech, such as examples that use the word "you" when obviously picking out only men, and even with lewd classroom remarks, which are not as uncommon today as people would like to believe.

In one-on-one student–professor interaction the male–
female and the teacher–student hierarchies become intensified. In these situations, male teachers can take advantage of
their authority and engage in mild to severe forms of sexual
harassment, from calling students diminutive nicknames such
as "honey" to discussing extra-academic and inappropriate
subject matter, such as in the following example:

*One time the professor asked this girl Ramie a question who
was a little bit plumper than I was, and I think I answered and
he goes, "Well, my Ramie, how your hips have shrunk." And I
just felt really strange that some man was noticing physically
what we looked like. To say that. It just didn't seem right.*

Professors also engage in inappropriate touching and even
in propositions for sex in exchange for good grades. One woman
related an example of a common experience for college women:

*He said, "Why don't you and I go . . . there's behind the green
doors, some other new type of porno films that I think would
be good research for you." And I just started giggling and laugh-
ing and said, "Oh, well, I've got to get home to my boyfriend"
or something. I just used that excuse instead of saying, "Up
yours. What are you talking about?" So he wheedled me into
it thinking that he was wanting to help me on the project. So I
just dismissed that as like no big deal. It wasn't anything very
aggressive; it was just kind of silly. But, again, I don't have
respect for my reaction. It wasn't to confront. I wasn't even sure,
well, was he being a good professor wanting to help me on this
project? No.*

A male teacher is more likely to ask a female student to
continue an office-hour discussion over drinks or coffee. This
offer usually does, and should, put the student in an awkward
position of not knowing but needing to guess at the professor's

true motivations. It happens much less frequently, but when a professor asks a male student out, most likely and correctly, the student will take it as a compliment to his achievement in the course or subject and will have little ambivalence about accepting.

In school clubs and academic extra-curricular activities, women are often found in deferential roles, such as the ones who do the errands or who take notes. Men are more often found in the active and more academically oriented roles. In sports and other non-academic extra-curricular school-sponsored activities, even where women are not actively discriminated against, they are often passively left out, or provided with inferior equipment, or given less desirable schedules, and in other ways generally discouraged.

Every way in which female students are not accorded full and equal standing on campus accumulates to result in inferior job profiles for women than for men. For example, less visibility and recognition in class can lead to lower grades and poorer letters of reference. Less visibility can also lead to a female student not being in a professor's mind when the department has a research or teaching assistantship open for a student or honors and awards to bestow. So, in short, there is a tacit sort of tracking system going on on campus.

In her third year, Emily decides to major in political science and minor in history. She intends to go on to law school and become a lawyer. Here another common feature of the female experience in college comes to the fore: the search for an enthusiastic mentor/advisor. Being a student in a mentor–student relationship can be one of the most rewarding and educational campus experiences. A mentor can serve as a role model for a student and give the student a glimpse into the professional realm she has decided to enter. A mentor can also guide the student to pursue her interests in greater depth and to gain insight into the breadth of the field. Finally, the mentor, even at the college level, can begin to invite and initiate the student into taking the first steps down her chosen career path such as choosing the best professional training and can facilitate her career by writing strong letters of recommendation and making inquiries on her behalf.

Being at a women's college, Emily's school tends to maintain a higher proportion of female faculty than the very low national average. Emily has a choice in the political science department of the mostly male faculty of all ranks and two female assistant professors. She feels naturally drawn to the more established and impressive professor who is also chair of the department. This male professor is highly regarded, not only in the department and on campus but also in the field in general. Part of his attraction is the professor's command of and creativity within the field. His attraction is also due to his high stature, but lastly, to his gender. Even students at a women's college cannot escape the power of the female–male hierarchy. Emily approaches this professor and asks him to be her major advisor. He consents with a lukewarm response, and they proceed to enter into the student–advisor relationship. He is not necessarily a bad choice for Emily, but he is probably not the best choice either.

In her last year at college, Emily prepares her applications to law schools and solicits the counsel of her advisor. He assists her and supports her through letters of recommendation, but he is not an ardent supporter. It may be that the professor just does not feel that Emily is an outstanding candidate for law school. But her grades and test scores are excellent, and her enthusiasm and diligence are high. One should wonder in such a case what is going on. It happens all too often that professors will strongly favor and promote more actively the male student over the female when the two are comparably matched in terms of grades, competence, and perseverance.

Emily is not particularly aware of the amount to which her advisor is falling short on her behalf. In the spring she is accepted to several law schools, and she is thrilled. Through the help of her advisor, Emily secures a summer job in a law firm performing rudimentary tasks. Emily graduates with honors and distinctions and sets out gleefully into the new world opening up to her.

GENDER LESSONS

Slowly and steadily, just as in her secondary school experience brought to a new level of sophistication, the constant focus on an all-male cast of thinkers erodes Emily's self-confidence and her ability to imagine herself in any of the exalted roles of philosopher, scientist, innovator, and the like. This impact complements and is similar to the effect on young children in school of the exclusive use of masculine pronouns to indicate hypothetical people and animals. It stultifies and skews Emily's imagination and throws a log jam into her perception of the range of her future options.

When the essentially biased nature of the college curriculum is viewed in tandem with the typical classroom environment, it becomes clear why female college students' self-confidence and future aspirations decline while those of males rise consistently. The classroom provides many opportunities for intellectual stimulation and motivation. It also contains many avenues in which to push the female student deeper into the hole of self-doubt. It is already the case that a female college student will enter the college classroom environment ready to preface any and all remarks and questions in class with self-deprecating disclaimers. Emily begins to notice in her last year in college that she has been doing this all along through her college career and finds it a bit curious. One college senior remarked,

I learned to realize that any time any woman opened her mouth she was going to be considered a bitch. That there re-

ally were differences in responses in the classroom. That if you made a remark, it would be "Uh huh," now on to the next person. But if a male student often made the same kind of remark,"Now, that's an interesting insight, Mr. Miller. Can you tell me more about that?"

Emily does not escape the student–student classroom biases. Her first year is filled with mostly all-female courses. But once she begins to take upper-level courses, the situation changes drastically. Many of her classes are fairly evenly mixed with female and male students, some have many more women, and a few have many more men. But, Emily finds that even in classes in which there are relatively few male students, that small subset tends to dominate the class. Emily finds herself speaking up less and less as she advances in her years at college. She also finds herself more hesitant in her essays and papers. She becomes more conservative in her writing style and takes fewer risks in her work.

Women seeking mentors are often caught in a double bind. On the one hand, the available candidates are typically males, many of whom disdain or feel uncomfortable taking on female students. And these men obviously cannot serve as female role models. Female role models are essential for the development of self-perception and self-confidence in the female students. On the other hand, in the still all-too-rare occasions in many fields in which there are female faculty members who can serve in an advisory position, they will generally have less clout and influence in the field. This fact does not make them worse mentors, but it does mean that their word will not yield the same edge in applying for jobs and to professional schools.

Moreover, all of the issues of fear surrounding Emily's college experience exact a toll on her educational opportunity. For example, she often had to miss what promised to be an interesting evening lecture by a visiting scholar when she could not find someone to go there and back with. The thoroughness of her school work suffered when she could not get to the library often enough in the evening to do a complete job, particularly when the library was the only place available to her that promised to be sufficiently quiet. And, she even ended up dropping a couple of courses that she would have preferred to take and that would have rounded out her college education because of the hours or remote locations in which they met.

Even though it is Emily herself making more or less conscious decisions in each case to miss out on something, she makes those decisions not because she is suffering from irrational delusions. Rather, she is making sensible choices that place her physical and emotional safety first. Virtually none of the institutions of higher education in this country supply their students with adequately safe campus environments. Moreover, this fact clearly has a disproportionate impact on female students.

Most of these gender issues affect Emily only indirectly and subconsciously. She remains, throughout her four years on campus, happy, vibrant, and stimulated. She perceives the issues as personal and not as systematic problems of pervasive bias. If her comments are not given much attention in class, she believes it because her ideas are not sufficiently interesting or that she didn't express herself properly. Thus, she does not walk the paths of campus seething with anger, nor does she see cause for remedial institutional action or protest. Rather, if anything, she experiences inward frustration at her own failings and incompetence. On the one hand, her interpretation galvanizes Emily to strive even harder to achieve, but on the other it also lowers her sights for herself.

GENDER COMPOUNDS

Suppose that Emily were up for an award or that she is applying for a scholarship to do foreign study and that the decision is largely in the hands of one professor. And this professor, who is male, is interviewing the candidates in turn. Emily has taken two classes given by the professor in her major for which she received good grades and has spoken to him about her work on several occasions during his office hours. Thus, Emily is relatively relaxed when she goes in for her interview.

As the interview proceeds, Emily feels increasingly that it is going well. The professor smiles frequently while she is speaking, and she answers his questions in an articulate and serious fashion. She thinks that she has a fighting chance of getting the award.

At the close of the interview, as both Emily and the professor are walking toward the door, she senses that the professor is about to ask her something further. He leans closer and quickly kisses her on the lips. Emily is stunned and bolts from the room. The professor calls after her to come back, that she has misunderstood. When Emily, in her shock, keeps on going, he calls out that he will wait ten minutes for her and that she will regret not returning.

There are countless variations on this theme that occur frequently and on every college campus in the nation. There is also a wide range to the severity and intensity to such incidents. Although the consequences are generally nil for the professors, both emotionally and in terms of being held legally accountable, for the student they are vast and long lasting. Emily will surely now question whether she was actually doing well in the interview and that her record is strong, or whether she was chosen and encouraged because that professor happened to want to get her into bed. She feels that she is a sham and a fake who has just been uncovered for who she is.

Emily also may spend many a sleepless night in the weeks and perhaps months to come. The incident will turn over and over in her head, and she may experience flashbacks. She is likely to be hesitant in or altogether avoid the one-on-one interactions with professors that can often be so rewarding educationally. She is also clearly deprived of receiving a letter of recommendation from this professor or in using him as a reference of any sort.

A college student related a similar incident:

Something happened to me in college with one of my professors, an organic chemistry professor, which was a course that I actually needed as part of my pre-med major. I was taking this organic chemistry course and I think I had a B average and then it came time to take the final, and I was sick and I missed the final. And so I made an appointment, and I went to his office. And I was telling him, "I missed the final, and I need to take a make-up exam." And he said, "Well you know you're the only student who missed the test." And I said, "Well I was sick. I had gastroenteritis. I can take it next week or whenever." And he said, "Well, I'll have to make up a new exam and everything."

So, after some talking and this and that, he came over to me. I was sitting. He was originally behind his desk, and I was sitting in a chair. Then he came over, he was standing right where I was, and he said to me, "Well, I could make up an exam. I could give you a make-up test, and if you do well, you'll probably get a B in the course because that's what your grades are." He said, "But I don't have to give you this make-up test because you missed the exam and you don't have a doctor's note. I can just give you an F." And I said, "What do you mean give me an F? You just said I had a B average. Why can't I take a make-up?" And he said, "Well, if I don't want to make up a new exam, I can just give you an F in the course."

So I got hysterical. I was upset. I said, "What do you mean an F? I need this course for medical school. I'm a pre-med, and I need organic chemistry. I won't get into medical school unless I pass this course. And you yourself just said I was doing okay in the course." I'm very emotional, so I was crying. And so then he comes over to me. I was sitting down and he came

*over to me, and he basically put my head in his crotch, and said,
"Oh, there, there," and he put his hand behind my head and
said, "Oh, there, there. Don't be upset. I'm not going to do that.
I wouldn't do that to you. I was just seeing what you'd say. I
was just seeing what your reaction would be. Don't worry, I'll
give you the make-up test. But I just wanted you to know that
that's what could happen."*

*I don't remember the whole conversation, but it was some-
where along those lines. And I got the impression, from the way
he was holding my head and the way he was standing there,
that he wanted me to have oral sex with him. So then I felt
uncomfortable so I stood up. I was still upset and crying, and
so he pretended to hug me and was patting me on the back
saying, "There, there. Don't be upset. It's okay." You know,
things like that. I mean nothing really happened, but it was just
that I got the impression that he was basically saying that he
had the control over what happened to me. I could either get a
B or I could get an F, depending on what he wanted to do.*

*And then he proceeded to get too close to me. Like he was
pressing himself against me. I just felt the distinct impression that
he wanted something from me. So I managed to get out of there.*

*He didn't press the issue that day. I sort of got the impres-
sion, and I could tell—he was pressed right up against me, you
know—I could tell he had an erection. And then he wanted to
talk to me again the following week. So I said maybe he's lay-
ing the groundwork and then he was going to go take it a step
further. I felt so strongly that he had something else in mind
other than just giving me this make-up exam.*

*So I went and spoke to my roommate first and I said, "You
won't believe what this guy did." And then she said, "Well, you
should talk to someone else." I talked to the dean of my resi-
dential college; he didn't want to deal with it either. He just
said, "Oh, look, I don't want to get involved. I've known this
guy for years and years." This guy was on the staff for thirty
years and he was a senior tenured professor, as big as they get,*

and he was the head of the department of chemistry. So, what are you going to do. So he said, "Well, why don't you bring this up with the commission of sexual harassment?" I didn't even know there was one. So I actually made an appointment and went and spoke to them, and that's when I found out that his wife, who is a lawyer, was one of the people who was a principal player in setting up this commission originally years earlier.

So I told them what happened, and they intervened and they actually approached him, told him that I had made this complaint and they said, "She needs to take this exam," They wanted to oversee it because I said, "Look, I just want to make sure that I get to take the exam and that it's fair and it's graded fairly now that I filed this complaint against this guy. He's going to make it really hard." So they actually intervened; they arranged it so that I could take the exam in a proper setting, and that he would grade it but then someone else would review the exam. Because I was just worried that he was going to chasten me after that.

And then what happened was he wanted to talk to me after that. He said, "How could you do this to me? I've been on this staff for thirty years and my wife set up this commission." I was alone with him but his secretary was there in the outside office so it wasn't during an off-hour.

But, that was that. At least I was on it right away. Because I was afraid, I was really afraid that I felt like he was saying indirectly either go along with what he had in mind or my grade was going to go down the tubes, and it meant a lot to me. I was a pre-med, I had to pass that course. It wasn't some bogus stuffed course; it was a requirement. Because I had missed the exam, I was totally in his control, and I was so scared that something was going to happen to me. And then after that whole incident I was so confused. On the one hand I felt guilty because I felt, well maybe I was just jumping the gun and I was like reading into it too much.

But, I don't think so. I know what he said and I know what he was doing, and he didn't say anything really blatant like

"Either you do this, or . . ." but it was just the way he made me feel. He made me feel uncomfortable, and he made me feel like he wanted something from me sexually. So I knew in my heart that I wasn't reading into it, but I felt badly that I had gotten him in trouble. But I just had to do something to protect myself. It was too important for me to let it slide. And this was an old guy, almost sixty years old. I didn't want to go out with him. It just made me nauseous, the whole thought of it.

After he spoke to me saying, "How could you do this?" is when I felt really guilty and bad about it. Because before that, before I went to the commission, I was convinced that that's what he intended, that's what he thought, and I just felt like he was a real bastard for doing this to me. But that's what I had to do. But then afterward I felt bad. I felt like I humiliated him. I mean even though whatever goes on in this commission is supposed to be confidential, it's not going to be on the front page of any paper or anything, but still I'm sure enough people knew about it that it could humiliate him, and he made it seem like enough people would know about it to humiliate him.

He basically tried to make me feel bad like, "How could you do this? And, I didn't mean anything by it. I was just trying to comfort you." He was trying to explain what he had done. But I also felt badly because I had liked this professor. I thought he was a good professor, a nice guy, when I would sit in class and listen to him. And I respected him, I looked up to him. So when he did this to me, I just felt not so much betrayed but it's like you can't judge someone just by the way they seem in public. It's like taking advantage of his position, basically, because he is supposed to be someone that you respect and look up to. So to take advantage of that position, to make a student feel so uncomfortable and so bad about herself is really, you can't respect someone after that.

That's the thing that gets me the most annoyed about the whole issue is that if it was just a man making a pass at a woman, that's one thing. But it's when the woman is in the

position where she really feels she doesn't have much of a choice,
she doesn't have recourse and she needs him for something. It's
almost like they know they have that advantage and they want
to use that to achieve their goal and that's what makes me angry
about the whole thing.

And I think that's the whole point that makes it harassment.
That the fact that they know you're in a position where you don't
have much of a choice. In other words, the choices are all bad
choices. I could have either gone along with what he wanted,
which is a bad move, or I could have flunked the course. If I hadn't
known, or if I was ashamed to talk about it, if I hadn't known
about the committee, if I had just spoken to my dean and he said,
"Oh, no, forget about it, I don't want to know." If I hadn't known
that there were some other avenues to go to, then I could have
been between a rock and a hard place, in a very bad situation.
And that's what makes this such an awful thing.

The additions to the Gender Framework and Trends found
in this chapter are

GF 15. Safety is an educational issue.

Trend 5. Classroom gender bias can result in lower grades
and job profiles for women students.

GENDER ACTION

There is so much that is so obvious that institutions of higher
education could be doing to achieve gender equity that it is
baffling that so little is actually being done.

First, begin with the curriculum. There is a huge resistance
to what is perceived as tinkering with a time-honored successful course of instruction, so much so that on campuses with
required courses in Western thought, even adding a discus-

sion topic on the role and status of women is balked at, let alone adding or trading some reading material on the syllabus.

Nevertheless, changes will eventually be made, and the sooner the better. Long forgotten and buried classics, written by women, need to be reintroduced. The long-standing staples can be re-examined in class, not eliminated but rather discussed critically with an eye to the view of the women portrayed. For example, in the classic texts of political science from Plato to Hobbes to Marx, professors and students in class can analyze the role and status of women found in them. They would thereby profit, gaining insight not only about the status of women but also about political science generally. Contemporary works by women in all fields of study can be given their due. This is not a matter of including lesser works for the sake of complying with some abstract concept of equity, nor is it about tacking any work by a woman on at the end of a course, if time permits. Rather, it is about broadening our horizons, it is about reintegrating valuable lost work into a good but skewed curriculum, it is about uncovering important discoveries buried by the myopia of gender bias, and it is about admitting new and exciting research that has looked at the issues from a different perspective.

Second, the administration can make concerted efforts to revise and oversee the hiring, promotion, and tenure practices for staff and faculty in every department. More women must simply be hired, particularly at the tenured faculty level. Nationwide, their ranks are horribly low, hovering between the ten and twenty percent mark.

Generally, departments are left more or less to their own devices when it comes to hiring and promotions. There is now lip service paid to affirmative action, and women often find themselves in the number two slot in the rankings. Faculty members like to give tenure to those they feel comfortable with, those who will fit in, those who are most like them; that is, to men. All of this can stop. With the rising numbers of women receiving advanced professional degrees, there is no shortage of capable female candidates.

Third, every campus needs a clearly stated and well-publicized policy statement on sexual harassment and sex discrimination and a grievance procedure that works: one that students and faculty and staff will be comfortable using. Such measures will help set the tone on campus.

And, fourth, the administration can take steps to ensure that the campus is a safe place for all of its inhabitants. Students cannot lose out on educational opportunities because they value their safety first. Hiring more guards, running a frequent campus bus service, or providing better lighting at night can easily improve safety and security on campus.

Professors in their own right can make strides in achieving gender equity on campus. They can each create equitable classroom environments for their students. They can accomplish this by using nonsexist language, by making sure that everyone can have a voice in the class, by encouraging female students to be bolder in class, and by fostering a cooperative spirit in the classroom.

Professors can also make an effort to canvass their female students when research or teaching assistant jobs come up. They can make sure to consider female students in the awarding of honors, scholarships, and fellowships. Once they have the female students' records alongside those of the males, they must make every effort to address and curtail the ingrained gender bias with which they have themselves been raised.

Emily herself can do much in her college years to enhance her self-perception and her educational experience. First, by continuing to think critically about her environment, she can begin to perceive the hidden curriculum in college for what it is. She can unravel the messages and assumptions present in the classroom situation that work against her as a female, and thereby stop believing that they are a personal reflection of her competence. To assess the accuracy of her hunches and intuition, she could even make a worksheet in which classroom incidents are checked off in columns according to kinds of gender bias. Emily may feel that a certain professor or a certain course provides a hostile environment for the women in the class, but if she tallies it up on paper her perceptions will be concretely confirmed. Thus, she can see that when she is cut off or hastily responded to that it is not personal, that her intelligence or work is not at stake.

Emily can begin to teach herself to be more assertive in class and to renounce her use of disclaimers. She can adopt the use of non-sexist language and use it in class as well as in other contexts. These two steps will require some training, but will reap great benefits. The more Emily is forthcoming and bold in class and outside with her peers, the more her self-confidence will grow. Her new use of language will change the way she sees the world and herself in it; it will no longer be populated by males with her as an outsider to the main events. It will foster many other subtle changes in the way she comports herself and the decisions she makes.

When Emily finds herself in an uncomfortable situation that she feels involves gender bias, whether in class, at a club meeting, at a party, or in a one-on-one meeting with a professor, she can try to step back and analyze what is happening. She should try to perceive how the situation would be different were she a man. This imaging is a powerful tool to carry around for the job of cutting through gender bias. Would the situation not be bothersome or not arise at all were Emily a male, then Emily is correct in perceiving gender bias. Awareness is the first, and in most instances, the most difficult, step in combating gender bias.

Another important step Emily can take is to keep a dialogue open and running with her female peers about their questions and problems of gender bias on campus. Isolation is one of the crucial components that keeps women in the trap of generating personal explanations for what is actually sexual harassment and sex discrimination. By talking with friends about the issues, Emily gains support, perspective, and confidence.

These additions to the Gender Actions are found in this chapter:

GA 17. Continue to question and modify the core college curriculum.

GA 18. Monitor faculty hiring and tenure sufficiently in order to recruit more women.

GA 19. Secure campus safety for all students, staff, and faculty.

GA 20. Have professors make a greater effort to obtain awards, grants, and research positions for their female students.

GA 21. Increase students' recognition of gender bias in their courses.

GA 22. Develop the habit of discussion of gender bias on campus with other females.

EXERCISE 6

Try this three-step method for approaching problems of gender bias:

1. Awareness: Learn to be aware of the obstacles that stand in the way of girls' and women's self-respect and access to opportunities.
2. Clarification: Look deeper into the situation in order to recognize the forces at play and the way in which we've been taught to think about girls and women and their role in society.
3. Action: Know when and how to respond to these larger issues and specific events.

PART III
THE RED SHOES

The choice repeatedly offered to Victoria Page, the lead character in the movie classic, *The Red Shoes*, was between dancing, and thus an alliance with Boris Lermontov, the ballet company director, and marriage to Julian Kraster, a composer and conductor for the ballet company. She already was a ballet dancer of international repute at the time she was confronted with the choice. "Choice" in this case is a euphemism for a battle that raged between the two men, Lermontov and Kraster. They fought it out over whether Page would continue in her profession or become a housewife, an either–or dilemma that Page herself did not see the sense in.

In a heated debate between Lermontov and Kraster, as Lermontov tries to forbid Kraster from seeing Page romantically, in this either–or mode, he spits out: *"Do you know what you are asking of her? Do you know what you are asking of her?"*

But Lermontov does not question or even acknowledge what *he* is asking of Page, that she must dispense with all other aspects of her life in order to work with him, that she must be completely under his domination. Lermontov sums up his

paternalistic attitude toward Page as his property while excit-
edly relating his plans for her career: *"I want more, much more.
I want to create something big out of something little. I want to
make a great dancer out of you."*

In the end, of course, Page exercises the only true option
left open to her within the framework of the movie: *she* solves
the *men's* problem by removing herself entirely. It is her very
existence and consequent attempt at self-determination that
cause the trouble. Dressed in full costume, as the final curtain
call is ringing out, with Kraster pulling her on one side and
Lermontov on the other, Page gathers her resolve and decides
to dance. The pressure of her (non-)choice being too great to
bear, as her dresser is walking her to the stage entrance, Page
frees her arm, bolts out a side door, and leaps off a terrace onto
the railroad tracks to her death.

If this story sounds fantastical or dated, this part will show
how more than fifty years later, the messages of *The Red Shoes*
resonate in contemporary working women's lives. The rheto-
ric of the exclusive either–or choice of career versus home has
not only not disappeared, but in recent years it has strengthened. There are several variations on the choice, which are
examined below through their impact on Emily.

Although the either-or choice has received increasing emphasis over the last few years, the framework in which it is
couched embodies a false picture. In the movie and elsewhere,
the concept of marriage is a code for the notorious second shift
of labor *as an exclusive, unpaid, and unsecured vocation.* What
this second shift consists of, the range of labor and energy that
it encompasses, is spelled out in this part. Professional women
do not, in fact, at any time face a choice between home and
career. This is due to the fact that the second shift is a job that
all women—those with children, those married, and even, as
is shown later, single women who live alone—are expected to
fulfill. Moreover, women themselves expect to fulfill all or most
of the tasks on the list of the second shift.

Because of this second shift that all women are expected to take on, the either–or life choice becomes a choice of career plus second shift or second shift on its own. Thus, the stakes are raised for professional women in such a way that makes it stressful and much more difficult to perform satisfactorily in a career than it ever would be for men. Moreover, a double standard about earnings has developed. On the one hand, women are not supposed to exceed male, particularly their male partner's, earnings. On the other, they are expected increasingly to earn a substantial portion of the household earnings. This expectation is a purported nod toward equality and fairness. Yet, the second shift has not altered, and that remains steadfastly the woman's job too. So women have more than double the pressure than before to perform in all ways.

In addition to the choice, the second shift itself and its impact on women's professional development are examined in this part. For these purposes, the shift is defined in all its details and is not confined to its usual characterization in terms of purely straightforward housework. The overriding concept of the second shift used here is the totality of all chores, tasks, skills, and other effort that women are expected to perform that are not work related and that men are not expected to do. Included are the issues, tasks, decisions, and time involved in child bearing and raising. Historically, the role of raising children while maintaining careers in the professions has transformed, but it has not yet evolved into a workable arrangement.

The generation of women now in their sixties feel that having children ruined their chances for sustained career involvement. Consider the words of two women with thwarted careers:

I didn't know what to do. I'm sure if it was 1995, I wouldn't have gotten married in graduate school because I was very involved in the subject matter and the work [she cries]. Let's face it, it was a mistake. I didn't really think about it; I didn't want to get married.

I wasn't going to stop my career at that point. When I got pregnant in my second year of graduate school, I realized I wasn't going to be an anthropologist because of the travel and deprivation involved. That was a big blow.

Many women in their forties with careers feel that children are the high point of their lives and occasionally dream of staying at home to care for them, although their children are more often than not found in more than full-time day care. Women in their twenties seem to expect to give up their training in order to raise their children. We are verging on returning full circle, or in a spiral fashion that takes certain modifications into account, to the situation of the past. All of these frameworks paint a false dichotomy. The point is that women cannot remain the virtually sole caretakers, planners, worriers for children if both women and men are to maintain full professional careers.

The placement of this part within the book posed a difficulty. The issues contained here are as pervasive in our culture and central to the lives of professional women as the frame of mind with which women walk into professional development. Thus, it was placed here after the primary basic issues were addressed and before the parts that contain the details of the steps involved in professional development.

8   The Second Shift: Before Children

THE BASICS

Emily's years in graduate school are divided fairly clearly into two distinct eras. The first was before she started living with John, and the second began when John moved into her apartment. During the first era, Emily was a student in good standing in her program and felt that she was on good terms with the faculty. Her work was received well, and like other enthusiastic students, she spent out-of-class time discussing issues with the professors in informal gatherings and chance meetings in the hallways. However, she also observed certain trends in differential treatment of herself and her male peers by the faculty.

In addition to the various relatively subtle cues of respect accorded to the male students by the faculty that were not extended to herself, Emily noted a range of flirtatious and diminutive behavior that was directed at her. Most of the behavior was covert enough that it was difficult to distinguish on its own. Nevertheless, in conversation, several professors would touch or pat Emily on her shoulder, speak in a solicitous tone, comment on her dress or appearance with regularity, discuss or mention her personal life in veiled ways that did not permit a genuine answer, and so forth. Emily did not observe the male students receiving any of these sorts of attention from the professors. In fact, she never saw one of the professors touch a male student, and she never heard a comment on a male student's attire or appearance, even though several of them seemed to cry out for it. Discussion of a male student's personal life was more likely to be about discovering if a student could be enticed to play volleyball or go running with the professor.

This differential behavior of the faculty toward female and male students shades into portions of the second shift for Emily at this stage of her life. Emily increasingly finds that her peers as well as her professors tend to come to her to discuss the personal problems that they are having. They seek out her ear and her advice. Frequently such discussions take the place of the work that a meeting was scheduled to accomplish. Instead, Emily would sometimes spend hours listening to problems that one of her professors in particular was having with his elderly mother. Although Emily was genuinely interested in these people and wanted to be helpful, she often walked away feeling vaguely dissatisfied because she had been prepared to discuss her work, only to find that the time had run out before the planned subject could come up. Emily did not notice male students being expected to play the role of a sympathetic ear to professors in this way.

In fact, similar patterns emerge in professional settings between supervisors and female employees. Consider the words of a seasoned executive:

In effect, they're searching for a mother in me. They come to me with this family problem and that, and they listen to my advice. I'm respected in this regard. But, when it comes to busi-

ness, I get blown off far too often considering my experience in the field. And, they take up so much of my time with their personal affairs that I can barely get enough work done at the office.

Emily has also noticed that when a male student gets married, he is accorded a higher degree of respect from the faculty than previously, as if he had just reached a new level of professional development or had joined a club in which the (male) faculty are already members. Emily observes that the newly married male student is hustled through the program more rapidly on account of his newly acquired responsibility for his wife and potential family. This is the case whether the student's wife had a well-paying job or not and is independent therefore from any recently acquired actual financial need. If a male graduate student has a child, this sequence is accelerated.

Emily found that the opposite came true in her own case. When she and John decided to live together, it became public knowledge throughout Emily's program. John began to appear with her at social occasions within the department, and she had mentioned her new arrangements to several faculty members and students to whom she is close. Far from being accorded enhanced respect or being perceived as someone who had taken on new life responsibilities, Emily had the feeling that she must have, in part, turned to sawdust in the eyes of the faculty. Although the flirtatious behavior from the faculty in large measure stopped, she began to hear what she considered rather bizarre remarks about her future. For example, when her mentor was discussing her work responsibilities for the following year, he expressed hesitance at assigning her even the same amount of work that she was currently sailing through with. He explained this decision by pronouncing that he didn't feel confident that she could manage the work and a marriage with children at the same time!

Understandably, Emily didn't know what hit her. She was not married nor planning to be, was not pregnant nor was she planning to be. Yet her mentor, someone with whom she felt she had been developing a close and mutually respectful professional relationship, someone whose shoes she saw herself as someday filling, downsized her workload based on the assumption that because John was in her life, she could not be as effective as a professional. This was quite in contrast to the assumptions made of the male students in similar situations. In other words, because of assumptions about the ownership of the second shift, even when the factors are not imminently relevant, a student's relationship to her work, to her mentor, and thereby her future is easily undermined.

As Emily grew closer to finishing the program, she and John did in fact decide to marry, another personal choice that Emily did not hide from the faculty, although in retrospect she wished that she had. Now the differential treatment she began to receive intensified. When she turned her attention to finding her first job, she began to hear strange remarks that she never heard directed to any of her male colleagues. For example, she was asked by one of her advisors what her hurry is to find a job. After some perplexity, Emily determined in conversation with the advisor that the sentiment was that she doesn't need one because of John. It was also remarked several times in passing, despite her affirmations to the contrary each time, that Emily needed to stay in the area. Because John had a job there, therefore, *Emily* could not move away.

Similarly, one woman relates her experience serving on a hiring committee for a senior-level position:

We were all sitting around the conference table, eight men and myself, discussing the candidates. There were five of them, but only two were serious contenders—a woman and a man. We were talking about the top candidate's work records, when all of a sudden the conversation took a turn. My colleagues started to comment on the woman's husband and how he has a job where they are now, and how we couldn't possibly find him a comparable job nearby. They continued with questioning why the female candidate wants our job anyway since she already has one, and since her husband can't come, neither can she. No comparable comments were made about the male candidate, his wife who does in fact work, nor about the fact that he also has a job where he is. I didn't know what to do; I just sat there in horror.

Emily also noted that her professors began to identify her as "Mrs. Johnson," Johnson being John's last name. Emily had not changed her last name upon marriage. In the letters of recommendation for Emily, many of the professors were careful to spell out that she is married by using "Mrs." in front of her name every time they used it, whereas as far as she could determine from her friends, "Mr." was not carefully placed in front of male students' names in letters of recommendation. Emily had the distinct impression that her marital status was an important part of the letter, serving as a cue to her potential employers.

Marital status and the female possession by the male, the husband, go hand in hand on a subtle level, and often this drama is first played out over names. Will the woman, the new wife, change her last name to that of her husband? Emily does not, but this remains today a raging debate between new couples. As a psychoanalyst describes her experience with this issue,

I didn't want to change my name when I got married. We had terrible fights. Freud was quoted to the effect that I wasn't committed to the marriage. My husband was persistent, and I gave in.

Emily had heard of women who removed their wedding rings upon entering job interviews and generally withheld all information pertaining to their marital status and personal lives as much as possible while seeking employment. Emily did not understand why until several days after her first job interview. It took her some time to clarify what had happened because the experience ran so contrary to her expectations of what it would be like. In her first interview for a very attractive job, Emily found herself being asked multiple personal questions about such topics as her plans about children, maternity leave, her feelings about being at work and away from her home and children, and so forth. Emily, of course, did not have any children yet and did not plan to. She loved her work and felt fulfilled by it. She expected to continue to excel at what she did upon entering the workplace and did not envision any room in her life for children.

Emily's interview experience is replicated frequently. Another young woman related her interview experience thus:

I was interviewed one-on-one by a partner of the firm. We immediately went to lunch when I arrived. He tossed my resume and file aside, which I had painstakingly prepared, and began to barrage me with questions as he ate his lunch. Did I have boyfriends? Was I planning to get married? Do I like to cook? And on and on. I never had a single bite of my food, my stomach was so twisted into knots. I hated the situation, but what could I do?

Emily felt like getting up and bolting when she was confronted with a stranger who held out the possibility of desirable employment but who was querying her about her future life with husband and children. She also felt like blurting that she was not interested in children, that there is no issue about conflict with her work. She wanted to get on with the real interview. But something in her—two factors, in fact—held Emily back from such an exclamation.

First was a sense of integrity to which Emily clung. She felt that she was a worthy candidate for the job and shouldn't need to disown her potential to bear children or even discuss it as admission to the doors of being considered for a job. Emily had a strong sense that the conversation ought to be irrelevant and that it was degrading, although these were perhaps not entirely explicit thoughts in her mind at the time.

Second, and this was not necessarily explicit in Emily's mind either, Emily had the instinct that if she had disowned her birth-given female potential to bear children, if she had expressed her lack of interest in the entire enterprise of creating a family out of her marriage with John, her candidacy for the job would similarly be disqualified. To express such a disclaimer would be to render herself *unnatural* as a female in the eyes of the interviewer. Emily would thereby place herself in the threatening realm of androgyny, of a woman who is trying to play it tough. Several of her interviews proceeded similarly, and Emily had to try constantly to politely maneuver her way out of these difficult situations without offending the interviewers or blowing her chances of being hired.

At home, because the second shift was grafted onto Emily's other responsibilities, the seeds of inequity were present in her relationship with John from the beginning. Emily's home life changed in many typical ways once she began living with John. John was a few years older than Emily and was already advanced in his career by the time Emily started living with him. Thus, he often went away on business trips for two to three days. Each time John went on a trip, Emily found herself thoroughly cleaning their apartment, whereas otherwise, she and John would give the place a quick once-over straightening. Even for the lighter job, Emily found herself doing the bulk of the picking up and putting away sort of household maintenance, often of John's clothing, towels, and so forth. Emily also found herself regularly leaving work early in order to do routine food and household shopping as well as to pick up items at the dry cleaner, for example, before it closed. In contrast, John might occasionally go to a specialty food store to pick up something unusual for them to cook or use if an idea struck him.

An unacknowledged component of the second shift is so-called beautification. Emily, unlike John, is expected to maintain a certain standard of so-called feminine beauty. This too needs to be scheduled in and around and to the detriment of Emily's work. She finds herself applying facial masks also while John is away. She diets when she is not with him so that she can relax and enjoy the kind of rich meals that John prefers when they are together. Emily schedules manicure, leg waxing, hair cut, and facial appointments and expends a significant portion of her time obtaining and maintaining appropriate clothing for work and social occasions. In the morning, it is no simple matter for Emily to get dressed, apply make-up, and attend to her hair.

For work, there are unspoken parameters concerning her appearance that are more complex and contradictory than any that men must heed. She definitely must tread a fine line when outfitting herself. Although she cannot appear masculine, she must neither appear too feminine for fear of being treated as someone devoid of mental capability. Thus, any nail polish other than clear or a very faint color is off limits at work. The same goes for brightly colored make-up, although wearing no make-up at all suggests that she is not attractive, that she is not a real woman, that she is perhaps trying to be a man, or that she is old. Her clothing cannot in any way be sexually suggestive, such as are short skirts and tight blouses. Yet, often, loose blouses and longer skirts are also considered suggestive. Pants are problematic unless they are clearly feminized, for the threat of masculinization that is otherwise implied. Heeled shoes are seductive, yet flat shoes are too casual. Bright colors are frivolous, yet dull colors are unattractive and suggest age. An attractive figure is seductive and suggests she has no intelligence; yet, if she is too thin or too fat or too tall or too short, she is also viewed disparagingly and is often the brunt of jokes.

An assistant professor in the humanities expressed her care with appearance thus:

When I get tenure, that's when I'll paint my nails red and wear make-up. If I did that now, it'd be professional suicide.

A colleague quickly retorted,

No, you won't do it then either. You'll still need to maintain respect. In fact, you'll be fighting even harder for it. That's if you ever get tenure; women don't in this field, you know.

For social occasions or when at home with John, she is supposed to do a 180-degree flip and be more stereotypically attractive. Emily tries to keep her body to a certain standard of thinness and firmness, which requires that she work out with regularity and that she diet. But if she goes too far and spends more time than somebody else would like working out, or if she eats too little or too much, then she is labeled as sick, either under the title of anorexic or some other of the myriad possibilities. In contrast, John goes through virtually none of these hoops of appearance and judgment at work or at home. In short, this segment of the second shift, which pertains to Emily's physical appearance, is one for which she can never fully meet all the requirements, no matter how much time, energy, and thought she devotes to it.

Overall, what developed in the course of their first year together was that Emily quickly began to take up mental space and physical time with household chores, errands, and maintenance, much more than she ever had living alone. Whereas John's time demands for household considerations, as compared with when he was single, decreased dramatically.

Emily also began to find that her person was being subsumed or absorbed by the outside world and by John into John's person—that where two independent people had been there was one plus something rather amorphous. This developed through subtle, small alterations of the manner in which friends and colleagues spoke to her and expressed different expectations of her. For example, it was tacitly assumed by friends as well as by John that Emily would be in charge of their social calendar. In fact, Emily took on this responsibility without even noticing that she was doing so. And she found that friends, even friends of hers who predated her relationship with John, assumed automatically that to see her socially now meant that she would appear with John. This was a trend that Emily noticed distinctly and caused her some distress, because she could not convince her friends that she also liked to see them individually in John's absence just as they had for years before.

There is another common asymmetry. This one concerns responsibility between John and Emily with regard to work-related social situations. Emily is expected as a matter of course to attend social functions for John's work and is expected to enhance his standing by maintaining a certain comportment at such events: to be demurely flirtatious with the right people, to be moderately and pleasantly interested in the activities of John's colleagues, and to relate in a traditionally female way with the wives of John's colleagues.

The reverse does not usually hold. John is not expected to fill this slot in Emily's life. In fact, there is no comparable slot for John to fill. He might attend social functions related to Emily's work, but he would not be tacitly required to do so. If he did attend, he would be likely to be queried and talk about his own career, and not be there to bolster Emily's professional standing.

Similarly, Emily is expected tacitly to bolster John's career in myriad ways that John would not be likely to reciprocate. It would appear unseemly for Emily not to be eager to listen to John's work stories and to be attentive to difficulties he is facing. She helps him problem solve when that is required, celebrates his accomplishments with gusto, and generally finds daily ways of supporting his advancement through encouragement, discussion, and action where possible.

All of this could be considered as just a natural part of a caring relationship between two adults engaged in professional endeavors, if not for the fact that it is largely a one-way street. Although John may not actively try to sabotage Emily's career, which many male partners in fact do, he is likely to feel competitive with her and only feel comfortable when she is at a lower level of achievement than he is. This holds true even though they are in different professions. John is unlikely to spend any amount of time thinking about promoting Emily and assisting her in her professional achievement. In fact, there is a vacuum surrounding the subject of her career, which the two of them spend little time discussing or even acknowledging.

In addition to assuming the roles of the social director for herself and John as a couple and of midwife to John's career, it quickly unfolds that it is Emily who must manage the relationship between herself and John. If there are problems, she is the one generally to bring them up and attempt to discuss and resolve the issues. She is the one who must assume the role of coach of their "team." She must be tough on them when that is called for, and soft and forgiving when that is what will get the job of relationship adjustment done.

Sex is a murky subject in the lives of American couples, and few people like to admit that it can be a problematic aspect of a relationship until sexual problems have reached disaster proportions. Managing the sexual relationship in a couple is definitely part of the second shift, and Emily has not escaped responsibility for this component. Like many women involved in a sexual relationship with a man, Emily keeps an ongoing monitor in her mind of the sexual activity between her and John in which his needs are considered first. If John wants to have sex more frequently or less frequently than she does, Emily accommodates to John's comfort level in the name of maintaining a good relationship. Emily also makes an effort to supply the kind of sexual experience for John that she thinks he wants, but does not consistently pursue a kind of sexual activity that would enhance her experience. Sex becomes, for many women, one task on a list of many that comprise the second shift. In fact, one woman, dismayed at how the work that she does outside her career for her family is not only not appreciated but even unacknowledged, listed the categories of services that she performs. One item was sex, in these words: *"And, plus, in addition to all of that, I give him really great sex."* Again, trying to please one's partner sexually could be considered a natural part of a healthy relationship if the concern were reciprocal on balance.

In short, much of what has been discussed above could be placed under the general category of mothering behavior. The fact is that Emily is expected to engage in nurturing, mothering behavior in virtually every aspect of her life. She must be mother to peers, advisors, mentors, and bosses; to the household; to her relationship with John; and to John in regard to his career goals. When she adds her own actual children into the hopper, the burden of this multiple mothering flies off the charts. At that point, something has to be broken off, and too often, it is the career that is sacrificed.

GENDER LESSONS

There are two arenas from which to draw Gender Lessons in this chapter. The first concerns the actual treatment Emily receives because she is someone for whom the exclusive either–or *Red Shoes* dilemma applies, and the second arises from the second shift of labor that Emily is expected to perform..

First, Emily is, of course, infantilized by being pushed into the false choice of career or marriage. This is because she is being *told* what she can and cannot handle, in paternalistic, seemingly well-intentioned advice from her professors or superiors about what are her life options. A choice between career or marriage is one that nobody would imagine imposing upon a man in Emily's position. Emily, of course, can disregard the command to make a choice, as many women do, but the diminishment of her self-concept has an impact nevertheless. For just being talked to in such a manner, and repeatedly throughout her training and career, as if one were a child or incompetent can easily become self-fulfilling to an extent. And, even while disregarding the impetus to choose, in the back of everyone's mind, including Emily's, is that there is a grain of truth in the choice as presented because of the way society is structured. A man does not need to confront the choice because he is either single and free or he has a wife equivalent at home to organize his life for him. Emily, and other women, outside the still rare exceptions, do not have wives to take care of the necessities-plus. Moreover, she *is* the wife equivalent who performs the domestic services in addition to her career demands. Thus, she will find herself at a competitive disadvantage professionally as compared with her male colleagues.

Second, a woman cannot win with the false dichotomy in place. Whatever her choice is, she will be condemned for it. If she rejects any sort of domestic alliance and throws all her life energy into her work and building her career, then she is kept at arm's length distance by her male colleagues because she may appear overly masculinized or because she just seems odd, not a real woman, someone who is unnatural and threatening. And, of course, if she does enter into a domestic relationship with a man, then she is considered spoken for and without sufficient time at her disposal for her work.

Third, it is harder for a woman to achieve professional excellence with the dichotomy constantly held over her head. She is demoralized by the attitudes that it promotes in herself and in her colleagues, both female and male.

Fourth, she must waste time and energy solving the men's problems concerning her choices. That is, she must convince both colleagues and bosses, as well as her partner, that she can perform each shift as if it were the only one. It is the new ethic of loyalty and monogamy, where the competition is not another potential partner or job, but of job and partner competing with one another.

Emily's second shift of labor causes two principal problems. The first is that, while at this point in her work and marriage, she can manage work, professional development, and household responsibilities, both the expectation that she will perform this second shift of service and the actual fact that she does fulfill it take a toll. The toll is more widespread than is often noted, even by Emily herself. First, the second shift requires a physical toll that leaves Emily with less energy for her work and for the rest of her life. Shopping, cleaning, cooking, errands, and home, personal, and relationship maintenance all require energy, muscle, and time. The amount that Emily expends in these ways clearly detracts from her energy pool for her career.

Perhaps even more critical is the mental toll of the second shift. Quite simply, Emily must reserve a large amount of mental room for household tasks and social organization. Even if she keeps a log book or calendar for such items as dry cleaner pick-ups, shopping, errands, tasks, and social engagements, she must use up mental energy creating the lists, calendars, and so forth. In addition is the glaring fact that John does not need to use his mind or his body this way for more than a small fraction of Emily's expenditure. This fact alone can eat away at Emily's psyche as an unjust consequence of her romantic and domestic association with John. At some point, the pent-up resentment and bitterness will begin to erode Emily's own self-confidence.

Moreover, a vicious cycle ensues. Both because John is more advanced in terms of his career, and thus makes more money than Emily, and because Emily spends a large chunk of her time and energy in ways with which John does not concern himself, Emily cannot advance as quickly as she might have if she were not responsible for the second shift on her own. And this is true for two reasons: because of the sheer amount of time and energy involved and because of the sub rosa psychic damage that is developing. This is another factor in Emily's consequent drop in self-esteem.

GENDER COMPOUNDS

Complications arise if in fact a woman is married to a man and their work requires them to live in separate locations. With good jobs in the professional sector becoming increasingly scarce, couples are forced to accept the fact that in all probability, they will spend segments of their shared life actually living apart if both are to be able to remain reasonably competitive in their chosen fields. Often, however, in order to stay together or at least within reasonable commuting distance, it is the woman who will sacrifice advancement.

When a couple lives apart because of job location, it is more than likely that it is the woman who will make more than most of the accommodations to this living arrangement. She will set up and maintain all of one and the bulk of the other household. She will do more of the commuting, and she will have even more restricted work hours because of these factors. And although the woman will be a presence at the man's business location, and will therefore be available for work-related social events, the reverse will not in general be true. Thus, whatever benefits accrue to one's career from being available socially as a family unit will be present for the man and not the woman. Thus, in this mode, the woman's second shift leavens, while her time, energy, and, most importantly, her enthusiasm for her career shrinks.

GENDER ACTION

Emily has her work cut out for herself. She must find her way out of the responsibility for the second shift, and she must navigate the either–or *Red Shoes* choice being laid out for her. This navigation is both external, involving her colleagues and superiors, and internal, within her own psyche.

Restructuring her interaction with colleagues, professors,

and bosses is a difficult path to tread because much of what goes on, subtle or otherwise, occurs largely unnoticed. Thus, in attempting to transform the situation, it is easy to appear overly sensitive and harsh. Moreover, with the plethora of gender battles that Emily may to choose to take on, she is not sure, for example, if addressing the issue of listening to her mentor's personal trials is worth it. But taking the entire second shift picture in at a glance, it is probably essential to the progression of her career to make some changes in the structure of her professional interaction.

In fact, simple changes often reap great benefits. For example, if Emily were to walk into an advisory meeting prepared to redirect the conversation to her work, only subtle conversational cues would probably be necessary. The same holds true for conversations with colleagues and other professional interactions. Professional settings in which Emily is being placed in the role of personal confidante, rather than peer, student, or employee, are some of the few instances that are relatively easy to modify toward appropriate professional discourse.

The best time to address the second shift at home is before it begins. Thus, when choosing to live with John and later to marry him, one of the early subjects for conversation ought to be the division of labor for the household. Not only should the labor itself and the chores be split equally but also the responsibility for *creativity* with regard to the home and social life must be shared. This means that it is not acceptable for Emily, for example, to sit down each week, plan the social calendar and the shopping, errand, and chores lists, divide them, and hand John's half to him. And, as is often the case inside many American homes that get this far in the division of labor, she might then need to keep a copy of John's list in order to make sure that he accomplishes his part and to be able to supply him with a fresh copy when he inevitably loses it. In such a case it is still Emily alone who must occupy her mind with the second shift; it is she who still remains responsible for its smooth functioning. John is merely carrying out a set of tasks for which he holds no responsibility for their effectiveness in the overall plan.

Of course, even this minimal sharing by John in the second shift would constitute a vast improvement in the lives of many American women. But it is not acceptable as an end state. This sort of arrangement can only be labeled as John "helping" Emily, as so many men are fond of saying that they are helping their wives out in a pinch. Men retreat from responsibility for the second shift, and women take it on as a matter of course.

Why this is, that women almost willingly assume the second shift, is interesting in itself. Educated, busy, professional women simply proceed to perform the jobs required at home. When asked why, many women declare that after trying to achieve an approximation of equity in the home with their husbands, they found the effort and conflict required were greater than the amount of energy needed to just go ahead and do the chores themselves. One woman relates,

First I had to tell my husband what to do. Then I'd have to remind him a few times to do it. Then, if he did it, and that's a big if, in general, I'd have to tell him how to redo it, you know, return the wrong product and get the right one, or whatever, even though I had spelled out the item in painstaking detail. And ultimately, I'd have to go ahead and do it myself. In the process, I'd build up a lot of resentment and anger. It wasn't worth it.

Some women do not even consider attempting to share the second shift with their male partner; they simply assume the responsibility as their own from the start. Partly, this is training from early childhood, and partly it is a form of guilt. Mixed in with a feeling of entitlement to fulfilling careers on equal footing with men is a measure of twofold guilt concerning, on the one hand, usurping a spot in the professional world that is not actually theirs to take and, on the other, failing as a woman and domestic partner.

Thus, not only must the woman work toward a genuine sharing of the responsibility for the second shift but she must also do battle with her internal conflict over her role in life. She must remind herself on a daily basis that the price of being allowed to enter the professional realm is not excellent performance of the second shift. On the contrary, this kind of guilt-provoked rationale for the status quo is precisely one of the ways in which women are undermined and participate in their own demise professionally. By keeping their hands and minds mired in domestic tasks, they keep themselves in chains. They participate in fettering themselves, away from the freedom to actively pursue a career to the fullest extent possible and to achieve their professional goals.

The second shift can no longer be considered women's work if this country is to continue to grow and function to capacity. Nor can individual women allow their lives, personal and professional, to be occupied to the extent that they usually are with home maintenance. Letting go of the second shift will not only free the woman's time but it will also free her mind to have interesting thoughts in the place where shopping lists and chore assignments once reigned. It will also elevate her self-esteem, as she will no longer have an implicit feeling of inferiority or unworthiness as a result of being the one who exclusively or largely performs the grunt work for the home. Instead, she will have the satisfied feeling of a shared life and mutual respect. She will literally be able to look in the mirror and smile at herself.

9 THE SECOND SHIFT: AFTER CHILDREN

GENDER BASICS

One of the most momentous personal decisions professional women must make is whether to have children. The second is when to have children, if one has already decided that one does want to have a family. Emily is no exception. Before Emily began living with John, she assumed that she would not have or want to have children of her own. She had never been around children, at least since her teenaged days of babysitting, and was completely immersed in her studies and plans for the future. She was ambitious and planned on achieving the highest rank in her career.

John, on the other hand, like most men, operated on the assumption that he would eventually marry and have a family. For men in this culture the decision is much simpler. As matters stand, the man's life changes very little in the passage to life with children. His professional life continues as it had, or accelerates, and he is not likely to take on extra chores at home. Rather, he will gain enormously in a certain respect without sacrificing anything of import. He will gain the joys of fatherhood in the amounts that suit his existing schedule; he is likely to gain respect at the office and often a promotion and salary increase. The actual work of parenting will be left largely to the woman—the diapering, feeding, waking in the night, purchases, pediatric visits, and so on.

Just like other components of the second shift, the bulk of the burden of child care and the tasks surrounding the raising of children falls to the mother—from carrying and giving birth; nursing; feeding; diapering; supplying the baby equipment, food, clothing, toys, and diapers; cleaning; playing; educating, including seeking out the educational options; arranging for child care and for contact with friends and family; and generally supplying the child with an appropriate physical, social, emotional, and intellectual home environment. Although only the mother can carry, give birth, and nurse, the rest of the child care tasks are not an innately female province.

Even fathers who have the option of paternity leave after the birth of their children do not often exercise it; most do not even consider it. A biochemist explained the impact of their first child on her husband:

I know of fathers who at least handle part of the night shift sometimes, particularly in the beginning when the mother is so worn out and overwhelmed. My husband was overjoyed when our son was born, but he was unprepared for the reality. He doesn't see why his life as he's known it until now should change. He needs to work, and he needs rest to work. So I sleep in the baby's room so that I can quiet him instantly so that my husband won't lose sleep and be tired for work. I love my son dearly, but he's 2 months old, and I'm so exhausted that it's going to seem like a vacation when I return to work.

In order to have children, mothers, in contrast, make great sacrifices personally, socially, and professionally. Their lives change drastically and forever. Their professional life is likely to undergo several transitions, partly stemming from the attitudes and behavior of colleagues, superiors, and clients. Women are penalized enough on the job for merely having the potential to create life; when they actually do so, their professional lives can be altered forever. In the words of a successful executive,

I had built the marketing department, and I was really pleased with that. Then I left to have my baby, and when I came back they wouldn't give me my job back. They had built a really cohesive team in the interim, and they found that they loved my part of the job. It is sort of glamorous; you get to go to all the meetings at the front end when everyone's all enthused about a project and nobody's fighting about money yet. So they really liked that. They liked being in the offices with the executives and stuff.

So, all of a sudden, I found that I was being accompanied on all trips. And I wondered what am I here for, what's my value in this case. If they're going to do the job, then they don't need me. And so that was bugging me. Because I had kids, the perception was I'm not as committed as they are. And they also had babies at the same time as me so they knew the demands of a baby, and they knew the demands of the home, but they both had full-time wives at home. And they just never gave me back my responsibilities and back my area. And it became marketing by committee. And I just felt we were wasting a lot of time, their time, and my time was all redundant.

So I spoke up. I attempted to have conversations about it, but it was just real subtle. They would say they would give me back my job, but they didn't. And when it came to a head, when they just saw me as a mother and it was, for example, six o'clock, they would make jokes. You know, if I was in a meeting with them, "Oh, well, she has got to go. You can't expect her to stay past six." And it was all kind of good-humored, but it was like,

"You're not committed. You're not really here. You want to be with your kids." And that was much more damaging to me than any of the other kinds of sexual harassment I encountered. My sense of purpose, my self-esteem plunged. I was really unhappy because I wasn't given my responsibility, I wasn't listened to.

They would have meetings without me on subjects that had to do with the marketing department. So I decided to turn things around and get involved in another project. I developed a new project for the company. And then I was told, "That's not your job. You maybe better write a job description." So seventeen years at the place and I'm supposed to write a job description. So those were like subtle forms of trying to push me out I felt.

Because of the real fear of losing seniority, status, and one's job itself, many professional women conceal their personal lives to the greatest extent possible. In the words of one mother of three small children,

I am careful not to keep pictures of my children and my husband in my office, and I avoid all conversation that verges on becoming personal. I just know that colleagues and clients will think less of my capabilities automatically if they know that I am a mother.

Of course, yet again, professional women are placed in a no-win situation with respect to revealing the specifics of their personal lives. If they let it be known that they have children, superiors and colleagues may think less of their capabilities and of their commitment. They may be actually demoted or phased out or may suffer pay cuts. Clients and associates may also patronize them on this score and feel less secure of their professional performance. Yet, if they let it be known that they do not have children, then they may be treated as if they are on the verge of having them, with all the consequences as if they already had them, or under the assumption that as soon as they do, they will quit never to return to work again. Or they might be greeted with suspicion, calling their very identity into question. One woman expressed her frustration with this issue:

I feel like because I don't have a family to trot out and display for my colleagues, I'm considered as less. I am devalued in my work because of personal choices I've made for myself. And I get passed over for comparable raises to my peers' salary increases because I'm perceived as not needing the money.

A childless lesbian of international repute in her field spoke with great bitterness about the treatment she received from colleagues when she was up for tenure. It was a promotion that should have come to pass readily in her case were the process based on merit:

The tenure battle was over me as a certain kind of woman. If I had been married with children it would have been very different.

Once a professional woman has a child or children, her professional life will likely undergo change due to her own attitude and behavior. There are two branches of the new mother's transition: one branch concerns the alterations in her routine caused by the real demands of the baby. The other branch concerns changes in the woman's life pattern as a result of her response to becoming a mother, a response that she could not fully anticipate beforehand.

Many women who have the option to do so do cut back their work schedule or stop professional work altogether for up to a period of years after the birth of their first child. Some of these women would surely choose to do so, even if they lived in a perfectly egalitarian world. After all, there are few things as rewarding and enjoyable as nursing, playing with, and caring for one's own infant and toddler. There is also virtually nothing as demanding and taxing as doing so in the vacuum in which most American women find themselves as mothers.

Many of these women, however, decide to restrict or stop work altogether or in some other way to rein in their professional advancement because social norms and patterns make doing so appear to be the path of least resistance. That it seems this way is, of course, only possible by ignoring the potential emotional and professional damage done to these women's lives. Because our culture, wrongly, does not value the job of raising and caring for children, child care is something appropriate for women to do. It is easy to envision a high-powered female lawyer leaving her job to care for her baby, but virtually impossible to imagine a high-powered male lawyer taking a three-month paternity leave to care for his baby.

Even women who have had the option of cutting back their work in order to be available for their children fall into the trap of devaluing the work of mothering. And work it is. Not accidentally, the only element of an extremely demanding job that it lacks is a salary. Thus, when a mother who has cut back her work is asked what she does, she will more than likely spin into a bout of self-deprecation, doubt, and confusion. Virtually inevitably, her audible reply will consist of a response about her professional work whether she is currently actively pursuing it or not. One mother described her dismay over her response to the question thus:

When I get asked what I do, I try to pump myself up. I've found ways of describing my professional achievements that mask the fact that they are not absolutely current, since I started to stay at home half-time to take care of my two boys.

But each time, I feel like a notch is taken out of my gut: I don't give value to being a mother. I don't say, "Well, I'm a mother, and I really love being able to spend this time with my kids, and I do a very good job at being a mother and devote a lot of my energy and intellect to it." I don't say any of that. I know I've adopted the male model of value and it kills me.

Although some professional women do have and exercise the option of cutting back their hours or of stopping work altogether to raise their children at least to school age, there are emotional, professional, and financial costs to the choice. Because the care and maintenance of children are considered part of the second shift and thus are not considered to be valuable work, and because child care comes as a package with all the drudgery of housework, women who have professions who take on the task of mothering suffer particularly large drops in self-confidence and self-esteem.

These declines in self-concept arise in part from the manner in which these women are treated by the outside world, which takes a large enough toll as it is. They also arise from the pressure within the woman's own mind combined with a set of demands she places on herself that are impossible to fulfill satisfactorily. If she has cut back her work hours, then the myth of squeezing a full-time and demanding professional job into part-time hours would create tension enough. Add to this demand caring for an infant or young child in all of its myriad aspects, even with hired child care present, and one has a recipe for multiple disappointment if not outright failure. This is where the myth of the supermom shores up its debt and cashes in on the back of the woman trying to accomplish more than one human can.

In Emily's case, she decided to go on a half-time schedule at work, an option that was only grudgingly conceded to by her boss. Emily made that decision because she feared that full-time work, in which she regularly worked fifty- and sixty-hour weeks, would leave her too depleted to get to know her child. Taking an extended leave scared her both financially and professionally, in terms of weakening her professional contacts and standing. Even in retrospect, Emily felt that she made the best choice of the alternatives, but that does not mean that she was necessarily happy with her situation. Her half-time work often amounted to full-time hours, yet brought diminished respect because of her new status. When meetings and other professional obligations were scheduled during hours when she was supposed to be home with her daughter and did not have child care coverage, she was frustrated with an array of bad choices. Not attending was an option that left Emily feeling out of it and unprofessional.

Makeshift child care arrangements often did not work out and, in any case, caused a good deal of anxiety. And the few times that Moria attempted to bring her baby along with her, she often left virtually in tears, feeling like she had made a spectacle of herself in the process. It happened on too many occasions for Emily not to begin to take it to heart that she scheduled meetings only to need to rearrange or cancel them with virtual predictability. Many days passed with Emily wishing that her daughter would grow up faster so she could bypass as much of this phase rapidly, only to catch herself and break down into tears at the thought. Because of this tension, Emily was unable to enjoy the time she was with her daughter, and this saddened her more than any other factor. Emily had been surprised at the love she felt for her baby as soon as she was born, and she genuinely cherished her and loved to play with her and watch her try new things. To have these incredible experiences marred by the specter of losing her grip on her career depressed Emily and left her feeling doubly less competent. She felt that she was failing as a mother, as a professional, and as an adult managing incremental stress.

If she had taken an extended leave of absence from professional work, then the emphasis of the internal pressure would shift, and calculating the timing of re-entry to professional work would be difficult. Re-entry into the professional realm after a partial or full-time absence because of the birth of a child is a tricky matter. Not only do many women return to find that their job has been filled or eliminated, but even when their position has been held for them, they return with a different status. Whatever respect and standing in the field they had managed to gain before are, more often than not, significantly diminished if not dissipated altogether in their absence. They are no longer viewed the same way, and as in the case of the woman quoted above, their commitment to work is seriously called into question regardless of their actual performance upon return.

Timing, in fact, is an overarching issue in the careers of professional women. They constantly are trying to juggle multiple life schedules in their heads to coincide with an optimal career plan. First, they must often try to fit in the time demands of their own training and work pattern to accommodate the professional schedule of their husband or partner. Second, they must calculate as best they can the timing of children in order to cause the least amount of damage to their professions. Whereas a generation ago women had children in their early twenties and developed a career in their thirties or forties, now women train in their early to mid-twenties and launch careers, have children in their early thirties and then attempt to continue professionally at some point thereafter.

Many women attempt to wait to have children until they have reached a level of professional development that minimizes professional risk. Thus, a professor might want to wait until she has achieved tenure, a lawyer until she has made partner, a doctor until she has an established practice. In trying to make all the relevant calculations, Emily's head spins. Conception is not the kind of event that can be planned precisely, nor is pregnancy, the birth event itself, the kind of child and specific attention that it will require after birth, nor the mother's feelings and desires after the birth of her first child. Emily begins to feel dulled at the prospect of trying to plan, as if she is in preschool attempting to fit a round peg into a square hole.

GENDER LESSONS

The second shift with regard to child rearing has vast implications for women's careers in the professions, and there can
be no parity between women and men until women are no
longer exclusively responsible for it. Whatever lip service is
currently spent on fatherhood, the fact remains that women's
careers suffer and men's careers often are enhanced by the
birth of their children.

A high-level executive, whose career went through many
twists and turns while raising her three children, blurted out
angrily the following in response to the question of how she
envisions her life differently had she been born male:

*I certainly would have a more consistent career, because I
would have a wife at home doing everything.*

Barring steadfast determination not to miss a single beat at
work and thus also to deny the true demands of motherhood
even at their most minimal, every mother's professional career
is shunted aside. Mothers' careers are checkered in ways that
men do not even need to consider, let alone tolerate and adapt
to. For example, a psychologist reflects on her feelings early
in her role as mother:

*I thought my career was postponed like all women. I thought,
"Look how healthy I am that I can do this. I'm a mother. I'm
normal. Aren't I great?" It was so natural to me to think that I
should take care of the children and do all that. I took that for
granted. I expected help; that was the most revolutionary part.
I expected that their father would participate in their upbringing.*

That is, women not only must adapt their careers to the
demands of motherhood, but our cultural myths have also
convinced us that a woman ought not feel whole and normal

without bearing children. The anguish that many women endure in the decision not to have children is testament to the force of this myth. At the same time that women are not permitted and do not permit themselves to feel adequate without having children, our culture also devalues the work of mothering. It is a Catch-22 situation that causes professional women to suffer tremendously.

GENDER COMPOUNDS

An older woman who already has a family when she enters a career will face increased prejudice. First, the woman has none of the qualities that we admire in this culture in a professional. She is not male, she is not young, and because she has started or raised a family first, she will have to go to great lengths, greater than other women, to be perceived as professional. To gain admission to professional programs, the older woman with children will have to supply much more impressive credentials than a single woman of average entry age and conjure more convincing displays of commitment to the profession. One such older woman relates her experience in applying to professional programs:

I was very self-conscious when I was applying to architecture programs. I felt old, and was at least ten years older than most entrants. And I had three kids. I just didn't feel like people would see me as a viable candidate because of this picture. I spent months, literally, painstakingly putting together the best portfolio and application I could. I went and schmoozed at every opportunity, open house, or whatever and spent a great deal of time cultivating contacts at my top choices. All just to get into a program I was maybe even overqualified for. I knew that the true linchpin, though, was that I look young and could dress young. And I hid the fact that I'm married, and I hid the fact that I have kids, and I hid the fact that I live in a suburban-style home and have a family life. It wasn't easy evading all the personal questions, but I was determined.

Many graduate programs openly acknowledge that they admit certain candidates whom they consider to be risks and not of quite the quality to make a successful graduate of the program simply and solely to financially support the program. Thus, applicants such as older women are often not given financial support according to merit, but are put in a risk category for the purposes of paying faculty salaries, not to train these entrants and give them a fair shake.

Thus, admission is the first hurdle, but completing the program successfully can be even more difficult, particularly when the faculty have no real expectations that such students will do so. Thus, piled on top of the real constraints of trying to complete a degree or training program while raising a family, and more than likely performing both the labor of the second shift and of paid employment full or part time, the older female student will have to contend with the negative expectations of her held by the faculty of the program.

Applying for and maintaining jobs in this circumstance are similarly problematic, yet only more difficult because in this case, one is asking to be employed and paid for work. The issue of professional commitment will be held over her head like a weapon as if to say, "There, you exercised your potential to bear children; *they* are your commitment. We can't let you mess up here for us because you won't be serious enough or focused enough about this job."

Another compounding factor arises were Emily to get divorced while her children were still in school or younger. She would face additional problems that would affect her professional life. Not only would Emily need to contend with the stress and realities of the process and aftermath of a divorce but she would also be put at a professional disadvantage in

almost exact inverse proportion to the advantages professionally that John would gain through a divorce. Emily is more
than likely to suffer a drop in her standard of living, whereas
John will entertain an increased standard of living. To alleviate her new financial burden, Emily is likely to make short-
term professional decisions that would be detrimental to her
overall, long-term career development. John would not need
to consider this kind of career move.

   Moreover, while the divorce will more than likely free up
much of John's time that he can now devote to his professional
development, Emily will experience the reverse. Because she
will have retained the bulk of the responsibility for the children and they will live with her, her time, even with increased
child care help and freedom, will be substantially restricted
as compared with the pre-divorce arrangement. Thus, Emily
will need to forego many opportunities for advancement.

GENDER ACTION

*I was really scared about having children, I didn't think I
wanted to do it because I was afraid of sacrificing my career.
But when my husband assured me that we'd share the responsibility fifty-fifty, I was thrilled.*

   No one can know how she will experience parenthood nor
truly grasp what the demands of it will be before the birth of
the first child. Nevertheless, it is essential for the woman working in the professions who is considering becoming a mother
to discuss with her partner in detail how the added responsibilities resulting from children will be met. She and her partner must set aside ample time and energy for discovering what
their goals are for parenting, household management, and
maintaining professional standing through the years with a
young child or children. The less that is discussed and planned

for, the greater the chances that the woman will shoulder the bulk of the new responsibilities and find herself overwhelmed and bitter.

The woman, based in part on the projections she makes with her partner, must then try to make realistic career goals that match the household plans she is making. It is amazing how women set themselves up for disappointment or failure by ignoring the obvious. If she plans to continue her career development as she did before having children, then she is going to require more than full-time child care and home maintenance backup. An assessment needs to be made, given the specific profession and position that the woman holds, of what is possible professionally. She needs to go beyond the leave policy she's entitled to and review what other women before her, if there are any, have tried and with what degree of success.

Above all, it is important at this juncture for the woman to reflect on who she is and what her own personal goals are, to the extent that she can honestly do this. Women are caught in the dilemma of professional success being valued above all else as the measure of achievement while child bearing and care are devalued, and at the same time, women are virtually required to desire children of their own. The woman who knows that she does not want children almost necessarily becomes conflicted and guilty due to the tide of social pressure and mores. It is certainly easier to create a compromise plan based on the real facts of her profession and of her partner and household situation, if she first knows what her ideal choices would be.

PART IV
FATHER KNOWS BEST

Advanced degree programs are often run like the small household fiefdoms such as those found in the old television serial, *Father Knows Best.* The pervasive atmosphere of paternalism and patronization found in *Father Knows Best* exists within degree program departments, and occasionally the indulgent benevolence present in the family life on the show is extended to at least some segment of the students. In any case, advanced professional degree candidates are treated much in the same fashion as the children in the family on the television program—as if they are not free agents and decision-making adults, but rather quasi-competent beings.

This picture holds for all students, female and male. The female professional degree candidates, however, are accorded an increased amount of infantilizing and discriminatory behavior from the faculty and staff than are their male peers. And their standing as future professionals is more precarious than is that of their male colleagues. This part provides an overview of the institutional training process for aspiring professional women, from admissions to completion of the degree.

10 ADMISSION AND FUNDING IN ADVANCED DEGREE PROGRAMS

GENDER BASICS

In her senior year of college, Emily applies to graduate programs. She has a strong academic record, excellent letters of recommendation, and she has scored fairly high on the necessary standardized tests. In addition to a formal application and her dossier, most of the institutions to which Emily is applying require an interview. In some cases, the interview is carried out by the director of admissions, sometimes by the director of the program, and sometimes by a faculty member whose area of expertise covers the interests that Emily expressed in her application.

Emily is nervous about the interviews and worried about presenting herself to her best advantage. She is also looking forward to being able to meet with the interviewers to gain information that she could not otherwise collect about the programs. She prepares her questions carefully for each interview and walks into each feeling as confident as she can.

In some cases, Emily is pleasantly surprised at how congenial and relaxed the interview is. In others, Emily is somewhat taken aback by the questions posed to her. In one case, Emily left the interview reeling. She had traveled a substantial distance there and back and, in the aftermath, spent the better part of the week pondering what had happened and what she did wrong. In this particular case, it was the director of the program who had conducted the interview. After telling Emily about the program and how well it compared with what is being offered elsewhere, the interviewer launched into an interrogation of Emily's ability and dedication.

He asked her why she is applying to graduate programs at all, what she thinks her qualifications are, and whether she believes that she can last through the entire program. In a sense, these are legitimate questions to ask any applicant. Yet, afterward, Emily had the feeling that there was a level of hostility in the air, and she felt under siege. Emily interpreted the event as a result of her own failing—that she had started off badly and had answered incorrectly. She felt she had presented herself as undecided and perhaps not as interested and committed as she actually was. Emily wracked her brains about how to rectify the situation, but could not come up with anything that felt reasonable and that wouldn't merely serve to underscore the fiasco. Thus, she resolved not to let that happen again, as she had three more interviews to go to in the next two weeks.

It is possible that Emily was having an off day and that she did not present herself in the best possible light. Nevertheless, even though women are being admitted to professional degree programs in greater proportions than ever before, they are still occasionally being discouraged from even applying. Women who have gone through the admission process report similar experiences to Emily's. For example, a mathematician reports an interview experience that she will not forget:

I remember taking the train out to this university to be interviewed by a mathematician whose work I knew well and admired greatly. I had studied many of his proofs in great detail and had read all of his papers. So, I was really excited to meet him in person, and the prospect of working closely with him in the program was thrilling. And he had a reputation for treating his students well.

I got there and he took me to lunch; it all seemed friendly enough. But, when we got back to his office, he quickly proceeded to tell me that I was wasting my time applying to graduate programs, that my best creative years were over. If I hadn't done anything remarkable yet, I never would. Oughtn't I try marriage instead, he'd even suggested at one point. I started to feel dizzy and was trying to calculate quickly in my head what I had said over lunch that had caused this weird turnaround.

I was really thrown. I mean, I was 20 years old, graduating younger than anyone else I knew and getting every honor and award in mathematics my college had to offer, including scholarship money for graduate work in the field. All of my professors conveyed the sense that I was going to go on and do solid, interesting work. So I didn't entirely believe him, but it did sort of throw me into a whirlpool of self-doubt for awhile. It took the wind out of me. I mean, I had felt very big when I walked in his door and felt very small when I walked out. I withdrew my application from that place out of anger. I'm not sure I should have, in retrospect, but I did know I'd have other options.

In spite of experiences such as this one, admission procedures are fairly equitable relative to other aspects of professional development. This does not mean that bias does not creep in from several entry points, however. Women's achievement still has to be significantly higher than men's to appear to those evaluating it that it is comparable. Thus, in all of the details of an application that are not strictly measured such as grades and test scores, the female applicant's features must be undeniably better than a male's in order to be ranked higher. Thus, letters of recommendation must be substantially more outstanding, the number and quality of awards and honors must be clearly higher, and the personal essay must be sparklingly perfect if a female is to be selected over a similarly ranked male. Much of this sort of bias is not intentional, but is subconscious in many of the ways that have been discussed in previous chapters. Word for word, achievement for achievement, parity in female and male applications would, with virtual certainty, lead to the male's application being ranked higher because of the lingering perception of males as more valuable, more serious, more intelligent, and, more stable.

And, even if the admission portion of the process were precisely equitable, this would not mean that encouragement to actually join a program after acceptance is even. Such encouragement can range from faculty members contacting the potential student to the offering of funding for tuition and/or living expenses and the designation of prestigious awards or work status as part of the admission package.

In this situation, it may be a conscious move for a program to appear to be equitable in admissions by, say, admitting women and men in equal numbers or equal proportions to the applications, and yet to undercut this potential for equity by offering more attractive packages to the men admitted than to the women. Generally, however, reasons for offering inequitable packages relative to merit more likely stem from unconscious factors. Men are perceived as being more needy of financial assistance because it remains part of our collective framework that men are the breadwinners. Even though at the level of the admission of college seniors to graduate programs, the consideration of supporting a household is virtually irrelevant, it is part of the underlying assumption that those in charge of the decisions draw upon. For, in fact, this consideration, if genuinely applied, would bias the awards in favor of women, who tend to go for graduate degrees at later ages than men possibly after having had children and thus are in need of, if anything, greater support.

Similarly, in the award of prestigious research or other work as part of the admission package, it remains easier for men to be perceived of as not only capable of the task required but as also needing and filling it. A faculty member, for example, will automatically conjure a picture of a male graduate student filling his research needs when he imagines the ideal candidate, much in the same way that almost all of us conjure a male image when we use the term "astrophysicist."

GENDER LESSONS

Admission packages are another instance of the status quo maintaining a strong grip on the future, even in the absence of deliberate discrimination. In programs in which women are admitted in equal numbers, they are not extended financial assistance and other necessary enticements in equal amounts to men. Largely, this inequity is due to ingrained perception. In the words of a law professor,

> *You have an array of subtle barriers that make it harder for women. It's filled with stereotypes used against women. It's pernicious.*

Thus, admissions packages to advanced degree programs must be regarded with a degree of skepticism. We are so far away from realizing the public perception and fear that women are being admitted and funded because they are women, not because they are qualified. The reality is that women are often awarded attractive admission packages *in spite of* the fact that they are women.

GENDER COMPOUNDS

Consider the case in which Emily is in middle age or close to it and is seeking entrance to a profession degree program. Assume it is to be her second career, and she is trying to make a career shift. In this case, many of the stereotypes used against women entering professions are highlighted.

First of all, her dedication and seriousness will be called into question even more so than if she were fresh out of college and launching a career path. Regardless of the fact that many men entertain and carry out career changes at every stage, it is not part of the ideal male professional model. The idea smacks more of the picture of the fickle or indecisive female dilettante who tried her hand at one thing, perhaps had children in between, and now wants another round at something else. In this picture, she's probably married and, by assumption, therefore does not need an income.

The age factor can bear on the prejudices at play here as well: Emily is substantially older than the other applicants. In such a case, her usefulness for the profession will be called into question. Emily may come to be viewed by the admissions committee as merely part of the tuition pool that creates revenue for the institution, but she will not be viewed as a serious contender for degree completion. Characterizing the general role of female graduate students are these bitter words of a university professor:

Women students are used to create jobs that male professors will have. Women's tuitions are used for the income for these male professors.

By the mere age factor alone plus gender, Emily may enter a professional degree program with multiple handicaps attached to her candidacy. She will have to work much harder than her female peers who are younger, less experienced, and less knowledgeable than herself in order to convince the faculty that she is worthy of their time and attention. These problems may ramify as Emily proceeds through the program. Even if she manages to convince one or two faculty members of her worth, she will face the disrespect of the rest of the faculty and probably her peers, female and male. Thus, all course credits, qualifications, theses, dissertations, degree awards, and letters of recommendation from faculty for jobs will be more difficult for Emily to obtain at fair value than for her peers.

GENDER ACTION

To obtain the best admissions package possible, Emily should ensure that she has made everything about herself as explicit and clear as possible. She must instruct college professors about her intentions and desires, as well as her accomplishments, so that they can write the best and most useful letters of reference for her applications as possible. She also must not be hesitant to ask these professors whether the letters they will write will be of the highest quality or if they can only recommend her as one among many.

In filling out her application Emily must take care that she presents herself in the best light possible and not be shy about asserting her achievements boldly. Men are trained to do this and take for granted that they will present themselves forcefully. Women learn this self-assertion at too late a point; it does not come as second nature. Women, on the contrary, are trained to be modest, to hold back positive information about themselves, not to step out into the light as individuals, and to be ashamed of surpassing others. Privately, of course, many strive to outpace others, but are coy about admitting to successes publicly. This is not a useful trait to cultivate. If women are to compete, they must display themselves boldly.

An application should also spell out Emily's professional aspirations in clear and optimistic terms. She needs to state clearly what her future goals are for herself in the professional realm. She must flesh out her interests and what she has accomplished to date in exploring these interests. She must set out her acquired competence and what her skills or abilities and work experience are to date that would be of use in an admissions committee putting together a package that would suit her, such as the inclusion of a special fellowship or research position. Emily must also make her financial needs crystal clear and not leave the matter up to the assumptions of the members of an admissions committee.

Before Emily accepts admission to any particular program, she must do her homework. Ideally, she should visit the institution and speak not only with faculty members and administrators but also with the students already enrolled. Preferably, she should speak with women and try to get a sense of the gender issues pertinent to that program.

11 COURSE WORK AND QUALIFYING EXAMS

GENDER BASICS

Having selected a graduate program, Emily enters in the fall with great enthusiasm. Her first-semester courses are interesting and even exhilarating at times. Emily has made friends with several other students in the program, female and male, and she feels that she will be able to forge meaningful professional relationships with members of the faculty.

In contrast with her college experience, Emily senses a different atmosphere even though she is again taking courses, with a clear list of requirements for the degree and little room for individual variation. Nevertheless, the students and the faculty operate with a different level of seriousness, and there is an assumed background of knowledge for the subject matter that Emily is not confident she shares to the same degree as her peers. She has the sense that her college course of study did not prepare her adequately. Emily goes so far in her first year as to suspect that she is not up to the challenge of the program.

Many women in professional programs share these types of feelings. In part, the atmosphere encourages this insecurity, and partly it is the result of how females are brought up to feel less skilled, less intellectually capable even when they clearly surpass their peers. One exceptionally bright young professional described the predicament thus:

I always saw myself as comic relief. It was very hard for me to think of myself as someone who could actually be efficient or successful. It didn't fit into my picture of myself. I liked school, but I was always afraid that I was getting away with something. That feeling, "Oh, I've gotten away with people thinking that I'm good at what I do for so long but at some point they're going to find out that I'm not." And I continue to live under that. That seems to me that it's something that guys don't do as much. If somebody says something bad about their work, then they attack the person who says the thing that's bad. Which is probably a good reaction. But instead certainly me and a lot of women I know tend to internalize all of that and say, "What's wrong with me? How come I couldn't do this?"

If women in professional programs have difficulty taking themselves seriously as legitimate contenders for the degree, faculty members as well as peers have an even harder time doing so than they did in the undergraduate environment. The reason is simple: an advanced degree program is designed to train the professionals of tomorrow. And, if we, as a culture, have difficulty mentally picturing women in high-level professional roles, such as brain surgeons, those at the top of the professions themselves, a group consisting virtually solely of men in almost every case, have even more difficulty with this thought experiment, let alone with the reality. As one woman so aptly comments, the system can be self-perpetuating through the generations:

I don't think that that's acceptable in a university, especially when you're dealing with young people all the time. Both men and women are affected and are learning patterns of behavior. I see a lot of male students being reinforced in things I would like to see them dislodged from by their male professors. So that it's not as if it's something that just affects women badly; I think it also affects male students badly. It's like bringing up your son badly. You don't want to bring him up in that same pattern; you want to make some kind of changes.

The ambiance of an advanced degree program for the students is made up of several components. For women, through all phases of the program, it makes a difference whether they are one among a sea of male students or there are other female students. This is so for a variety of reasons. First, if there are very few women, companionship of a certain nature would be wholly missing, as the statement of one epidemiologist attests:

My program had an official policy of admitting women for half of the entering class each year, and that made a huge difference to me. If I had been one of only a couple of women students in the department, I don't know if I would have made it through the program. Just the presence of the other women students was important because these were people to talk to. You learned that you weren't the only one having these little crises over interpreting the behavior of the professors. You found out that other women were having these experiences with members of the faculty. It was really important just having other women there.

When there is a balanced student body in terms of sex, then even in the absence of female faculty, women will have an easier time imagining themselves as future professionals because they are likely to be working with other women on projects, studying with them, and attending courses and seminars with them in which they give reports, and so forth. Had Emily been one of a mere handful of female students, she may have had a harder time, if not immediately, than in the long run, as the following observation describes:

It actually took me years to notice that I was virtually the only woman in the program. There were others, but we were all at different stages of the degree process. I was so wrapped up in my work, I loved it so much, that I didn't see that I was being treated as a curious anomaly. I mean, I was supported by the faculty in my work, but I didn't know that they saw me as a circus freak of sorts. I guess it's because I perceived myself as an individual, and that's not how they saw me. So, it took extreme behavior from the faculty for me to wake up to sexism. Then it was a shock, like the world had caved in.

And, of course, many women who are virtually alone in degree programs face and acknowledge trials because of their sex on a regular basis. Incidents may involve being effectively shut out of class discussions as well as from informal conversation with faculty. Students may be harassed inside the classroom, as this law student describes one of her experiences:

I always got asked the questions that involved sex cases in this particular class. I was the only woman in it. It was horrible. It was absolutely horrible. Whatever the case was, rape or whatever, the professor would ask me for the discussion.

Once when we were discussing a rape case, the professor wanted to discuss what the word "penetration" meant, and he called on me. I got so angry about it that I said it's not penetration unless it's six inches in. Or maybe I said eight or ten inches. Whatever I said, he was so upset by it, he couldn't catch his breath for a few minutes and I was happy.

It is outside the classroom that much of the harassment of advanced degree candidates occurs. Consider the following Ph.D. candidate's analysis of the situation:

Where I went to graduate school there were people who were notorious. They were the professors that you were warned against. Like, "Oh, he really doesn't mean to do anything like that, but just make sure you never sit next to him at an event because he'll put his hands on your knees. He'll start rubbing the back of your neck. If he gets a little drunk, he can get really sloppy. He can . . ." But it was always as if there was some eccentric uncle or something that had to be protected. Nobody said, you know, "How dare you allow this kind of guy in the classroom!" You just had to warn everybody away.

So it was this sort of electric fence idea where you couldn't actually see the barriers that people were setting up, but, if you were lucky enough to be warned off somebody like this, you were warned off them early. But this was somebody with a fair amount of power. And I knew women (I was lucky enough not to be one of them) who ended up in his classes who hadn't been warned, who were new students. If you happened to sign up for a class like that as a new student, you don't find out for three or four weeks into the course what kind of a creep that you're actually dealing with. And how could they know what to do? They're really in a trap.

Do you go to the head of the department? Then you seem like this whiner or you get told, "Everybody else can deal with him." And the systems of protection really are amazing. And I think, I don't know if I'm crazy or if this is something that other people's experience reproduces, but that one of the things I find most difficult is when somebody's behaving in incredibly inappropriate ways. They're putting their arms around you and keeping them there. I mean it's not just a hug when you walk into the room if it's an event or somebody you haven't seen in a long time, but somebody who's clearly moving beyond appropriate behavior.

Then when you go and say to somebody, "Can you . . . ?" This guy just did this to me. He just slapped me on the backside. It was like, you can't do that to me. What am I going to do? And then you're hoping for this sort of shared outrage from whatever sympathetic listener you think you're talking to. And then what they tell you is, "Oh, his wife left him last year. Oh, you know, he's really . . . he's just . . . he's in AA, he's trying really hard, he's just trying to . . . he's deeply insecure." They play on your sympathy, so you're supposed to feel bad for him and that's why you're not supposed to get upset. I haven't come across somebody saying, "He has the right to grab your ass if he wants to."

It's not somebody who is going to defend this act, but they're going to explain to you why this poor soul deserves your pity, not your outrage. That seems again a weapon to be drawn against women. And for me it was sort of horrifyingly effective a lot of the times where people would say, "Oh . . .", because all these people were in absolutely miserable circumstances. But you can say that about anybody. That's like if somebody is incredibly obnoxious and they say, "Oh, he's not really obnoxious, he's insecure." I wish he'd be a little more insecure. I think that's an excuse only so far, and then people have to start taking responsibility for their behavior.

But all of these guys who were really being jerks were the ones who were the most pathetic people. So we were supposed to forgive them for anything they did. And that was really annoying. I think that's a really subversive tactic.

Women who are harassed in advanced degree programs are caught in a double bind from which it is difficult to extricate themselves. On the one hand, the behavior directed at them is not personal. It is not about the woman in her own right, but rather is a reflection of the professor's mental frame of mind, his disposition, or his beliefs. In such a case, the woman is likely to feel extremely frustrated because her future is being curtailed due to reasons extraneous to her performance and personality. Moreover, the impersonal aspect serves to reinforce women's already shaky sense of self and personal integrity.

But, of course, harassing behavior, at a deeper level, *is* intensely personal, and those who attempt to deny this ignore women's reality. As one woman captured this camouflage,

The other line of course is "You can't take this personally."
And any time anybody says that to you, you know you have to
take it personally. I mean that's the line; it's the flag that has
to go up. So that if somebody says, "Oh, he's just misogynist, it
has nothing to do with you," [laughs], you know there's trouble.

Because the behavior has real-life consequences for the future of the woman who receives the harassment, it is surely personal. It is one among many mechanisms that make it harder for women to gain access, maintain presence, and advance in their professional goals.

Although, just as in college, it is more difficult for women to receive fair grades and even test scores than their male peers, the informal, much more amorphous aspect of the professionalization process and evaluation of students that must take place in virtually every form of advanced degree program is even more riddled with the stereotypical undervaluation of women. The faculty approval and cultivation so necessary for advancement to the degree and to professional life thereafter evolve through courses and formal work, but to a much greater extent through informal discussion and other forms of casual interaction between faculty and students. Just as in other areas of life, it is easer for the faculty members to feel comfortable with, and therefore approve of and evaluate highly, those students who share common ground with them; that is, generally, with the male students over the female students. A medical student was keenly aware of this part of the curriculum at her institution:

I did well in medical school, but I was very aggressive. I wanted people to know that I was good. You can't be a wall-flower. You can't just coast. You do notice that some people do better because they kiss ass more. They suck up to the residents or interns a little more, and they'll get ahead. Among your colleagues you'll know some people who aren't that bright, who don't work that hard, but they always do well because they schmooze. They know how to talk. They know how to chum it up with the right people and they get ahead. So there is that subtle influence there. You're graded based on evaluations from preceptors and residents, so not on exams but on what people think of you. And you notice this.

Chances are that those students who can advance with inferior work skills but a superior facility with banter are male. For a woman to truly stand out in a program, not only does there have to be faculty receptivity to this possibility but her work must also surpass the others *and* she must be gifted at informal interaction with faculty. The last component is quite often essential for her future, in terms of having a mentor, getting strong recommendations, and securing assistance in seeking a first job. Yet, it is often the very aspect of advanced degree programs from which women are effectively shut out.

Whereas a professor may ask a male student to join him for a jog or to shoot some hoops after work—in other words for casual, social *interaction*—that same professor might think it appropriate to ask a female student to babysit while he and his wife go out; that is, he will ask her not for interaction but for *service*. Or he may look at her primarily as female and tacitly conclude that the social interaction would be sexual. Even with some universities maintaining statutes against it, ongoing sexual relationships between faculty and students are rampant. A casual glance at male professors' wives would reveal that a large proportion of them were former students. In the words of a professor:

Essentially the woman graduate students are used to prop up the numbers, and they become fodder for the instructors as a date bank.

Moreover, in casual professor–student interaction different conversational styles are used by faculty members with female and male students. Consider a typical gathering of a handful of students and a professor in the hallway after a class. The professor is chatting pleasantly and professionally with a few male graduate students, listening to their ideas and views and challenging them to pursue the underlying issues to the fullest extent. Thus, part of the professional training process at its best is underway. Enter a female student, Emily, who is also in the class and is of equal competence with her male peers who are present in this conversation. Emily is curious to hear the discussion and joins them. The professor acknowledges her presence with a nod hello and reaches out to tap her shoulder or place his arm around her shoulder briefly, saying, "Hello, Emily" in a solicitous tone.

This is already stifling for Emily, though a small act on the part of the professor. He has singled her out and set her apart from the others with cautious, delicate attention, as though she required it. When Emily speaks up to enter the conversation proper, she is again marked. The professor responds to her remark as one would talk to a child, with slow, sweetened speech. Emily knows that what she said had merit and relevance to the subject at hand, but the treatment she receives makes her feel as though not only has she blundered, but that she was expected to do so. Typically, this causes her to second-guess herself and mull over the conversation many times throughout the remainder of the day.

Thus, informal interaction between professors and students is often like a souped-up version of the classroom. At least in the classroom there is a more or less fixed agenda and some form of rules of procedure, however loose. But out in the hallway, on the campus walk, or in a cafe, the format of this crucial sort of contact is social more than institutional, and this fact does not serve the needs of female students. It is even easier in these contexts for the professors as well as the students themselves to relegate the women to their socially accepted roles. Their comments are seen as cute or are ignored. The female students themselves are viewed as cute and are accorded entrance into these gatherings only on a second-class basis—as the entertainment or as nuisances, as the case may be.

GENDER LESSONS

Women in professional programs are confronted almost continually with a very important lesson about the mechanics of the working world. They get a profound glimpse of the contextual nature of evaluation and merit and of the virtual impossibility of a fair evaluation of work. It is part of the ideal of a training program, or of any other educational program for that matter, that students feel free to express themselves, their ideas, and questions in an atmosphere in which the faculty facilitate the students' thought processes and foster their ability to problem solve in the most expedient fashion and to learn to grasp the salient features of the subject matter in all of its ramified aspects. In the name of learning and growing as young professionals, students are ideally to be accorded a large measure of leeway in self-expression in order to be able to find their own professional voices and special abilities.

There are many programs in which this atmosphere does not exist at all, and the rest attain it with varying degrees of success. Yet, even at an institution that accomplishes this goal for the majority of its students, it is the male students who are accorded the leeway and the females who are scrutinized and judged with every sentence they utter; that is, when they are paid attention to at all. Women in these programs are not generally accorded the luxury of learning under these circumstances; rather they must mull over every remark before even attempting to voice it. Needless to say, this fact stifles the learning process and women's growth as professionals in training.

Women in professional programs often see that even when they do comparable or better work or receive comparable or better grades than their male peers, they are not rewarded accordingly or acknowledged in equal proportions as their male peers. They can see when their remarks are shooed away and when a male student utters the same thing it is applauded. They can see when they receive inferior grades than their male peers for virtually the same or, in some cases, joint work. They can see when they are not given comparable awards, fellowships, or jobs to inferior male peers. Female students can see all of this and the myriad variations on this theme. Even when they know their work is comparable or better, this is a bitter victory, and their psyches are damaged. Their professional resolve and ambition can suffer as a result. It is demoralizing to be put in second, third, or fourth place for first-place work. One woman tried to make sense of the situation:

I remember, a year or so ago, trying to figure out why this was happening to me. And, this will sound crazy, but it struck me all of a sudden, that all of this was happening because my genitals had a certain shape! I felt like screaming; it seemed like science fiction where a monster jumps out at you. That's how I felt.

I was angry after that, but I also kind of crashed. I think I collapsed mentally for a while, like, if that was the case for real, what could I do about it?

Some women develop a passive attitude about the situation, as is evident in the following observation:

It used to happen all the time. You just get used to it. It is hard, but it's something you just have to get used to. You can't get upset every time somebody does that. It would happen every single day.

GENDER COMPOUNDS

Suppose that English is not Emily's native language, but is her second language. She is fluent in spoken and written English, but she retains a strong accent from her native tongue. As much as women generally are closed out of casual interaction with faculty as well as the benevolent atmosphere of free exchange of ideas and information, this exclusion will apply to Emily specifically all the more so. It will also be even more difficult for her to receive a semblance of a fair evaluation of her work than it is for her American-born female peers.

Simply because of her accent and origins, Emily will be viewed as apart from the others. She will likely be treated with even more condescension, her work will be evaluated even lower, and she will be even more likely to be required to perform work for professors for which they will exclusively receive credit. In this situation, chances are Emily is also more likely to be viewed as easy, sexual prey by her professors and by her fellow students.

Moreover, Emily may well be caught between two cultures with differing standards of behavior. If American women are held to contradictory constraints, Emily may be operating under another cultural system as well. Thus, in addition to grappling with the demands of the professional program itself, she also may be attempting to straddle different and opposing norms of acceptable female behavior. Thus, in order to persevere, she will need to have even more resolve, reserves of self-confidence, and clarity of purpose in the program than her female peers.

GENDER ACTION

Again, everything that was outlined previously about making one's intentions, interests, experience, and talents clear and well articulated to the faculty and other relevant parties is of particular importance in degree programs. Emily must make sure to be prepared to promote her own work at every available opportunity. This is a habit that comes as second nature to most men because they have been encouraged to do this virtually from birth. In contrast, it is a habit that feels false or inappropriate to most women. This is because they have been trained and reinforced in the idea that they should, in a variety of ways, put themselves at the back.

In any case, self-promotion is a habit that Emily must cultivate if she is to achieve her goals to the fullest extent. She must also keep herself visible as a member of the community of the program; she must be a vocal participant in the activities and events that surround the course of study proper. Moreover, Emily must attend conferences and other professional gatherings with people in the field who are outside her institution. It can often be crucial for a female student to forge ties with professionals at other institutions who can know her and her work in some detail. For one woman, these ties are what saved her career:

I was getting the complete runaround in my department. I felt that my work was good and that it was relevant to the field, but no one was paying attention to me. Then I decided to send one of my reports to someone who had worked on a similar topic a few years back. I was really bowled over when he wrote me back right away, expressing great enthusiasm and encouragement. Through him, I started correspondence also with two other people with similar interests. It was those three who backed me up when I needed it, not members of my own faculty, not the people I'm actually paying to help and teach me.

Another approach often voiced by successful professional women is embodied in the following scientist's remark:

If there is prejudice around it's not only hard but it's also self-destructive to start looking at it. It focuses your energy on something that's kind of tangential. You have to use your energies to work, not to pick up all these little things. . . . What's the big deal? No, if you're going to get really annoyed by it, then it's quite distracting.

In a similar vein, a lawyer remarks,

I've really never experienced gender bias. Maybe I've been really lucky, but more I think it's just that I let it roll off my back. If I'd stopped to ponder it, I wouldn't have been as successful.

This is a choice that professional women face every day and one that presents a horrible dilemma. If the goal is to succeed professionally, and turning a blind eye to gender bias is one route to that success, why not do just that? This is particularly true in light of the glaring fact that acknowledging the bias for what it is, even privately, requires a great deal of energy—first, energy in learning to become aware of incidents for what they are; second, for acknowledging the myriad impact of the pervasive bias on one's own life; and third, recognizing the psychological toll that it takes and the effort expended trying to correct for that.

And, if you look around, many of the women who did succeed did so by playing by the rules, by accepting the male model, by accepting and keeping quiet about any bias, and by trying to blend in as quietly and as best as possible. So what is wrong with this approach? At least two key factors speak against it. The first concerns the more global picture, with the individual as only a part. The longer we stay silent about problems for women in the professions, the longer it will take for things to change. If those women who are forging their way to the top, those talented and motivated women particularly stay silent, then it makes it all the more difficult for women with lesser status, talent, ability, and drive to speak out. Clearly, the sooner we refuse to accept the status quo in the professional realm, the sooner we can begin to implement change.

Second, on a more individual level, this strategy cannot promote the well-being of its advocate in the long run. It forces a rift between herself and other women, as if to say she is not one of *them* but is an individual apart from the realm relegated to women. In this dissociation from a class of which she is in fact a member, the woman can only be postponing her awareness of the situation and her role in it. In so doing, her crash is likely to be the harder, and her fall the more precipitous.

12 THESES AND DISSERTATIONS

GENDER BASICS

In most professional degree programs, there is a quickening of the professionalization process in the second half of the program. The process of procuring the Ph. D. provides a clear model of this in dividing the program into the first half, consisting of course work and qualification exams, and the second half that consists of the dissertation. It is in the producing of original work for the dissertation as well as in the developing of a working relationship with a mentor, usually the principal advisor on the dissertation, that a degree candidate moves from being a graduate student to a professional in her chosen area of expertise. In medical school the equivalent is the internship, and in law school it is in the final years and the election of course work in a specific area of the law.

Of course, the professionalization process continues after the degree has been completed, as one advances through the first years on the job. Yet, the level of earnest seriousness that is attributed to one's standing is first accorded in the degree program. If women are made to feel uncomfortable and out of place at the beginning of their graduate work, at the point of quickening, they can be virtually entirely closed out altogether, held in a holding pattern at the midway point in their studies, having finished the courses or introductory courses but not yet allowed to progress much further. One young doctor described her observation thus:

In medical school there is a subtle type of sex discrimination. In the first two years of medical school, mostly you're in classes. You're getting lectured and taking exams. It's similar to college; it's all didactic. But when you're in the third and fourth year, you're mostly on the wards. You're doing clinical rotations where you're working in the hospital and you have preceptors, and you're following patients and learning how to take histories, do physicals, surgery, deliveries, all with supervision.

There is a subtle sense that other doctors, either professors or the doctors that you're working with on the ward, the residents and the interns, think by and large that women aren't as good. You just get that impression. So you really have to work twice as hard. You really have to work twice as hard and be aggressive so people think that you're good.

This state of limbo is particularly easy to accomplish in Ph.D. programs. In such a case, one can be held up literally for years simply because no one agrees to sponsor—that is, be the principal advisor—for one's dissertation. And this can occur for any reason at all, as one unhappy philosopher discovered:

I was told by the professor who was the logical choice to be my advisor that I simply wasn't bubbly enough, and so he didn't think he could work with me. I was also told that he didn't want to work with me because I'm a "quiet, ugly woman." I look around me here and don't exactly see a bubbly, beauty standard being held up for the men.

The point of professional quickening in degree programs is the point at which women can hit a wall. Even if there was fairly little differential treatment of the female and male students in the first half of the program, it is likely that as the stakes get higher, as professors actually need to take individual responsibility for students and form one-on-one relationships with them, as soon as the faculty needs to begin to see the students as actual near-future professionals and colleagues, women's advancement toward those goals will slow down and, in some cases, come to a grinding halt. And this is not for lack of merit of the performance of the women who are effectively stopped.

It is a clear measure of how little we have progressed in gender equity to note that even in cases in which women have been accepted to this second level of the professionalization process in degree programs and sometimes even welcomed wholeheartedly, they then have opportunities closed to them that are freely offered to male peers as a matter of course. That is, their abilities and the merit of their performance are acknowledged to a high degree, and then these women are asked to step aside, to sit the dance of professionalization out while the men continue waltzing. Consider the experience of a linguist:

There were three graduate students working on this professor's enterprise, two men and I. The professor valued my work highly, but I always made half the money the other two students made. Doing exactly the same work.

Then, a fourth graduate student was hired on the project, a man, and the three of us knew that he wasn't as well trained as we were and he didn't understand the project as well. The professor was putting together a big volume at that time, and the two graduate students who had been there when I got there were writing a chapter for the volume. When the new guy came on, the professor invited him to write a chapter. When questioned why he invited him to write a chapter when it wasn't going to be very good, the professor responded that the new guy needs the publications for his curriculum vita. When I asked if I could write a chapter for the book, I was told that they had already scheduled all the chapters and there was no room left in the book.

So, I made half as much money, and not only was I not encouraged to publish, I was actively kept out.

Occasionally such treatment of female graduate students is malicious. Most often though, this attitude stems from a vision problem. If professors just don't see women as potential professionals in *their own field*, then what comes to them automatically with regard to their male students will not occur to them for their female students. That is, those in the positions of advisors and supervisors have not been "retrained" to view their female students' futures in the same way that they envision their male students' futures. In part, this situation is beneficial to those in command. They can select the best and the brightest women in the program, have them perform endless amounts of work on their own projects, as in the case above, pay them less, and give them less credit for the work. Like a miniature production factory, the female students can apply themselves to their professors' work, for smaller rewards than their male peers, who often do less work for greater recognition. Science labs, for example, are notorious for this gender bias. A scientist's career is based on the lab teams he has built, which are usually composed of an empire of graduate students busy at work producing experimental results that further the work of the professor.

Whatever explanation is in operation—whether it be that the women are going to marry, produce children, and drop out of the profession and thus do not merit the same kind of personal investment that the more committed male students do, or some other similar rationale that works on a deeply ingrained level of thought that most often does not require articulation on the part of the advisor—the effect for the women is the same. They are treated as if their sex defined their work lives. They are treated *as women*, not as students in the program, as the men are. It is the familiar case of the men supplying the norm or standard, the given, against which everything else is differentiated. Thus, it is harder for women in these programs to receive the essential critiques and response to their work of a quality that is useful for their progress. Much of the interaction between professors and female students, even at the second level of training or perhaps especially at this level, is unprofessional and sloppy, with a blurring of the social and professional realms. As one woman observed of her experience with her advisor:

My advisor was flirtatious, and that mattered for my getting grants and fellowships.

Women in these programs are too often forced to play the role of the female cocquette in order to receive even the minimum attention that is due them. They are put in a position of pleading in order to get almost any kind of response to their work, and all too often the response that they finally wheedle out of their advisors is patronizing and offhand.

GENDER LESSONS

The overriding gender lesson of this chapter is that those professionals doing the training in the advanced degree programs, a group that overwhelmingly consists of men, simply still do not have it in their mental framework that women are becoming professionals in greater numbers every year. They thus do not *see* women as potential professionals; they make assumptions based on a standard that is rapidly becoming extinct. Consider this doctor's experience:

There were a lot of subtle things that went on. When you're on the wards, interns or even patients and nurses, talk to you like you're one of the nurses. Because you're a woman or you're black, they assume you're a nurse. They don't think you're a medical student; they don't think you're a doctor. You know, they say, "You, get me that bedpan." And I always had an attitude about that.

I can remember one time; I'll never forget this. I was sitting at the nurses' station. It was like the front desk. There's a clerk there, and usually the interns and other doctors will hang around that station checking labs on the computer or writing notes or something. So, one of my preceptors was a black woman who was an attending physician. I was sitting next to her, and the two of us had a patient's chart open in front of us and were discussing the patient's chart and our plan of management. I had a stethoscope around my neck, and I was wearing a white coat. She was wearing civilian clothes.

So we were sitting there talking, and this intern or some guy— he was either an intern or a resident—came around. He was mulling around, looking for a piece of paper in the clerk's filing desk. . . . So he interrupts us. We're in the middle of talking. He doesn't say, "Excuse me." He just says, "Can I have an x-ray form, please?" So I said, "Well, I don't know where they are. I'm sorry." So we went back to our discussion. So then he comes around behind us and leans over, looking for this form and says, "Look, I can't find these forms." So I said, "Well, I suggest that you ask the clerk," which was kind of obnoxious at that point.

So then a few minutes later, he doesn't quit. He's looking for the form, and he speaks up. He says, "Look, I'm looking for this form. I need to get this form for my patient, and I don't see why you two can't stop what you're doing and help me." So my preceptor who was an attending said, "Listen, I'm Doctor X and I'm having a discussion with Doctor Y about a patient, and why are you disturbing us?" And he said, "Oh, I didn't know you're a doctor. I'm sorry." And then she says, "You know, just be-

cause we are black females sitting at the nurses' station doesn't mean we're nurses and it doesn't mean we're clerks. And even if we were nurses or clerks, you should at least have the courtesy of saying 'excuse me' if you're interrupting our conversation." And the guy bolts out of there.

This is a perfect example of the way it is. He never thought for two seconds that we could be doctors because we're black women. And therefore he could talk to us however he likes. That's something that we have to face all the time. Even to this day, I hear it all the time. When I go to the hospital and say I'm Dr. Y, they say, "You're a doctor?" Most of the time they'll say, "Oh, you look too young to be a doctor" or something like that. But you know if I were a man they probably wouldn't say that. There's just a subtle sense that you get that people are always questioning your ability and who you are.

It is almost a personal problem for these senior male professionals, namely, that they do not *see themselves* as being peers with women. They do not see themselves as working alongside women, writing papers with them, doing research alongside them, running casework with women as equal peers, or as performing surgery possibly under a female chief surgeon. The focus in gender bias is traditionally on the women—that those in power do not see them as capable or committed enough—but in the case of training programs and future work, the attitude of men about themselves as potential peers to women needs to be examined in equal detail because it is a large piece of the equation of gender equity.

In a way, this part of the dynamic can be looked at as men fearing a certain overpowering by women if they are to be admitted as equals in the profession. They fear being overpowered because women are typically more verbal and actually have a greater capacity to focus on an issue without distraction. Generally, women do not have the luxury of time to be able to flail in different directions and eventually get the job done as do men, who do not typically have responsibility for home and children. Thus, women on the whole must be directed and must concentrate intensely in order to produce the necessary work. Men in a certain sense fear the keen organizational and verbal skills that women, for whatever reason, excel at. After all, it has been part of men's life experience from birth on that females are powerful and often more talented and skilled than them at a whole range of important tasks, even if this is not explicitly acknowledged in our culture.

Consider the perspective of a young child, an infant or toddler. That child, female or male, is likely to view the mother as more powerful than anyone else. Even if both parents work full time outside the home, it is generally the mother who also maintains the home operation, makes the decisions that the child is aware of, and is the one who says yes or no to the child on virtually all issues. In preschool and elementary school, girls develop fine motor skills younger than boys, read sooner, use toilets younger, and are verbal younger and to a greater degree. The fact that all of this is compensated for by a value system that places the attention on boys and boys' competencies does not diminish what must be a strong impact on the boys and men of this even subconscious observation that in fact girls are more skilled than them at a range of important tasks and activities and that women (mothers) are very powerful. This is not a feeling or observation that fades with age because it is continually reinforced. Think about high school and even college. Although it is the boys who are being praised most, it is the girls who are the better students and get better grades and who tend to be more serious and scholarly. It is girls who (in the cultural myth anyway) are the gatekeepers of sex and sexuality short of rape. And mothers still are fairly powerful, although by this age the father may be also. Yet, with the growing numbers of absentee fathers, the strength of the father does not begin to compare with the power of mothers. Most teachers are women, at least at schools below the college level, and they are authority figures as well.

Thus, at the same time that we are training our youth to devalue females and to value males, there is a strong counter-current that has not yet been taken into account. This countercurrent generates in men a sensation of being outstripped by females. One consequence may be the strong hold that men maintain over entrance and genuine acceptance into the professions: a grip that they somewhere know they will be forced to loosen sooner or later. Ironically, men have always known this. It speaks to the feeling that they have always had that females can overpower them at almost every human endeavor.

GENDER COMPOUNDS

A common compounding problem for women in professional degree programs arises when they choose their area of specialty. Perhaps by virtue of women's status in our culture as outsiders, they are far more likely than men to choose non-standard subjects or perspectives within their areas of specialization. And this choice is not exclusively tied to women taking on a woman's or feminist perspective of a subject matter. Rather, in general women are more likely to choose work that involves a break from tradition. A mathematician observes,

I think that because I was a woman I was freer to review the theories I was working with with a fresher eye than my male peers or advisors. I came up with a view of the current research that led me to pursue thoughts that ran contrary to the accepted doctrine, but that seemed more fruitful and interesting to me. I think that if I had been a man I would have been more likely to go with the flow and work on a more fashionable angle.

For one's intellectual integrity it is an advantage to be able to think for oneself and choose one's own work, unfettered by the accepted doctrine of the moment. But, from the point of view of a woman seeking approval in a degree program in which the deck is already stacked against her, her problems multiply with her non-standard choice of work. All of the problems that she may face in receiving adequate, consistent attention and being evaluated fairly will be compounded. Anyone, female or male, who makes choices that break with the prevailing opinions will be accorded a grain or two of skepticism, but a female in a degree program who does so may be scorned or ignored as, at best, a fringe player.

It is almost incumbent upon any woman who does so to make sure that she finds sympathetic ears for her work, whether they be part of the staff or students of her program or outside it. One woman in such a position eventually searched the country until she found people who were keenly interested in her work. She remarks,

In getting my Ph.D., it was key that I found an advisor independent from the department I was in.

GENDER ACTION

Developing a professional persona inside and out is crucial in the course of a degree program. Often for women doing so has meant following some standard of professional dress that fits an accepted mode, such as the woman's bow tie of the 1980s. And thus, typically, women's battles have been fought on the level of appearance. But developing a professional persona is in fact much more an internal issue than anything else. Women in the course of their professionalization process must begin *to think of themselves* as future professionals. There is little in their upbringing that prepares them for this thought experiment, and they are not provided with the positive reinforcement in this idea that the men are in the course of their advanced degree program. At this point, this persona is something that women must cultivate for themselves, in spite of the discouragement in its many forms that they are subjected to every day.

Women must seek out sympathetic people in positions of authority and people who are genuinely interested in cultivating them as future professionals. They may not always be women, as one woman so keenly observed:

Women on the faculty were of no use, and that's not accidental. There were no tenured women on the faculty. The junior women were told, when they were hired, not to even think of getting tenure there, that they never will. They knew they were ultimately going to have to look for other work, and they were therefore dependent on their colleagues for recommendations. There was no way they were in a position to stand up for students in any way. They were powerless in that environment.

Peers, both female and male, can be an invaluable source of assistance during professional quickening and often prove to be assets in the future. Of course, the female/male interaction among peers is not uncomplicated from gender bias, but it is a population within which to begin to try on a professional persona. Even when the atmosphere in the professional program contains intense competition, the fact remains that those students nearing completion of the program are all in the process of developing the foundation of their future work and are cultivating themselves as young professionals. The greater the interaction and camaraderie among this group, the more each can not only learn from each other but also build a collective feeling of being the next generation of professionals.

13 Degrees, Dossiers, and Interviews

GENDER BASICS

The actual completion of a degree, even after the formal work is done, is fraught with tasks and rules that must be accomplished one by one. Emily discovered that there was much more for her to do after she completed her dissertation and painstakingly arranged for her defense meeting, tasks that her advisor should have carried out. There were guidelines about how and when and where to submit revisions should they be required, there were sets of instructions for printing and depositing the dissertation, there were deadlines for depositing it in order to obtain the degree on time, and there were rules and deadlines for compiling a dossier in the office of career services without which she could not even apply for jobs.

Emily discovered each piece of information about the steps she needed to take on her own. Nowhere was all the information written down and spelled out for all students to read and retain. None of her three advisors sat her down and listed steps for her. Rather, she felt that each step led to another one and each office that she had to deal with on campus, and they were numerous, had its own set of requirements of her before she could proceed to the next. She finally got it all done, but felt all the while that she was groping in the dark at every turn. She did not notice her male peers in the same sort of quandary; they seemed to know the procedures.

Moreover, Emily had to orchestrate her own job search in spite of the fact that a faculty member in her program was designated to take the students through the job search process until they were placed successfully. Every time Emily met with him, she found herself correcting misimpressions that he had about her candidacy. First, he could not get her degree date straight in his mind, even though it was written down in her file. He kept insisting that she wasn't going to graduate for another two years. He also maintained that her job search should be limited to the immediate area because of her husband's job. He also consistently set his sights for her on third-rate institutions, he said, because he didn't want Emily to be rattled by too many rejections. Emily always left his office angry and confused.

She knows that she's a good student, that her work is well regarded, and that she expects to have her pick of jobs to the extent that jobs are available. Emily finally resolves that it is a waste of her time, not to mention destructive to her psyche, to return to that office, and she begins to manage her own job search. She knows that she needs to have a completed dossier, and she sets about to create one. She writes up her curriculum vita, describing her studies, her work experience, her educational information, and her future goals for her career. She then takes the recommendation forms from the career services office and brings them to five faculty members, including her three advisors, whom she thinks will write outstanding letters for her with enthusiasm. They all agree, and Emily requests that they write them within one month in order for

her to be able to compete in the first round of job announcements. The month comes and goes, and Emily has not received
a single letter for her file at the Career Services office. She then
goes back to each faculty member who has her form and
reminds them politely that she needs the letter of recommendation in her file very soon.

All are apologetic and say they'll complete it immediately.
Meanwhile the first round of job announcements comes out,
and Emily sees several job openings she'd like to apply for. She
brings the announcements to her principal advisor and asks
for his advice about how to go about applying. She leaves with
little information or encouragement and still does not even
have a letter of recommendation from him. Another couple of
weeks go by, with Emily checking her file every day now, and
only one letter has found its way there, a short letter from the
one professor who knew her least and is least relevant for a
job application. Now, she schedules appointments with each
of the four faculty members who should have written her letters. She sits down with each one of them separately and tells
them that she must apply for jobs now since she is about to
graduate and she needs their letters, if not further assistance,
to do so. This is information that, of course, they have, should
they have turned their thoughts to Emily at all. She asks each
what she can do to facilitate the process so that she will not
miss deadlines for some of the better jobs.

One of them suggests that Emily draft the letter herself so
that she can include all the details that she would like to see
in the letter, and then he will rewrite it for style in his own
words. Emily feels uncomfortable with this idea, but knows that
it is almost standard practice, and she needs the letter to be
written. It takes this professor two weeks after Emily hands
him her version to get the letter into her file. The other three
professors are more difficult, including her principal advisor.
One of them finally writes the letter, in pen, while Emily is

sitting in his office waiting for him. She then is instructed to take it to the department secretary and have her type it and get it to the Career Services office. The secretary's work is backed up, and it takes her three days just to type the three scrawled paragraphs. Emily had asked to do the typing, but because she was required by the professor to sign a statement waiving her freedom of information rights to read the letter, she cannot.

In the following weeks, Emily does finally get all five letters in her file, after several more rounds of badgering and pleading. She then sets out to submit applications for jobs, finding that she only missed a couple of deadlines. She knows that she will have to go out on interviews if she passes the first round of cuts in the applicant pools and so decides to go back to the professor in charge of student placement in her program to seek advice about the interviewing process. She learns that he has been holding mock interviews for all of the students who are applying for jobs this year, but no comment is made about why Emily was left out.

No amount of practice with faculty members prepares women for the varieties and strength of humiliation that they may undergo in the interview process for their first professional job. As one university professor recalls her feelings,

I had a number of interviews. I remember walking into one of them. There were nine men in the room, no women. You know, these interviews are in hotel suites. So you're walking into these bedrooms. I walked in and said, "I feel like I should jump out of a cake," because I wanted to address the issue that I'm the only woman in this bedroom. It is a weird thing. And there's a bar. I mean, the liquor is out.

I think that probably a guy walking in would have felt very differently. It's just not the same experience. It really isn't. It's like I don't exactly know what a hooker feels like, but I sure felt as close to a hooker as I could get walking into what seemed like a stag party.

Emily feels as though she is waffling through the placement process as best she can, given that it has a strong quality of vagueness. It is only toward the end when she does in fact obtain a job that she is pleased with what she begins to understand as the highly subjective and arbitrary nature of the hiring process. That is true for women and men alike. But, for women, it is murkier still. Because of ingrained and lingering bias, it is close to impossible for women to be viewed fairly. As one lawyer describes the situation,

Men are seen as brilliant, women are seen as able, committed. Never on the same plane.

Thus, when it comes to hiring meetings, the deliberations are necessarily skewed when women are being considered alongside men for the same positions. As one senior-level woman remarked,

The men will tell them what drives the women crazy, "You won't have any trouble getting a job. Everybody wants to hire women." We're certainly getting ahead, but I don't think the women are coddled at all. There's a perception in the community that everybody is out trying to help these poor young women. I don't believe it. I think there's deep prejudice. And that's in spite of the fact that I have more than my share of honors. I really have.
I think that it's very subtle, but the women do get shoved to the side. The hiring process here has the appearance of being even-handed, but I don't think it's even-handed. What happens is that there's a crucial moment when you're deciding who will go on the short list, or you're deciding how to rank the short list, and people are making very sharp judgments about the quality of somebody's work and the strength of it.
And then a little remark will be made, and it gets pushed to the side. And it's a remark that nobody could pick up or could

say it's prejudiced. And you don't know. Is it an opinion, is it an honest judgment, is it prejudice? And it's just when you look at the sweeping picture that you say it has to be prejudice.

GENDER LESSONS

The overriding theme of the professionalization process that takes place after its quickening until the securing of a first professional job is that women still are not being promoted or encouraged to the same degree that their male peers are. While it is often not entirely intentional, mentors, dissertation advisors, and even career counselors rarely have the female students at the forefront of their minds. It still comes most naturally to pick out the male students to encourage, prepare, and advance through the process to securing a professional job.

Moreover, implicitly, at the same time that female students are being infantilized as students like their male peers, they are also put, metaphorically, in the position of being mommies. Such being the case, it often does not occur to advisors to inform female students of the steps they need to take for completing the degree and for placement. Female professional degree candidates are then caught in the double bind of being assumed to be self-sufficient and capable at the same time that they are also undervalued by and dependent on their advisors. Thus, in order to progress at the same pace as their male peers, women must find multiple ways of advancing that supplement the basic path to the degree.

GENDER COMPOUNDS

Suppose that a professor in Emily's program has taken a dislike to her over the years, for reasons that Emily has not been able to figure out. It is not based on her work since she has never taken a course with him, and his field is far removed from the specialty that she has chosen. His behavior toward her is subtle enough to render a response from Emily difficult without her appearing to be oversensitive. Yet, it is frequent enough to show unmistakable hostility toward Emily. Thus, when it comes time to complete the degree and apply for jobs, Emily is fearful that this man will attempt to upset her future employment prospects.

Although no student would welcome having a faculty member against them when it comes time to find a job, it is a greater problem for women than for men. In many cases, whatever the actual disapproval comes from, many outsiders will assume that the problem was of a sexual nature. Although this will not put an ounce of tarnish on the professor's standing in all probability, it will enhance the already existing gender biases that work against Emily obtaining a first-rate job.

GENDER ACTION

What Emily finally learned by the end of her degree program is that she ought to have approached the degree, and not just her work, as though it were a business transaction. It is natural to succumb at many points in a degree program to emotional aspects of the process, such as the relationship one has with advisors, issues surrounding one's own identity as a future professional and thus as an adult, and the exposure involved in one's relationship to one's work as a public entity. Nevertheless, while grappling with the personal issues, it is particularly important for women not to lose sight of the fact that *a degree program is a business transaction.* Students are paying the professors and the institution to train them by means of the program and to confer upon them a certificate of competence once they have achieved a level of proficiency, as laid out in the requirements for degree completion. Women have the right to obtain clear guidelines about degree requirements and formal steps to its completion. It is then up to the women to stay abreast of them.

Women must also treat the opening and maintaining of a dossier in the same fashion. They must be clear about the job interview process, ask for mock interviews if they are not given as a matter of course, and try to ascertain what to expect and about how much assistance one will need from the faculty of the program. Above all, women at this stage of professional development must acknowledge to themselves that they have pursued the degree with determination and hard work, and that they deserve and need to obtain as much institutional back-up in order to secure the best first job possible for themselves. With this conviction clear in their minds, they will be able to pursue the necessary attention from their advisors and others in the final stages of their formal training.

PART V
THE TWILIGHT ZONE

A mentor can provide the backbone to one's professional life. Mentors provide guidance and assistance in all phases of professional development that may be crucial and invaluable. Yet, many women go through professional degree programs and the rest of their professional lives without the advantage of having had a mentor, whereas most men readily acquire mentors with little effort. The myriad reasons and factors that contribute to this disparity are discussed in this part.

The point in professional development at which it is customary and appropriate for one to enter into a relationship with an advisor, professor, or boss as a mentee varies from profession to profession. A common thread to the commencement of a mentor–mentee relationship across professions is that it occurs at the point at which one's professional development enters a new level of seriousness. It is also the moment at which whatever system is in place that promotes greater equity than in the past begins to break down. The ranks begin to close in tighter, admitting only those who appear familiar. Women at this stage can begin to be effectively shut out.

Thus, this part, more than any other in the book, is about *shape*. Simply put, women have been deemed to be of the wrong shape to enter many professional spheres. This explanation sounds absurd on the surface, like the disconcerting uncanny feeling one gets from watching an episode of *The Twilight Zone*. Yet, this part explores the various ways in which the social meaning attached to women's mere shape does, in fact, color the possibility of a meaningful mentor–mentee relationship.

Many women achieve professional satisfaction and success without mentors, but positioning oneself to create the possibility of having a mentor can be important. This part provides an overview of the current situation and addresses the differences between women and men in the mentor role. In the Gender Action segments, it is shown what women can do to change the current situation and enter into a meaningful mentor relationship. Supplements and alternatives to having a mentor are also canvassed so that the young professional can begin to cover all the bases toward a fulfilling career.

14   MALE MENTORS

GENDER BASICS

When Emily entered a Ph. D. program after college, she had
nothing but the highest expectations for herself in the field.
She was welcomed into the department as a new student, was
given fellowship money, and was assigned to an undergraduate course as a teaching assistant for the professor who would
probably come to be her dissertation advisor and mentor.
Entering into a mentor relationship with not only one but also
several faculty members was smooth and exhilarating for
Emily, as is detailed below. Because of what eventually transpired in her graduate career, this chapter begins by exploring in general terms what a mentor relationship can be like
and how it can evolve over time with a female mentee and male
mentor.

At one time or another, every college student is assigned to
an advisor. The advisor is there to help the student select a
course and study plan that best suits her educational and career
goals. The advisor may also try to help with specific problems

the student is having with the program, with a particular subject matter or teacher, and, occasionally, even with personal
problems that are interfering with the student's course of work.

A mentor is much more than an advisor. A mentor–mentee
relationship is something that develops over time and is not
arbitrarily assigned. The success of the relationship has a lot
to do with the psychological make-up of each party. When a
match between a potential mentor and mentee works, it can
be a lifelong and mutually rewarding experience. Both people
may strengthen and broaden their skills, talents, and ideas
through the relationship.

A mentor is often someone who views the student as pursuing similar interests within the field and who may even be able
to carry out segments of the mentor's work. Ideally, a mentor
takes a deep personal interest in the student and guides her
through her studies and professional development. The mentor may be instrumental in working through career decisions
with the student, in introducing her to the professional world
and its inhabitants, and in assisting in a variety of ways in selecting and securing the best possible job once the student is ready.
The relationship generally does not stop there, but rather can
be lifelong and mutually rewarding.

Mentor relationships outside the educational realm are similar, whether they be in the world of business, medicine, or law.
The form and nature of the counsel and assistance vary according to the situation at hand, but the underlying tenor is the
same. The mentor is the established and experienced professional who guides and enhances the mentee's career path.

The point at which a mentor relationship becomes appropriate for a mentee in the process of her professional development is when she has achieved a level of standing as a young
professional. In the case of graduate work this is usually once
one has passed all of the course requirements, qualification
exams, and tasks that lead one to begin down the path of seri-

ous, original professional work. As one graduate student describes the transition,

My graduate experience changed over time. I had been quite successful as an undergraduate. I chose a graduate institution because I had been so strongly encouraged there, and I had a large scholarship. I loved the graduate course work; I was given an extraordinary teaching offer as a graduate student. Then, when I approached the dissertation phase everything went downhill rapidly. So it was like two phases of the program. The first phase is canned stuff; everyone's taking the same courses. And the interaction with the faculty is easy; there's nothing that's at stake. There's no reason for anyone to be making subtle distinctions at that point.

Things get more complicated when you're done with the course work. You become much more dependent on individual members of the faculty who are going to be your advisors, maybe your one advisor. The faculty members then become more uncomfortable. That's a much more difficult role for them than just sitting in front of the class and bantering with you. But when you go to someone's office and say, "I want to do my dissertation work with you," suddenly it's much more complicated for them. It's a different ballgame at that point.

In the case of other professions, such as law, in which there does not exist such a clear division within the formal training program, the point of intensified professionalization may come after a period of hands-on work experience during which mentor–mentee relationships may begin to develop.

It is important to note that the relationship is not a one-way street. The student or young professional provides many benefits to the mentor. She may carry out significant portions of the mentor's research or work program, and she may bring fresh ideas to it. Her excellence in her field reflects on the mentor, bringing satisfaction and recognition. And, of course, the relationship may bring both the genuine pleasure of comradeship as partners in a professional enterprise.

Some who go through their training and professional lives without the benefits of some measure of a mentor do fine and thrive. But benefits are exactly what they are, and there can be a vast difference between a career aided by an active mentor and one that is not. The process of obtaining a mentor is a murky one, replete with ambiguity and many of the complexities of other interpersonal relationships. What makes the mentor relationship even more complex is that it is at once professional and personal. Generally, such a relationship unfolds slowly over time, with accumulated shared experiences between the mentor and the mentee. Each gradually becomes comfortable with the other as each learns of the other's interests. Thus, there has to be a significant time-span during which the mentor and mentee come into contact with each other.

Professional programs are perfect breeding grounds for such relationships to blossom. A student may attend several courses with the same professor, seek out private consultations with that person, and attend the same seminars, lectures, and conferences. The constant exchange of ideas and exposure to each other in a variety of settings enable the potential mentor and mentee to size each other up and test the waters. Many other situations are also ripe for the development of the relationship, such as when the young lawyer comes into contact with a partner on cases, in and around the office, and at conferences.

Because men still occupy the vast majority of seats in the upper echelons of professional life, it is men who are most of the mentors. This is not so for potential mentees. Entering postgraduate and professional classes are approaching equity in terms of sex. Yet, men still have a significantly easier time entering into and maintaining relationships with mentors. For women, it can be difficult to achieve the entry-level opportunities necessary to forming the foundations of the relationship.

One reason for this difficulty is that the mentor–mentee relationship is not something that people pursue as a goal in itself. Rather, it develops as a piece of a complex, amorphous web of exchanges, some professional and some personal. On the professional side, many factors come into play that contribute to women appearing to be less viable mentee candidates than men. Women still have lower professional profiles than do men. Several reasons taken together explain why this is so. One is that our cultural socialization prepares women to behave deferentially and men assertively. Another is the deeply ingrained, sometimes unconscious belief that women are intellectually less capable than men. And yet a third reason is that women are believed to be less committed professionally than men. Once these and other patterns are set in motion, they become part of a vicious cycle. Consider one woman's experience:

I got interested in a particular field and wanted to work with a particular member of the faculty. From the start of the time that I tried to go for a direct working relationship with this guy, the whole business was extremely confusing to me. For example, there were all these odd episodes. I was writing a paper for a course that was supposed to be turned into the first chapter of my dissertation. This was my first big step toward being an active Ph.D. candidate. And I wrote this paper, and for months I tried to get it back from him. He told me he read it and he liked it, but he never gave it back.

I remember once I was sitting in the graduate student lounge, and he came in and called me aside and said he read my paper and that he thought it was very good but it was not quite what he really thought was outstanding. But it was very good; it was close to that. He was standing in the student lounge—it was strange that he had come in there, the whole set-up was strange—

and I asked if could he tell me what he saw as the limitations of the paper. Well, no, he said, he couldn't; he was still going over it and he was going to write me extensive notes and give it back to me. For months I tried to get that paper back from him. I never did. The closest I ever came was once I was sitting in his office, and I saw it with his handwriting all over it. I said, "Oh, can I take that?," and he said, "No, I'm not done with it," and he hid it away somewhere. I never did get that paper back from him, and I never did find out why it wasn't an A paper. The whole thing was so peculiar.

I didn't know what to make of it. It was odd enough to make me uneasy. I think it's a very common theme in faculty dealings with women students, and I've seen it in other contexts. They say that their work seems great but somehow is not quite up to it. I think, to put it crudely in my case, he just couldn't bring himself to give it an A as he would have for a male student. That's all there is to it. He just couldn't perceive this work as really first rate. He didn't know why; he couldn't even say why. I'm sure he really didn't know why. But I know why.

This vicious cycle is accelerated by the crude fact of pervasive sex bias in our country that impairs everyone's vision. Nowhere is this more apparent than in the professional realm, where women are caught in one of many familiar dilemmas. If a woman is not deferential, then she is perceived as aggressive and strident. If she clearly has great intellectual capacity, she is considered a threat. And if she demonstrates her commitment to her work, she is chastised for not fulfilling her natural potential as a nurturing mother.

Men do not face these obstacles to professional acceptance. If a man is married or has children, his commitment to his work is not questioned. On the contrary, it is often felt that a promotion is in order because he has a family to support. He is generally assumed to be equipped with the necessary intellectual ingredients for his chosen professional goals unless he proves otherwise time and time again. If he is assertive, he will be seen as a go-getter, enthusiastic, ambitious, and quick on his feet. If he is quieter, he is likely to be assumed to be cautious and circumspect. Less important than the professional male's abilities is that he is perceived as a team player.

Easy access to acceptance is not always, however, the best path to the development of professional skills. Thus, women, who have to make a greater effort and achieve more in general than their male peers for comparable recognition, can inadvertently benefit from the obstacles to finding a mentor. Women often must do a vast amount of professional preparation on their own as compared with men, and thus they tend to develop a higher degree of expertise and independence. Because of these equalities, even without mentors, women can and do break out of the molds that they are expected to fit.

One large piece of the puzzle of matching mentors with mentees consists of the personal elements that can round out the relationship. For example, many "extra-curricular" activities such as jogging together or playing tennis can help foster a warm alliance. Yet, such avenues remain generally closed to women as potential mentees. Most often it would not occur to the male mentor to ask a female student or employee to join him for an early morning jog. Even when it does, the male is most likely to feel uncomfortable at such a thought. For example, here is the experience of a young business executive.

Sports are a big factor in business relationships. . . . I have always been an athletic person, and enjoy running in competitions for fun . . . . In my graduate program I remember feeling frustrated that my advisor had closer contact with a lesser student than myself simply because they jogged together in the mornings. When I once suggested I join them, my advisor turned red. Now I'm working at a firm where I'm the only woman at my level or above. I organized a lunch-time jog twice a week with some of my peers and a partner who is an avid runner. Even though I'm out there leading the pack and they are all happy I got them out and moving, I feel like I'm treated as a young cute thing because of it. You just can't win.

Mentors pick mentees with whom they feel comfortable on several levels. In general, people tend to feel more comfortable with those whom they feel are more like them. And because our culture draws a sharp line between the sexes, men perceive other men to be more like them and still perceive women as different.

The mentor–mentee relationship is already one based on power and authority. When one adds the male–female hierarchy to the picture, the situation becomes more complex. Conversations about the mentees's personal life, for example, can be construed differently by the mentor, depending on whether the mentee is female or male. Just as the male may be rewarded for a marriage or birth of a child and the female looked upon with suspicion, the male may be comforted through a divorce, whereas the female mentee may be treated with scorn or as fair game.

Private discussions or consultations between a male mentor and a female mentee can also present problems. A substantial amount of tension may be created by one or the other party not knowing or feeling uncomfortable with the boundaries, as is related in this woman's common experience:

I would go to my mentor's office to discuss my work, and he'd say, "Let's not talk here, let's go for a walk." And we'd be walking and he'd say, "Why don't we go in for a cup of coffee or maybe a beer somewhere." The dialogue would be going through my head that he's a chatty guy; he does this with male students and I knew that if I were a male student I wouldn't

have had to think twice about it. But he was also known to be
involved with an undergraduate student at that time, and the
whole thing made me nervous. I just wanted to sit in his office
and talk to him. I didn't know if he was only expressing inter-
est in my work and being my advisor or whether he had some-
thing else entirely in mind by way of a social relationship.

He started calling me up to have dinner. I remember once a
friend was over when this happened and I was a wreck. I had
no idea what the invitation meant, and I had no idea how I
felt about it. In a way, if I had known it was a truly social thing,
I would have been thrilled. You know, he was really smart and
interesting, and in my world he was a powerful, accomplished
figure and I would have been very flattered. And on the other
hand, it's the usual thing that I had to wonder if that meant he
didn't think my work was good and so forth.

The male mentor may not feel as comfortable sitting alone
in his office with a female mentee. Whether the door is open
or closed, for example, becomes a major issue. Perhaps he
has borne the brunt of crude jokes from his colleagues about
his true intentions with this particular mentee. Perhaps somewhere at the back of his mind he believes that women are
fragile, unpredictable, and emotional. Perhaps he is concerned that the mentee is interested in him sexually. There
are infinite variations on these themes that can play out in
the mind of a mentor that could make for a strained and
impaired relationship.

Similarly, the mentee may be put on guard for a multitude
of reasons. Perhaps the mentor has made, what are to him,
incidental remarks about her appearance or her personal life
or about women in general that nevertheless make her feel
uncomfortable and incompetent. Perhaps she has reason to
believe that the mentor is interested in her sexually, or perhaps she just assumes this based on our underlying social dicta

that hold that male interest of any sort is tantamount to sexual interest. And, perhaps, as is most often the case, the situation is idiosyncratic enough to warrant a double-take and hold the mentee in a constant state of uncertainty. Consider the protracted experience of one graduate student who took steps to clarify the groundrules for working with her mentor:

He never came out and said anything directly. He never made an actual advance. He would withhold things. At a very crucial moment, I needed a reading list for my dissertation work for the summer. He was at that point in Boston, and he said, "Don't worry, come up to Boston; I'll make out a list, and we'll get everything." I went up there, to his office as we planned, and he said, "Let me take you on a tour of the campus." He did. "Let's go out for dinner." We did. And I kept saying, "Can we talk about what I need to talk about?" And he kept saying, "Don't worry, don't worry." We talked a little over dinner, and I got out a pen to write it down, and he told me to stop, that he'd make out a list. He asked if we could have dinner the next night; I couldn't and then he asked about the next night after. I said I had to leave town and go back home by then. Anyway, I went all the way up to Boston and ended up leaving without a reading list.

I wrote him a letter expressing my uneasiness and saying that I had really needed that list and I wasted a lot of time without it, and if he has some problem working with me as my advisor he should let me know and I'll find someone else to work with.

He wrote me back a very business-like letter with a reading list, and I thought, great, now we've gotten everything straightened out. And then I got back from the summer and what really did it for me was when he told me that he had spoken with my other potential advisor Y, without consulting me, and that he told Y that he would be my primary advisor. And I realized then that if he said, "Go to bed with me or else," there was no way I could go to Y and say, "I want to work with you now" because once that happened, I had been roped in. That I wasn't going to have any options if things got worse. I don't think he was scheming anything, I don't think he had a plan, but he might as well have.

And consider the words of a graduating medical student as she signed the contract for her first job with a partner in the practice who had begun to fill the mentor role for her.

So the night of the signing of the contract, three of them [partners] were supposed to be there, but I got stuck in traffic and I was late. So X and I were alone in the office. I signed all the papers and we were going through a lot of little other things: applications for privileges and this and this and this. I had to sign a lot of things. Then he said, "Listen, have you had dinner?" And I said, "No, not yet." He said, "Well I think we should go out and celebrate." And he had already said previously on the phone, a couple days before, that after we've been through all this negotiating and finally signed the contract we should go out and celebrate. So when he had said "we," I assumed he meant everyone.

So that night he said, "We should go out and celebrate." And I said, "Well, I don't know." And he said, "Oh well, we have to eat dinner anyway. You have to eat. So, you know, just something casual. We'll go grab a bite to eat somewhere." I said, "OK." Now this was going to be my boss, so I didn't think anything that bad at that time. We went out to this restaurant. A local place, very casual. He ordered something to drink, and I ordered a glass of wine. We started talking, and he's saying he's so happy about the contract, about me joining them, and he's really expecting things to just go really well. And he just has this sense that things are going to work out so well, and he felt that this was the start of something very good for me and for them. He was going on and on and on, pontificating about how great things were going to be. That was the general theme.

And then, later on, we had another couple of glasses of wine, so then he starts getting all personal and he's saying, "You're such a beautiful creature," or something like that. "And you're so intelligent. You're this, you're that. You have such a great career ahead of you. And you're beautiful." And then he said, "I just hope that the two of us can be very friendly. I want us to be close." He said, "I work well with these other two guys, but I don't socialize with them. We don't have a lot in common outside of the office. And, you know, they do their thing, I do my thing, we don't have much in common. But I'm hoping that you and I can be friendly. We can be friends." And he starts telling me more about his wife and their divorce, and how he's been lonely, how it's just hard for him because he's been with her for 21 years, he doesn't know what to do with himself, he can't imagine being alone now. All this crap.

So I thought, Oh my God. This is getting too much. I don't know how I'm going to handle this. This is such a hard situation because on one level I think it would be nice if we could be friends because I am going to work with the guy. The guy seems like a very nice guy, he's very intelligent, but he is my boss. But you think to yourself, it's nice to be able to be friendly with someone whom you work for, to have a good relationship rather than a relationship where you can't even talk to him. But I just was worried that he was thinking something else.

A mentee can also become uncomfortable, not because of behavior directed at her personally, but because of the general demeanor of her mentor with regard to women. Consider the mentee experience of a lawyer at a large Wall Street firm:

There were people who, in their tone and words, everything they would say, the jokes they would tell, or the stories they would tell, were totally sexist. And I had a mentor in particular, I hate to say it, he was a good friend, but he was totally sexist. This

*person was also a big supporter of mine, gave me lots of oppor-
tunities, was very nice to me, except for the sexism. Was very
smart, was very witty, was clever, was a very good friend to me
and made paths of opportunity for me all the time.*

*He was also totally sexist. So in his demeanor, in the way he
thought about things, relationships, men—women, I was considered the exception, but this is another pattern of a lot of people
who are sexist. I justified that side of his beliefs by being the exception. But I could see the way he talked to women, the way he
acted, everything he did, was utterly sexist and disgusting really.*

*And I shouldn't have accepted his behavior. I shouldn't have
accepted it, and I shouldn't have been his friend, but I was
and I accepted it and I had a lot of nice lunches and dinners
with him and a lot of other people. He was a bon vivant, and
whenever you'd stay late and worked with him he would be
this big spender; he shouldn't have been but he was, because
it was charged. He took his entourage out to dinners, and I
would always be a favored person with him. But he was very
sexist.*

In these cases, and many others like them, the mentee is not
being overly sensitive. Rather, she is reacting appropriately to a
complex situation. For example, she is unlikely to believe explicitly that women are inferior intellectually and that the interest
in her expressed by the mentor must have an underlying sexual
nature. Yet, if she cannot help feeling that this must partly be
true, it is not because she is an insecure, weak person. Rather,
it is because such themes are so deeply ingrained in our culture
that she cannot avoid playing them somewhere in the back of
her mind when she experiences even very subtle, yet repeated
incidents of sex bias or stereotyping, whether addressed directly
to her or to other women around her. When these experiences
are taken together with a few inappropriate remarks or gestures
on the part of the mentor, real self-doubt can sink in.

Business trips, lectures, and conferences also pose problems. Whereas a male-male mentor–mentee pair can comfortably travel together and attend meetings together, when the mentee is female, the dynamic can change, as the following words attest:

> *I was often passed over for the more juicy assignments because my boss was worried about what his wife would think if I went with him on business trips.*

Partly, the problems arise when the mentor worries about what others will think, do, and say and partly the problems can arise when the mentor isn't sure how he feels himself.

For the male mentor working with a female mentee, a whole range of issues concerning more blatant sexual abuse can accompany this powerful relationship once it is set in motion. Here is one example:

> *In my department, there was only one professor who would take on female Ph.D. candidates at all as their advisor. He was very famous, so on the one hand, it was an exciting prospect to have him oversee my dissertation. On the other, I quickly learned that a requirement to meeting with him was sitting on his lap.*

This woman's range of options is certainly slim from this point on if she continues in the doctoral program.

Women's voices in graduate programs could ring out like a Greek chorus on the subject of potential mentors. Consider two other experiences:

> *I knew that not many women had gotten Ph.D.'s from this program, and there were two other women ahead of me and they were very intelligent, serious, and hard-working people. There was no question that they were first-rate graduate stu-*

dents. I was aware pretty early on in my graduate career that they weren't making headway in their dissertations. And it must have been hard to keep them from getting degrees, I figured their advisor was responsible, so I stayed away from him.

In my department of all the four faculty members who would have been appropriate as my dissertation advisors, they were all out of the question. For one reason or another, I don't think any one of them would have actually helped me get a degree because of their track records with women.

It is clear that different standards are applied to men and to women when being considered as potential mentees by persons in a position to mentor them. Although merit and need are the relevant considerations when applied to men, often appearance and personality features are used as considerations for potential female mentees. One woman reports the following reason for not being accepted by a potential mentor:

He told me that he would have trouble working with me because I am not sparkling. A friend on the faculty told me that he was in the faculty dining hall and heard the same guy saying that he couldn't work with me because I have bad acne, which disturbs him.

In corporate America, obtaining, staying with, and thriving under the tutelage of a mentor constitute virtually the only path to advancement. When the relationship is an abusive one, the woman often faces the stark choice of putting up with the abuse or losing her career and livelihood. The latter is so rarely an option that everyday women make conscious "decisions" to go along with the whims of their mentors. Speaking out or filing a complaint is generally equivalent to being ousted from the field and thus does not remain a live option. Surprisingly, even with all the media attention to the more blatant cases of sexual harassment on the job, it is still true that the complaint will often be in vain. For example, an established male social scientist, speaking of a peer who was forced to resign from his post because of multiple charges of sexual harassment against him, described the situation thus:

Competing institutions couldn't wait to snatch him up once he was a free agent.

Even in the more extreme cases of abuse of the authority of the mentor relationship, women have found and continue to find many paths out while maintaining their careers. Because too often each woman has struggled in silence on her own as if her case were unique, professional women have had to virtually reinvent the wheel with regard to problems with their mentors.

Emily had a rather extreme experience with mentors during her graduate career, as described in this section. It is included in the Gender Basics section here because, in broad outline, it describes aspects of the baseline experience of many women. Once women become serious contenders in their chosen professions, once they attain a level of professionalization at which they would, in effect, be accepted into the ranks of the outstanding leaders in their fields, then the system that promoted them to this point begins to break down irreparably. One obvious and common breaking point is in the mentor relationship. It is through this relationship that much of the career advancement is filtered and channeled.

In Emily's case, because in many respects she was in fact navigating new territory, she needed to create a path for herself, alone and anew. Emily's problem was not in obtaining a mentor. Because she was interested in the interplay among a few subjects and because she was talented and dedicated

enough to handle such a vast area, she quickly arrived at what
at first looked like an ideal situation for a graduate student in
the dissertation phase. She had two principal advisors, both
of whom acted as mentors and were well known in their respec-
tive fields and thus of influence in the professional community. She also had two other advisors, eager to assist her in the
development of her ideas and goals for her dissertation and
beyond, who to an extent also acted as mentors. Thus, where
many of the brightest and talented women struggle to get one
person to agree to supervise their work, Emily had four enthusiastic supporters.

Emily set about quite contentedly to pursue her research
goals and freely made use of the abundance of faculty input,
including meeting with one of her principal advisors once a
week to report on her progress and discuss her work and having multiple meetings a week with the other principal advisor
also to discuss her findings and analyses. If there was an early
discontent, it was that Emily noticed that her advisors were
not perhaps fully reading the written material she supplied
them with to report on her work, and thus they did not always
make useful comments in her meetings with them. She marked
this lack up to the sheer amount of material she was giving
them plus the fact that, even at this stage, she was rapidly
becoming the expert in her subject and surpassed the knowledge and understanding of it that her advisors had. Thus, although she was getting plenty of attention, she was perhaps
not getting as useful critiques and comments as she could have.
This treatment, she felt, was no different from that of any other
graduate student, female or male, and was perhaps even natural
to some extent.

However, she did feel peeved at the scanty response she
received when she devoted a chapter of her dissertation to a
subject that one of her principal advisors had written about
extensively. She had carefully critiqued his analysis of it and

came to different conclusions than he had. In this case, she had expected some useful dialogue to take place between them, but it did not.

When Emily was close to finishing her dissertation, she took on an adjunct faculty position at a nearby, prestigious liberal arts college. The department there had wanted to hire Emily full time for the following year, by which time they expected her to complete her Ph.D. When Emily consulted one of her mentors about this offer, he responded that she should pass it up because she should go for her first job to a first-rate, full-scale university and not get bogged down overloaded with teaching duties when she should be actively pursuing her research. Flattered, Emily took the advice.

A few months later when she was closer to completing her work for the Ph.D., Emily discussed applying for jobs for the following year with her mentors. They all concurred that this was a good idea and they wrote very strong, powerful letters of recommendation for her and personally recommended her for specific jobs at prestigious universities. They did not, however, prepare her for the job search process or the interview process, as they did their male students. Emily was unaware at that time of the preparations and practice that her male peers were undergoing. Thus, she walked into several intimidating interview situations insufficiently prepared.

Emily began to notice that her mentors as well as other members of the faculty were making some strange remarks to her. The director of the graduate program kept insisting that she could not apply for jobs outside the immediate local area because of John's employment. And he continued to assume this despite the fact that Emily protested this idea and tried to make it clear, verbally and in writing, that she was more than willing to relocate for the right job. Emily was also told by one of her mentors that she really didn't need the degree because she was married and so didn't need to apply for jobs either.

Worse still, that semester Emily had begun to co-teach a graduate-level seminar in her area of expertise with one of her principal advisors. Of course, he was paid for doing so, and no one even considered paying Emily for the work she did nor even to give her an official title for it. Nevertheless, Emily had expected to enjoy the experience and to learn and profit from it. It happened, in fact, that the topic they chose jointly for the seminar was one in which Emily had become an expert and her mentor was considerably less well versed in it than she. Part of the reason for this choice was so that the mentor could learn more about it from one of the world's leading authorities on it, Emily herself.

Very early on in the semester, it became clear that the mentor was uncomfortable with the imbalance in expertise between himself and Emily. The seminar sessions degenerated after the second one into attacks on Emily and her work. At first, the attacks concerned Emily's theoretical analyses, in which the mentor would turn beet red in the face and splutter out semi-coherent objections and comments. After a session or two like that, the mentor's attacks became personal. Each seminar meeting would follow what became a predictable path. The first few minutes would start off reasonably on the subject matter, with Emily leading the discussion. Then, the mentor would begin to make comments, at first concerning the subject at hand, but within minutes he would be off on another dimension, with a loud voice and red face. Emily tried to make the subject matter more and more neutral in an attempt to circumvent the confrontation, but to no avail. She felt like she was living in the Twilight Zone, with a mentor who had previously been rational, calm, and attentive, and interested in her work, despite theoretical disagreements that they had had all along who had become excitable and discontent, rarely getting out two coherent sentences at one time.

The attacks degenerated further into personal diatribes against Emily that had very much to do with her sex. At one point in a class meeting, he hurled out, "And you, you! You should be at home. You should have children and be at home. Women should stay at home and have babies!" The room was pin silent. The event was so bizarre that Emily had no idea what to do.

Finally, she decided to discuss the matter with her other principal advisor, who was the more senior member of the faculty of the two. He agreed to speak with the troubled mentor and try to rectify the situation. Although Emily knew that the two mentors did speak, she found no change in the problematic behavior and began to feel desperate.

Emily began to want to clarify her standing and move on, and she asked her principal advisor if they could set a defense date for her dissertation. He said that he could, that he just needed to finish reading her material, and that they should make an appointment for the following week to decide how to proceed with a date. When Emily arrived the next week for their appointment, the mentor expressed regret that he had not yet read her work and that they should meet the following week. This routine went on for seven straight weeks. When she spoke with one of her other mentors about her defense, he replied that she didn't really need to finish her dissertation and that he had an "eternal" attitude about her completion of the degree. When she pressed him a little further to discuss a defense date, he merely responded that he didn't like her attitude.

Emily got together with the other women in the program and compared notes. They compiled statistics on the status of women in the department, both in terms of faculty and students. The numbers were quite disturbing, and Emily and her female peers decided to try to do something to change the situation. The first step was to go to the director of the program and share the statistics as well as personal stories from women currently enrolled in the Ph.D. program. Subsequently, the women were intimidated so effectively on a one-to-one basis by members of the faculty that only Emily herself and one other women, another student, were left willing to stand up for equal treatment of women in the department.

Next, Emily and this one other student wrote a letter detailing Emily's treatment by her mentors, under the presumption that if Emily, their star student, could be treated in such a fashion, then lesser female students must receive worse. They also naively assumed that Emily was unassailable, that no harm could come to her because she was generally known and well respected in the field already. They both signed and sent the letter to the members of the faculty.

All of the members of Emily's colleague's advisory committee subsequently resigned from it, and Emily's own letters of recommendation were pulled from her file and replaced with mediocre letters that called the quality of her work into question. Emily was informed that if she insisted on a defense any time in the foreseeable future, it would result, at best, in a low grade pass. One of Emily's mentors announced to her that he would have trouble speaking with her.

Only by sheer force of will and obstinence did Emily and her colleague get out of that program with their degrees. Of course, they lost considerable prospects in their fields, had no mentors, and had inferior letters of recommendation in their files. Emily's mentor experience, which initially had all the makings of a fantasy come true, exhibits the extreme fragility of the male mentor/female mentee relationship. Such relationships must struggle under the constant threat of breaking down, rendering the female mentee with few resources to recoup professionally.

GENDER LESSONS

The mentoring system is the linchpin of entry into a field in good standing, and it remains a quasi-feudal system through which women are locked out. Because having a mentor can be a determining factor for a successful and rewarding career, the clear lesson to be drawn from the current situation is for the female mentee to proceed with caution, to make informed choices whenever possible, and to understand her situation even if she cannot make an active choice about her mentor.

There are two strong themes that dominate mentor–mentee interactions. First is the sheer amount of time and energy that women as training professionals must *waste* navigating and processing these situations, time and energy that men are free to use toward their professional goals. Concomitant with this is the second theme of female tacit complicity in the system. By trying to be polite and largely silent in these difficult maneuvers, the cycle of bias in mentoring continues. In these cases, women are truly caught in a Catch-22 situation.

Any and all of the problematic aspects of the male mentor–female mentee relationship can have a huge impact on the mentee and virtually none on the mentor. If the mentor is uncomfortable playing sports and discussing personal matters with the female mentee, it is of no consequence to his life, whereas for the mentee it is likely to lead to a diminished mentor–mentee relationship in the professional sphere. Similarly, if the mentor makes inappropriate gender-based remarks, he probably isn't aware of it. If he is, he may even derive some pleasure from doing so. The mentee, in contrast, can be led into a tailspin of diminished self-worth and a strained working relationship. If the mentor is hesitant to attend conferences or meetings or to go on business trips with the mentee, he is likely to have plenty of other candidates to accompany him. The mentee, however, may lose out on professional contacts, experience, training, and, possibly, promotion.

GENDER COMPOUNDS

One extremely common occurrence that vastly complicates the career of a professional woman is becoming too personally involved with her mentor. This involvement can take several forms, from the mentee becoming the personal confidante of the mentor, and thus filling a mothering role, to romantic and sexual involvement. Whatever the actual format of the arrangements, the fact remains that they are situations that male mentees would rarely, if ever, find themselves in, and these are circumstances that inevitably have deleterious effects on the female mentee's professional development.

It is fairly easy to understand the attraction of personal involvement with a mentor. If a mentor begins to confide his personal affairs to the mentee, the mentee is likely, at least at first, to feel flattered and to feel that their relationship is deepening. Thus, a mentee may even encourage this sort of development until it begins to go awry; for example, when the personal trials of the mentor begin to consume all or most of the time the mentee has with him, time that should have been spent on her work. The situation may also begin to plant a bitter taste in the mouth of the mentee if she feels as though she is a mother surrogate and is being looked to for nurturance—the very thing on a professional level that the mentor is supposed to supply. Thus, in this situation the mentee's time is being squandered on the personal tribulations of her mentor, who, in turn, is offering less and less in the way of professional advice and advancement. In fact, the deeper the personal involvement becomes and the more the mentee fills the slot of mother figure, the less seriously the mentor considers her work and career prospects. It is the old double-bind of men needing a woman to draw out their emotional selves and, at the same time, devaluing the person in every other capacity who fills that function for them.

When the involvement is sexual or romantic between mentee

and mentor, the problems can be more severe. Again, though, the attraction to such an arrangement on the part of the mentee is easy to imagine. After all, she usually greatly respects and is interested in the mentor, his work, and his involvement in the profession, and he is often powerful in relation to the mentee. Authority can be not only blinding but also attractive. This combination makes the mentor–mentee situation ripe for sexual involvement. In fact, it is not uncommon for mentor–mentee pairs to marry. It is almost as equally likely that such an arrangement spells the end of the mentee's career.

Quite often in these situations the quality of the mentee's work is devalued in the estimation of the mentor. This devaluation can happen in a variety of ways. Listen to the words of an executive who became involved with her mentor:

Before our relationship began, he consistently rated my performance very highly. Once we were involved, my work evaluations from him plummeted. He kept repeating, by way of explanation, that he had to be fair, he couldn't let our relationship influence him as far as my work goes.

Several psychological consequences ensue for the mentee who is personally involved with her mentor. Where before she only needed to navigate her actual world, once the personal relationship commenced, the mentee must straddle both her own world as aspiring professional and her mentor's accomplished segment of the professional world. Thus, she may feel distanced or cut off from those who are her actual peers and are a source of support and friendship. And, at the same time, she may feel awkward in the presence of her mentor's peers, now that she is filling this dual role of social equal yet professional trainee of one form or another. The mentee may feel adrift much of the time, caught in between the two worlds with only partial anchors in each. This is not likely to be good for her psyche. Chances are the circumstances will erode the professional self-confidence she very definitely needs to be building at this time. Her personal integrity may suffer at the same time. For, in both domains, she will now be measuring herself against her mentor–lover who is already accomplished in the same field as her own.

It would require two extremely unusual people to accomplish such a relationship that would not result in paternalistic patronizing of the mentee, an atmosphere that will not be conducive to her professional development. And she will find herself in the tricky position of being dependent professionally on someone with whom she is personally involved and on the mentor's peers who now see her socially and view her, to some degree, as a personal appendage of her mentor. They are given the opportunity to see her in social terms and to obliterate or devalue her work as a result.

A universal problem arising from sexual or romantic involvement with a mentor is getting out of it while retaining one's career intact, not to mention keeping one's sense of oneself intact as well. The best solution is prevention. Professional arrangements should be made *in advance of* personal involvement with a mentor. However, this is not always possible. It is not uncommon for such personal relationships to be subtly, tacitly coerced by the mentor.

GENDER ACTION

Although women can find it extremely difficult to find genuine mentors, even when they have them, the female mentee is most often constantly making trade-offs, whether explicitly or only on an implicit level. The trade-offs are often between benefits of the mentor relationship she is in and an amount of gender bias and often sexual harassment that she must endure from the mentor. It might be useful to make this trade-off process explicit, so that the mentee can make deliberate and sound choices. In such a case, at least the mentee acknowledges the circumstances and can take steps to eradicate the negative impact they may have on her psyche and self-confidence, which arises particularly when the dealings are left tacit and thus unacknowledged. One woman, a research health scientist, transformed a cycle of harassment she endured from her otherwise effective mentor by making it into an explicit trade. She describes the situation thus:

I was making a deal. I was going to put up with a certain amount of shit in exchange for which I was going to get my Ph.D. I was going to get more out of it than I gave up. I was going to get something really important, so to me it was a worthwhile deal. I understood the economics of it as an exchange. When I let something slide, it's not me being victimized by other people. It's a deal. I let this go, but I know that I profit. I know what I got out of the deal. My career goes forward along this path I've set. I get to do the work that I love and get paid for it.

Another woman might not be able to consider such a trade, being unwilling to endure bias in the name of her career, as is the case in the following statement from a liberal arts professor:

There was a certain point in my career where all of a sudden I recognized that my mentor was treating me discriminatorily because I'm a woman. I mean, he promoted me, but he was just applying considerations about me that he wouldn't have dreamt of if I had been a man. And it affected how he saw my work and how he saw me as a professional and future colleague.

I just knew I couldn't let it go without dispensing with my own personal integrity forever. The trade-off would have been too great; it would have been a form of emotional death. In the end, because my attempts to get him to stop the behavior failed, I switched fields.

A third view comes from a woman who experienced devastating gender bias, professionally and personally. Having rebuilt a career in a second profession, she adopted the following perspective:

A lot of sexism, you can deal with. It's not the end of the world. You recognize it and don't let it get to you. You learn to call it what it is. You can live with it if the circumstances are right.

I let certain incidents and events go now. If I hadn't? If I had called them on it, it would have put my mentor in an uncomfortable position. It would have resulted in a series of very unpleasant exchanges. And, in the end, the histories would have been rewritten in terms of lapses of memory and misunderstandings.

I've been more and more successful, the more I've been inclined to let things slide. When I let things slide, I definitely have an emotional reaction. I'll be driving home from the train station and people will be looking at me because I'm gesticulating wildly. In my car, I'm privately giving my division chief a piece of my mind. I get mad, but I have enough positive reinforcement that it's not devastating. It's not undermining. I see it as other people's problems, not mine. I've learned to separate sexist behavior and the evaluation of how good my work is. None of the treatment I get now is dispositive to my career advancement as it has been in the past. So, I can afford not to take it personally.

Unlike men, women have found that it is crucial to their professional success to cover their bases whenever and wherever possible. Thus, a woman, whether she is in a professional program or already working in her field, must make her work and herself known to as many people as possible.

The report of the job search experience of a graduate student in a Ph.D. program attests to the importance of making one's work known:

No, no. I didn't have a mentor in graduate school. There was nobody who knew the material. The best that they did, it was like laissez faire. They left me alone, and then they approved it. Which, basically, what it came down to is what I wanted. No, nobody read the stuff. My main advisor, who was a man, was very good. He at least read some of the novels by every author that I dealt with, which he went out of his way to do.

So there was nobody who was really involved in the same way as a mentor. I had a sense that I was going to have to work twice as hard as people who were coming out of programs where there could be phone calls made where someone could be placed. And so I really started to do stuff as an apprentice. I started giving papers at conferences. I started sending stuff out for publication so that by the time I graduated I had two books under contract.

But they left me alone to do it. They didn't necessarily show me how to do it, but at least I didn't get what I think a lot of other people got, which was interference. There was nobody actually blocking my way to doing that. And in the absence of that I realized how much easier my graduate experience was than a lot of other people's where there were actually people literally setting up blockades for whatever success they could have professionally. For my people, they didn't make it easier, there were no paths that were greased, but nobody took it upon themselves not to let me do what I wanted to do.

Not having a mentor, when I finished the Ph.D., my job search wasn't the sort of active process that I see at some places going on where I mean that's what people do automatically. . . . If I asked particularly for somebody to write a note, if I prepared something that was very easy for someone to do, they would then do it. This is where I learned that lesson. So that I would go with my cover letter with the form, and bring a piece of paper to the person saying, "Could you just write a couple of lines on this and I'll send it to the head of the department."

So, I would literally bring them the whole form, with the pen and they would then write a couple of lines. But I knew that if I gave it to them and said, "Give this back to me tomorrow," it would never happen. . . . So I was very self-starting. What I did was to make sure that I got letters from people outside. I mean I really hustled so that people whom I'd met at conferences, or whose panels I was on or whatever, also wrote letters in addition to the professors from my program. And that's where I learned to build up a community of people, not the people I was in school with, but from other places who shared similar interests.

The strategy of being extremely clear about one's needs, whether in regard to a job search or in order to fulfill work properly, is essential. Just as the experience of the woman above shows, it is often effective to communicate one's needs, both verbally and in writing, and as clearly and succinctly as possible.

It is also important, particularly in the absence of a mentor, to look to people outside one's professional program or firm for advice and encouragement. Broadening the exposure of one's work and oneself to the larger community of professionals in the field can be both rewarding and can fill in the gaps that a mentor might supply. It will certainly require a sustained effort in order to accomplish this exposure, but the long-range benefits can be enormous.

Some institutions have mentoring networks in place specifically for women. There are several mentor pools in operation across the nation, and more are forming every year. Some fields have nationwide mentor systems, such as the "Systers" network for female computer scientists. Its members range from undergraduate computer science majors to graduate students to senior faculty to seasoned women in the industry. The network has changed the field for the women in it, providing information about conferences, Systers' meetings, research, and career advice. Most fields now at a minimum have an association for the women working in it that can serve as a launching pad for obtaining information, advice, and respectful collegiality.

15   FEMALE MENTORS

GENDER BASICS

For mentors of graduate students it's still a good old boys' system. In order for women to think they can at least have a chance for performing in the professional world, they need female role models in their undergraduate and graduate education.

The dearth of women in the upper echelons of virtually every professional field means that it is a rare occasion when a woman can look to another woman as a mentor. Clearly, many of the problems in mentor relationships discussed above—from situations of ambiguous sexual or derogatory content to outright sexual harassment and abuse of power—vanish from the scene when the mentor is a woman.

The benefits to women of having female mentors are so clear, manifest, and well documented that this chapter focuses only on the potential problem areas. The first issue arises from the fact that women as well as men are socialized to hold negative and stereotyped views of women as a group. Thus, a woman in a senior position may disdain younger women in much the same way as her male colleagues do and be reluctant to take them on as mentees. Moreover, a female mentor may look down upon other women as prospective mentees and favor male mentees in much the same fashion that male mentors do. She may be just as likely as a male mentor to value a male protegee's work more highly than comparable work done by a female and to have lower expectations of a female's professional potential. In such cases, the woman may rationalize her attitudes tacitly by believing that she is the exception, that she is different and unlike other women. One lawyer looked back on her experience holding such views with bitterness:

For the longest time, I would laugh at sexist stories. I would be one of the boys. I would look down upon the stereotypical woman, so-called. And I had sexist attitudes. That was the thing that helped me survive. That was the only way to survive. I believed that I was an exception. That's the only way I survived, and that's the only reason I was a partner. Not the only reason, but I would not have been a partner had I not been so malleable and so adaptive to their model. The best thing for them is to have a woman who accepts their model.

Often during their training and careers, women are encouraged by the men around them to maintain such beliefs. They are often viewed as the shining golden girls. This attitude serves several functions. Chief among them is fostering divisiveness among women, causing the chosen woman to look to her male peers for professional and personal camaraderie and to shun the women in her field as "other" and unworthy. And with this attitude the males have worked out a rationale for why they do not need to consider women generally as viable professionals: the one they have is different. A further result of the exceptional golden girl syndrome is that often the woman is held up to impossible standards that few, if any, people could meet. Thus, in the end, she may be doomed to appearing a failure.

Because women so rarely make it even close to the top, they may be pitted against each other in another way as well. When a woman achieves some success in her career, she may be fearful of maintaining her position when other women appear on the scene. Knowing full well that scant one woman will be admitted near the top of the hierarchy, women often undercut other women within their profession. Consider the following observation:

It seems like women in senior positions are never given the same kind of job security that the men at comparable levels have. Whatever the reason, the reigning folklore is that, if you're a woman, the worst thing is to have another woman as your boss or mentor because she'll shut you out. She'll be afraid that you'll be tomorrow's competition if she trains you well, and then she'll be booted out the door.

Thus, several factors together can conspire to keep women from becoming solid mentors to other women and to promoting them actively. First are the cultural factors that pit women against each other and promote a poor evaluation of women's professional potential. Second is the real issue of competition and job security. And, third, ironically, women report having a dual attitude toward being the only or one of the few women in her field or at her level. They are, on the one hand, made uncomfortable by this situation and often know that they will bear the brunt of the gender bias in the field. On the other, they enjoy being novelties, held up for inspection as special cases, as the following remarks bear out:

In a technical field such as mine, it is rare to see women at all. If there is one, she generally does everything she can to keep other women out. They like the attention their uniqueness brings and don't want to lose it.

These feelings draw upon and play into the stereotypical formula of female jealousy of each other, with the cultural advantage being on the side of youth. Thus, a certain amount of typical female rivalry comes into play in the mentor relationship between females at the subconscious level. It is almost unavoidable, for example, that each will check the other out physically in an automatic and reflexive manner and that this evaluation may continue to be an underlying current that runs through the duration of their relationship and places an additional stress on it.

Moreover, because there are so few women at the top, there is intense pressure from all sides for this slim minority to serve as mentors and concomitantly as role models. Many feel genuine discomfort with this idea, as expressed in the following statement:

I realize there really is a lot I could do, taking women and working with them by helping them and teaching them. That is really concrete. But being called a role model is just awful. It's like the experience when you're a child and somebody says, "Why aren't you good like so and so?" I just hated it when my friends' mothers would say that. It was awful. Nobody likes to be pointed out as the one who is successful. It's icky and also it places some level of an obligation on you to not be stupid and to not have your own problems. To make it seem as if women should be looking up to you, which they shouldn't. The idea that to be told that you should be a model to somebody else is just uncomfortable.

Another reason why women may shun female mentees does not arise from sexist attitudes or single-minded self-preservation tactics. Rather, it stems from the fact that women still must work more and better than their male peers to achieve lesser recognition and pay. Often a woman will face the non-choice between her own uphill career struggle and fostering the careers of younger women in her field. This is a Catch-22 situation that men do not need to confront. If a woman pursues her career effectively and achieves the influence and status that would make her a powerful mentor, she will have little time to expend on her mentees. And, conversely, if she invests significant time on mentees, she will sacrifice her own career. Add to this the fact that women are still responsible for virtually all of the home and child care, and the situation becomes an almost hopelessly vicious cycle.

A distinguished university professor described the dilemma thus:

I could have an impact on female students if I wanted to make that my whole life. But I don't. It's just too exhausting. It's so demanding and I'm still ambitious. I can't spend my time that way!

Yet another and almost startling stumbling block to women taking on female mentees was expressed by an accomplished mathematician:

I just started working with women students a few years ago. In terms of having mentors the women are not coddled at all. One of the things that women suffer from is a terrible lack of self-confidence. And I guess I just really thought that two women will make a mess of it. So I avoided them. I really avoided them. Then, after a very long period of time, I started to think, "Gee what's the matter with me?" And I just acted a little bit friendly toward a female graduate student, and the next thing I knew the women started to flock to me. I was working with several women students.

That is, even women at the pinnacle of their careers manage to maintain low self-evaluations as a result of a lifetime of social conditioning, despite all of the evidence from their career to the contrary. It would be virtually impossible for such a person to genuinely believe in her female mentees' capabilities. In this way, the learned attitude about women's worth and potential is handed down to the next generation at the worst possible moment: the point at which an accomplished professional female could extend her hand to a mentee, raising both of them out of the self-perpetuating vicious cycle.

An overarching reason why successful professional women shy away from the mentor role is that, for a woman, the mentor role can readily become a maternal one. They find, for example, that excessive and often irrational demands are placed on them by mentees, that there is a fusing of professional and personal realms in the relationship in a way that demands the mentor to perform the function of the stereotypical caring and omnipotent mother.

The recollection of the following executive bears this out:

I had a mentor, and as I look back, I can see that I made her into a mommy. I even slept at her house with her kids. When I was at her house, she left my term papers under my pillow when she was done reading them.

She fell into the mother role, and I fell into that of the child. I think women expect much more of women than of men.

Male mentees may have two contradictory attitudes about a female mentor. On the one hand, they too will expect more from a female mentor than a male. They will expect her to expend greater effort on their behalf than they would of a male mentor. In fact, they may go so far as to feel that she should be devoted to their needs to the exclusion of her other duties, as they might of a mother. They also might expect a female mentor to perform certain tasks for them that they would never dream of a male mentor carrying out. For example, they might expect her to put together their dossiers and see to the various procedural tasks required. They might also feel more secure about personal infringements such as calling a female mentor at home, asking her personal questions, and revealing their own personal lives while seeking advice from her, in ways that they would not if the mentor were male. Generally, they may not wait for the mentor to provide the cues to the operation of their mentor relationship, but may take the initiative upon themselves in a fashion that is actually inappropriate to the actual nature of their relationship.

The flip side of this, which is almost a consequence of the male mentee's increased expectations of a female mentor, is a lower respect for the mentor than were the same person male instead. And, thus, they feel entitled to trespass over the proper boundaries of the mentor–mentee relationship. The mentee's attitude is bolstered by the fact that even when the female mentor is of the most senior level, she is often held in some ways in a less authoritative status than her male peers. And she is regarded as less in the eyes of her male peers, a fact that is rarely kept a secret from the community at large, including the woman's mentees.

The woman's female mentees may also regard her as less than her male peers, even when professionally this is not the case. That is true, even when on an objective plane the woman has clearly accomplished more or has acquired greater skill and knowledge of the field than her male peers. This perception too will be fed by the male peers' attitude about the senior female whom they may dually disdain and fear. And generally because of ingrained attitudes about women, the female mentee may not regard females as viable mentors. In addition, however, because of her subordinate status, even though she is a senior and established member of her profession, the female mentor may in point of fact have less to offer her mentees, female or male, than would a male mentor. For, if her clout in the profession is diminished, then she can accomplish less for her mentees. And this would be the case despite the fact that she may be an excellent teacher and a dedicated and gener- ous advisor to her mentees. Thus, she as well as her potential mentees will be in the troubling position of needing to weigh her strong mentoring skills against her lowered status in the field in a way that one would rarely need to consider for poten- tial male mentors. Additionally, because of women's learned self-perceptions, even women of great accomplishment may have decreased self-confidence and hold diminished expecta- tions of women. Consequently, such women do not make good mentors for the female mentee.

GENDER LESSONS

The myriad issues for women in the mentor role provide a stark lesson in the strength of our collective investment and belief in acquired, normative truth. That is, if we, culturally and implicitly, hold to notions about women in the professions that they are not competent or powerful enough, for example, then in a self-perpetuating style, women are not likely to retain enough self-confidence and respect to be effective mentors. A further consequence of the general disdain for professional women is that female mentors are not likely to hold potential female mentees in high regard. A pivotal result is the continu- ation of the cultural isolation of women from one another.

Whereas prevailing lip service is paid to the importance of female role models and mentors for aspiring women in the professions, in fact, the trends run in the opposite direction. Precisely what holds women back from appropriate self- acknowledgment and acceptance is what holds them back from becoming powerful forces in the next generation's pro- fessional development. As an alternative, senior-level profes- sional women need to begin to take seriously the lesson of the potential strength to be drawn from female solidarity in the professions.

GENDER COMPOUNDS

If Emily were Puerto Rican, for example, or a member of another ethnic or racial minority, she would be likely to be expected to fill the role of mentor to and champion of all potential mentees who are also members of minority groups, not necessarily the same one that Emily is. In effect, she would be held up as the accomplished minority representative in her profession. She would often hear herself introduced as the "outstanding Puerto Rican" professional in her field, not as unqualifiedly outstanding.

This ghettoization of minority members does a disservice to mentor and mentee alike. It reduces Emily's choice of protegees to a select and small group, and it channels this group into Emily's field, whether that is where the individual's interests lie or not. Chances are, Emily's own choice of specialization would have, in effect, been selected for her in a similar manner as well.

There are an infinite variety of ways in which this tacit tracking system can operate and sustain itself, and it surely does not promote the ideal sort of mentor relationship for which one usually hopes. In addition to the burden of being placed in the dual mentor–mother role by her mentees, Emily will now have to contend with being awarded with the title of champion of minority mentees. Since no additional authority is being given to Emily to accomplish some sort of equity greater than what is currently found in her profession, she is being set up for failure in this regard. Thus, she will be failing her mentees in crucial ways. And her mentees may well resent the situation they find themselves in and turn this anger on Emily herself.

A mentee may resent being implicitly placed with Emily because she is not in the area of the profession in which the mentee's interest lies. The mentee may resent Emily as a woman or being placed with someone who is perceived as a not good enough mentee–mother. Or, finally, the mentee, being identified with the cultural norms as most of us are, may not respect Emily simply on the basis of her ethnic origin. None of this contributes to a successful mentor–mentee relationship when the pairing was not arranged in anything resembling a freely chosen match.

GENDER ACTION

The more ways that are found to bolster and increase the self-confidence of women in the professions, the more likely it is that we will begin to see larger numbers of effective female role models and mentors. Thus, all of the suggestions found in the Gender Action segments throughout this book can have an impact on the situation of female mentors. Women in a position to be mentors must begin to break out of the vicious cycle they are in and learn what men have always known about mentoring: that, in and of itself, being a mentor builds confidence. Just as when one teaches, one often learns a great deal, so in a mentor role, one not only is likely to have the opportunity to explore areas of the field one otherwise would not have but also in the process one discovers facets of one's own talents, knowledge, and experience, thereby gaining increased self-respect.

Men have always known that mentoring can and often does enhance one's standing in the profession in many, and some unforeseeable, ways. The more one provides a successful mentor relationship to energetic and bright young people, the more one's own work will be carried on and disseminated throughout the professional community. And the more likely it is that, down the road, one's own proteges will provide opportunities for the mentor. Thus, contrary to feeling that the time and effort involved in mentoring detract from the building of one's own career, the reverse has proven to be true for generations of male professionals. The stronger the channels for building female-to-female professional interaction and relationships, the better women will be able to and will find it natural to fill the mentor and the mentee roles. Women with male mentors would benefit from this development because their sense of their own potential within the profession would be more likely to be supported by a backup system of female role models.

PART VI
SILENCE OF THE LAMBS

In this part, the work experience of junior professional women
is examined by looking at three general issues: the atmosphere
in the work environment, the key components of first jobs, and
career advancement. The movie, *Silence of the Lambs,* portrayed many of the salient themes in all three issues through
the eyes of Clarisse, a rookie F.B.I. agent who has not yet completed her training yet is on her first assignment. Just as with
professional women embarking on their careers, Clarisse is
continuously running up against the pervasive gender bias in
our culture—from her supervisor's lecherous glance as he's
complimenting her work in his course and giving her her first
assignment, to the psychiatrist at the prison where she must
meet with Hannibal Lecter who tries to withhold her visita-
tion privileges unless she goes out with him, to the fact that
she is called Clarisse while everyone else has full names and
titles, to the case she works on involving a man who starves
and skins fat women, to the attempt to deal Clarisse out of the
case just as it is about to be solved with an airy promise of some
kind of credit to her, and to the fact that she is told that she

was given the job because her femininity would appeal to Hannibal and the hope was that he would let down his guard in the presence of a (mere) woman. In short, Clarisse does not endure a single scene in the movie without being confronted with sexist and even misogynist attitudes and actions. They are the very air she must choke on and breathe at the same time.

Much like Clarisse, although in a completely different professional context, Emily has similar experiences. Yet where Clarisse is fairly clear and vocal about what is going on around and to her, Emily is less explicitly aware of the various components of her work experience. Thus, the result in most cases, but particularly in Emily's because she is not as conscious of the bias that she is digesting from every corner of her work, is a continuation of the process of demoralization. Even though Emily perseveres in her chosen profession and advances, it is much more difficult for her to do so than it is for her male peers because she is constantly interpreting messages and behaviors of which she is only partially aware. Clarisse, who is aware of the bias being pelted around and at her, also succumbs to the degradation of her professional energy by means of demoralization, if for no other reason than that she must constantly expend energy fending it off, responding to it, reminding herself that it is bias and not a reflection on her performance, ultimately doubting herself and her ability on occasion, and generally assessing the situation through gendered vision in order to try to determine the dynamic in play. All of this requires a great deal of effort in addition to that needed for the professional work that needs to be done. It is a job unto its own that requires incredible acuity, clarity, and vast stores of inner strength. These are the extra job requirements, among several others, that are demanded only of women.

16 PROFESSIONAL AMBIANCE

GENDER BASICS

The atmosphere of the work environment varies from institution to institution and firm to firm depending on many factors, including the personalities of the individuals who work in them. But they vary only to a degree. Work environments are in large part constructions molded by the social climate that surrounds them, and thus there are fixed components present in most of them. And because the factors present in the workplace are continuous with the rest of everyday life, they are often difficult to isolate and discern. To the untrained eye, they are part of the fabric of the everyday. Low-level sexual harassment on the job in the professional realm is constant, and the impact is all the stronger while it remains unseen. This circumstance, of course, leads the women who work in these environments to internalize the issues yet again and to seek solutions that involve modifying only themselves.

This is an accurate description of Emily's situation. Having obtained her degree and successfully landed a good first job, she has begun the work that she expects to spend her adult life developing. Emily is caught up in performing well and learning to navigate her way through the basics of the profession, even though she does feel that her training did provide her with the requisite knowledge and thus she is fairly confident about her abilities. As a result, much of the negatively charged atmosphere that surrounds her passes her by. Those pieces that Emily does pick up on as biased, she instinctively lets slide in the name of getting along and through the first stage of her career. To the extent that Emily thinks it through, she fears that publicly questioning biased behavior, no matter how minor or how big, would jeopardize her future. She doesn't feel that the risk is worth it. Perhaps later, she reasons silently, she will question the bias when she has achieved a different level of standing in the field.

In the words of an executive concerning the early harassment that she endured,

I never said anything to my boss about it. I felt I was so new, I was just learning the business, that I just had to be a good sport.

The ambiance at work has many parts, each with different levels of nuance and layering. There is general hallway banter between peers, there is mixed bantering among junior- and senior-level people, there are the mentoring and quasi-mentoring relationships that form between senior and junior members, there is the tone and comportment of those involved in work discussions, there is the differential treatment of non-professional staff, such as secretaries, there is also the general tenor of the field nationwide that affects the attitudes of the senior members of the field, and finally there are known overt forms of discrimination and harassment that cast a pall over the work environment and color every aspect of it.

In order to assess Emily's situation, let's move from the top down, and begin with the general tenor of the profession itself.

As in most professions, in Emily's field very few women have made it to the top levels. This would mean, on average, that women might have hit the eight percent mark this year. And, the bulk of this eight percent work in the less prestigious subspecialties and at the less prestigious companies or institutions. Thus, it is rare that women in the field are in a position of decision-making authority for hiring, making internal policies, or making policy that affects the field as a whole such as those decisions that might be made in nationwide society meetings. Very few of the officers of the various professional societies in Emily's field are women, though not for lack of women having run for elected office to these positions nor for lacking the necessary qualifications.

Thus, in this regard a vicious cycle is in effect. Because the senior-level women in the field are mostly working at the second- and third-rate institutions, and because they are not generally elected to the higher offices in the professional associations, they are less visible in the profession and are not part of the active decision-making process for the field. And because the women in the field are not accorded equal standing, they are not in the appropriate positions to have the pervasive patterns of gender bias examined within the field nor to have remedial measures undertaken. Thus, the status quo marches on with little if any alteration. As one psychologist observed of her own profession:

This is a terrible field for women in many ways. The men are condescending to women. They imitate Freud's attitudes. The more orthodox the psychoanalytic institute, the worse the attitude toward women therapists.

And if the system present in a profession is not conducive to respecting women as equals, then the individuals within it are not likely to either. That is, in virtually every profession the general tone of the profession combines with the biases of

the individuals within it to work together to create an atmosphere that makes it impossible for women to feel as if they
have equal standing and equal integrity with their male peers.
Thus, the casual cross-talk and interaction that occur in every
work environment will almost invariably involve frequent
episodes that are degrading to women. For example, Harrington (1993) notes that the 1989 Massachusetts Gender Bias
Study reported that sixty-four percent of female lawyers had
observed male lawyers in court making remarks or jokes that
demean women, forty-three percent had heard inappropriate
sexual comments, and virtually all had heard remarks about
the clothing or physical appearance of women lawyers and the
use of such tags as "honey" and "sweetheart" for female
lawyers.

Emily finds that there is a constant, daily, baseline level of
comments either directly about women or in the form of jokes
or cracks. Occasionally, she hears remarks peppered with an
afterthought chuckled out along the lines of "Oops, sorry, that's
not P.C. anymore is it?" This afterthought at the same time
emphasizes the degradation, makes a jab at the notion of political correctness, and gives the appearance of an apology. The
little exchanges and comments ascend gradually upward to
larger or more sustained forms of behavior and comments, as
the framework provided for this young professional attests.

*I was cute, I was young, I was there to bring light-hearted
joy to these guys who were working so hard. But I didn't welcome any touching or advances. And I always would escape,
move quickly and stuff. But there was a lot of ass grabbing.*

In fact, as reported in the Sadkers' (1994) study, a California State Bar Survey found that eighty-eight percent of the
female lawyers reported pervasive gender bias and sixty-two
percent believed that they were not accepted as peers by male
lawyers. One experience of a successful executive serves as an

example of the next step up the chain of disparaging behavior in the professional workplace:

There's the men that try to protect you, and put their arm around you and say, "Don't talk like that in front of her. She's so sweet. She's not like that." So there would be that kind and you'd gravitate toward them because they were brotherly. And then there were the men who were trying to pretend that they were these big sex fiends to each other.

One day I was in the hall, and I was really working hard. I had a lot of respect for myself that I had done this. I felt pretty aggressive. And they would give me plenty of work to do. They respected my work. But as soon as other men got around and it was a group thing, then they just became outrageous. I remember once we were standing in the hallway, and I was taking notes and there were five men around in a circle. And this production manager put his arm around me and I thought, well I'm not going to make a big deal because I don't want to draw attention to this whole deal. And all of a sudden I realized he had undone my skirt and my skirt fell to the floor.

Women in such situations are left with the task not only of attempting to preserve some vestige of professional decorum for themselves but also of keeping the peace and smoothing over such incidents so that no one is upset by them. Otherwise, as the women know very well, they are the ones who will be left out in the cold, not the perpetrators of the demeaning behavior. They need to decide what to do, and most often the chosen path involves silence, as the following woman's words confirm:

He was always saying like, "Oh, let's not have lunch. Let's go to a hotel. I know this hotel that shows porno movies. You know, come on, let's. Don't be so uptight. You're so uptight." He was this old ugly man. I was thinking, do other women actually go with him? Every day he would do that. I never said a word to anybody. Never complained because I felt, "I'm asking for it, I want this job."

The choice of silence over fury is the result, along with other decisions and factors, of professional women trying to blend in with the mostly male crowd to the fullest extent possible in order to succeed. The underlying sentiment is that the less their femininity is observed, singled out, and resented, the better their chances of getting by, getting along, and getting a fair shake in the division of work and promotion. Not all women make such a choice consciously. Rather, the play for invisibility can often stem from education, training, and a series of smaller decisions and behaviors that ultimately add up to the tack of assimilation. The following woman voiced her decision as though it were explicitly made, however:

When you work with men, this is what happens, and you have to be a good sport. You know, the language and everything, incredibly vulgar and vague in talking about who they laid and this and that. I was one of the boys; I was one of the guys from early on. Because when you work with all men, if you're not one of the boys, then they don't want you around. So I always just went along with it.

The consequences of going along with harassment, whether tacit or explicit, are manifested in a variety of ways, but they usually involve self-doubt. One lawyer described her response to the workplace ambiance thus:

I must have felt confused. But I also feel I was sure; I had the confidence of my convictions. I also felt that they never wiped away my convictions. Though I must say at the same time I felt confused at various times. It was awful. I would come home

and cry at night. It was terrible. It was a horrible period. I felt
very underappreciated, and I was.

Sexist language, jokes, and adolescent boys' pranks played
out against adult female professionals are part of the standard
fare of working conditions in the professional realm. In addition, it is almost commonplace for professional women, particularly at the beginning of their careers, to be stalked by a
single member of their field. This occurs with a regularity and
frequency that is astounding. For example, read the following
detailed description by a young English professor of her experience being persistently harassed by a colleague in the first
years of her first job.

There has been one gentleman who's sort of taken it upon
himself literally to examine every move that I have ever made.
He pulls out my grade sheets at the end of every term to see
what kind of grades I give, trying to show that I'm not a good
teacher because my students are doing well. So that my first
term here I was bright eyed and wanted to think the best of
everything. And so the head of the department, who again has
always been very supportive, calls me in and says, "We've just
gotten a sort of, it's not really a complaint, but an observation
from someone," and of course all these people are disguised.
It then became very clear to me who this was because he was
the same person who kept doing things over and over again,
but he was never named. "That so and so has looked up your
grade sheets and realized that you're two points above the
average for the department." What I said was, "Well, in part
that's because I probably spend 14 hours a day here, a lot of it
with students, rewriting, going over their rewrites, showing them
how to write, so that by the time they finish my class they know
more than when they came in so they can do well. There are
going to be kids who fail, there are going to be people who don't

do well, that's probably because they don't want to work. But if you get a classroom full of kids that you can make feel as if you have some investment in what they're doing and take their work seriously and respect what they're doing, then they will try hard. And then if you give them the time to do it and the right kinds of attention and the right kinds of support, often they will do well, you know. It shouldn't be shocking to you that I'm not failing a lot of people; that shouldn't be a disappointment. You should reward me for that as opposed to penalizing me."

But this as I say was only the beginning. Things kept going on. He did a collage. I have all these things in my drawer; I should have documented them. My picture was in the middle of the collage. I was in a local paper for something. He took my photograph out of the paper, and then around it he put quotations about women and sort of cartoons. And he put them in all of my colleagues' mailboxes. So I walk in and I see my face reproduced in the pigeonholes. This, again, doesn't seem to me appropriate behavior.

I then get told, "This man is very sad, he has a tragic life, he has this, he has that, how come you can't be nice to him? You're nice to everyone else in the department; how come you can't be nice to him?" And I said, "Because he's attacking me. Because you can't legislate whom I'm nice to. I happen to like most of the people I work with and so I am nice to them, but you can't tell me that I have to be nice to somebody because I am nice to other people. I have to have some sort of say in whom I'm nice to or not. I'm not leaving spitballs under his door. I mean I'm not not being nice actively; I'm just not being chatty when I see him in the halls, but that can't be my job. Okay, then I'll stop talking to everyone and then he won't feel bad because it won't just be him." I mean what are the implications of something like that?

And, again, I don't think that anything like this would have been said to a male member of the staff. They would not go up and say you have to be nice to somebody. It would not occur to *them to say it to a guy. This was because I'm not being femi-nine enough by nurturing somebody who is wounded. I mean somebody who's again being presented as a basketcase that I'm then supposed to help out. I don't see this as part of my job description.*

So his harassment of me has continued. I gave a talk at the Women's Center, on campus. And somebody said, you know this guy is going to come and everybody said, "No, no he's not going to bother to come out to this. You know he just does this stuff, because that's what he does. He does it to everybody. So this is nothing personal. He's just picking on you because you're new and you teach the same sort of things that he teaches. So he's just razzing you. It was like a hazing at a fraternity; you just have to pass the initiation." But I said, "But I'm not inter-ested in passing. I don't want to pass it. I got a job; I don't need to pass this."

But I don't have tenure. So again I was in this position. In other words, I'm trying to figure out what to do, and this guy for whatever reason has a lot of friends. I mean people who have known him for 35 years, and I think a lot of them don't like or approve of what he is doing, but they feel a kind of loyalty to him. So I go to give a talk at the Women's Center. You know, an innocuous thing. My students come and they are very nice, they bring flowers, they are very sweet kids. People brought their moms; I mean it was really nice. And colleagues came, and during the question-and-answer period this guy puts his hand up. I don't call on him; I'm calling on other people. There were several men in the audience, again several male colleagues and boys from my classes and stuff. But probably three times as many women as men.

I think that there should be sort of an affirmative action in questioning because a lot of men put their hands up right away because it's easier for them, they're in the habit of doing that. So I like to encourage the women, especially if I have just spo-ken about something that has to do with women's issues, to talk first. So it's not a guy saying, "I disagree with that" as the first question. Then we get to them. But I like to encourage the women to speak up.

And then actually somebody sitting next to him says, "Oh, there's a hand back here," because he was sitting in the back. And I said, "Okay," and then I'm thinking maybe he is really being encouraging. Maybe he's trying to change his ways and be supportive. So he starts and doesn't stop. On and on. With a prepared speech that's really half insane, has nothing to do with what I've just spoken about. I say, "Okay, since this is an open discussion maybe you and I could talk about this in the department." So I'm trying to be really professional about this, right. I mean, I really want to knife him, but I just say "Can we talk about this in the department because I'd really like to take other questions." I said, "No really, we can put this on hold. I promise, you know, honestly, I will answer this question but can we just . . ."

The mother of one of my students said, "I came here to hear her talk, not you. So be quiet." Then he stopped. . . . What he always does is to nail his own coffin shut. It was clear both that he was harassing me and that he was crazy. So, after that, people were sympathetic. "I can't believe you had to go through that, but again you should feel sorry for him. Isn't it amazing that he's going through all this trouble for you?" Oh, yeah. It would be nicer if he found a hobby.

And then the next day, not only in everybody's mailboxes but this was something that he was also handing out to graduate students . . . —a one-page single-spaced, a legal-sized piece of paper, talking about how absolutely foolish my arguments were in the talk. "Oh come on" was how it began. And, obviously, he must have stayed up until three o'clock in the morning. And then came in and ran it off. He was handing them out to people, not only putting them in everybody's boxes; he was handing them out to students. That's really unprofessional.

And still I'm untenured. I was furious. I went to the depart-
ment head. I got the people who were there to write letters to
the Dean to say, "We witnessed this man harassing this woman.
Something needs to be done in this department to stop this
behavior. This isn't professional. It's unacceptable." And they
were great; they all wrote. So I got this packet of letters. I didn't
want an apology; I just wanted him to leave me alone. I wanted
him to fixate on something else. By this time it was two years
of harassment.

And then there was a petition that got sent around—this is
the amazing part—only to the full professors. Nineteen people
signed, that to this day I can recite. I saw the list once; I could
tell you every single name on it. It said that I was somehow
organizing some move against this man. That he was being slan-
dered. That I was setting people up against him. That I was
ruining, undermining his reputation in the department. I was
flabbergasted. It seemed amazing to me that first of all, all these
people should be writing to protect this guy. Most of them
wouldn't take five minutes to talk to him anyway. But some-
how there was this solidarity; I was considered this threat.

And I went to the Dean and to the head of the department
and I said, "Look. I'm an untenured assistant professor. This
guy is a tenured full professor and has been doing all this stuff
to me, and I'm the one who's supposedly setting up a posse
against him? Don't you see something a little funny in the power
structure here that he needs protection from me? I went to the
woman who deals with sexual harassment. She told me it was
not a matter for the sexual harassment office because it was
intellectual harassment, she claimed. I think that she knew this
person. She said, "Oh, but he does this to everybody."

I said, "I don't care. At this point I don't care if he does this
to everybody. He's doing it to me; that's the only thing I care
about. Screw context, precedent, anything else. The rest of you
might have been wanting to deal with this; I'm going to do some-

thing about it." But she was useless. Again, I was looking for someone to support me. And I think that it was appropriate for that office, there was something to do. I don't think she wanted to bother. That was my impression. Because in fact the university won a payback to its female staff and faculty members because someone took them to court. Things have been done in the university to make things happen.

So then there was the only thing that I felt I really had recourse to, unless I was going to get a lawyer, which I really didn't want to do because I wanted to keep my job and I didn't have a penny to do it with anyway. I was really terrified. I really didn't know what to do. I went to one of the most senior, most well-respected, gentlemanly guys in the department, and I said, "Look, you have to help me. There's nobody else who can do this." His signature had been on the petition and that was one of the reasons I went up to him and I said, "You have to help. I have to explain this to you because then you're going to have to explain to everybody else because I can't do it." He said, "My signature, like a lot of others, that's only there because we wanted due process to happen. We didn't want this to be a precedent." I said, "Let me explain to you what's going on." So I then had a meeting with this guy, the guy who was harassing me, and the department chair. And we all got around and talked. And I said, "Look," to the guy who's been doing all this stuff, "now, I'm only interested in opening up avenues of exchange. It seems to me that the best thing about being at a university is that people have ideas, we can share them. I'm interested in what you're doing." He said, "I wrote that letter. You were very welcome to respond to that letter." I said, "Look, I'm trying to get tenure. I'm trying to write articles. I don't have time to write a letter." But that's really what it was; more than anything else he really did want attention. That was the pathological part of all of this. In fact I don't think he wanted to ruin me. He just wanted to make me into his adjunct or something. He wanted me to follow in his footsteps, or he somehow expected something from me that I clearly was refusing to give, was uninterested in giving. And I said, "Well, you have to stop doing this. You know you have to stop." And I finally got it through to this guy that he had to stop. It's lessened, but it hasn't really stopped.

Thus, it is part of this woman's not uncommon experience that she must walk into work everyday and confront, in addition to the low-level harassment and belittling remarks that her colleagues express on a continuous basis, the behavior of one man, a colleague who has decided to stalk her and harass her on a daily basis, both professionally and personally. He is a person who is also her senior and has decision-making power over her career to some extent. He has become, just like the students and the classes that she teaches, the papers that she writes, and the research that she conducts, part of the very air that she breathes. This man and his actions set the tone of her work environment.

A final and highly significant component of the professional ambiance for women and one that contributes to this sense of isolation, not only from male colleagues but even from other women, is often overlooked. This involves the treatment of non-professional women within the professional context. Non-professional women come from diverse groups; they are the secretaries, paralegals, nurses, clients, patients, students, wives, and daughters of the professional workers. The treatment that women from these groups receive has a direct and important impact on female professionals.

Doctors, for example, in part due to the general cultural norms and in part due to their training in medical school, have learned to treat both nurses and patients with condescension. Nurses are treated as though they are there merely to brainlessly carry out doctor's orders and perform the menial tasks that are beneath the doctors. Nurses generally are female, although the rare male nurse is treated with a level of professional and personal respect that the female nurse rarely experiences. Female patients are treated as if they have no knowledge of their own bodies and physical health, as if they cannot understand the details of a medical course of action, and as if they cannot make a sound choice about their own health care. That is, they are often regarded paternalistically by doctors as if they are children, without rational functioning and in need of detailed guidance.

The situation of the paralegal is much like that of the medical nurse, and female legal clients are treated by lawyers much in the fashion that female patients are by doctors. Lawyers are found not listening to their female clients and making decisions for them, believing their clients not to be capable of the potentially complex thought process involved.

Students, secretaries, wives, and daughters might be looked at as a single category, since they receive overlapping and similar treatment from male professionals. It is not entirely unfounded that one's natural reaction to a secretary–boss pair is to wonder whether they are engaged in a sexual relationship. It is a very common occurrence. So too are professor–student relationships often sexual. Most often, such relationships are fleeting and opportunistic on the part of the man in the position of relative authority. Yet, it is also common for professors to marry students and for executives, lawyers, and doctors to sometimes marry their secretaries. The basic explanation for this phenomenon is that not only is there a power relationship in place and the opportunity but often, this relationship is the only opportunity for the man in question. His range of choice might be narrowed to students or a handful of secretaries in his firm, because his colleagues are mostly male and those who are women may not appear to be sufficiently subordinate. His friends, to the extent that he has them, are mostly male or are women who are involved already in a relationship with one of these male friends.

GENDER LESSONS

The workplace ambiance creates a situation in which a large amount of what should be a woman's work time is taken up battling harassing behavior mentally, directly, and with other colleagues and administrators in a position of authority. Even though the woman may know that she is clearly in the right, the process of demoralization is working on her and eating away at her resolve. It is not a mystery that most professional women go the route of turning a blind eye, deaf ear, and mute mouth to the treatment they receive. What is a wonder is that women who are able to see what is going on maintain their confidence and their professions at all.

What many professional women feel as a result of the general ambiance of their profession is a growing sense of isolation. The fact that they are often left out of professional conversations, that the senior male members of the field gravitate toward younger male members as their proteges, and that even the kind of attention paid to a male colleague engaged in casual banter is different from the attention received by a female voicing the same idea all point to a feeling of being an untouchable, invisible, or diminished and unworthy.

Women who are aware of bias on the job and attempt to maintain a level of professionalism on a par with their male peers suffer from the strain of constantly needing to be on guard, as the following woman's experience relates:

Four of the other trainees and I were in a cab. One of them had a crush on me the whole time. But very innocent, very sweet. And so we're riding home, and the other guys are all kind of giggling; they had this little plan in mind. The plan was that this guy was going to kiss me. And so we're in the cab, they all start giggling and talking, you know, "Are you going to . . . go ahead, go ahead." So he like lunges for me, and I just said, "Wait a minute. What's going on?" And he says, "Oh, come on. I just want a kiss. I've loved you all this time and I think you're the best woman in the whole group and we all think . . ."

They gave me a big cheer. And they're really encouraging, but I felt that it would somehow have wiped out all that hard work I had done. I felt that there was a real power struggle going on here. I felt that if I kissed him it would've been left in their minds that even when a woman is as tough and strong as me, still she wants to get fucked, and still we can dominate, and still we can . . . you know, that really at heart, I'm just a sex object. So I made a big stand, "No." And they said, "Big deal, kiss him. So what. Give him a thrill. What's it going to cost me?"

I felt it was a woman–man issue, and I wanted to keep the respect that I had worked so hard to build. So I made an issue out of it, and I wouldn't let him kiss me. It soured the whole evening, and they were so angry. And I paid the cab fare because I felt so guilty for not kissing him. And they wouldn't walk back with me. The next day, they didn't even say good-bye to me. He was so humiliated, and they were so disappointed that I didn't go for it. And they felt very unempowered, I guess. To me it was a very climactic moment in the battle of the sexes. It showed that it's a tough one to really be friends with men, and be equal, and be respected, and not have sex. I mean if there's sexual attraction, that's normal, but not to act on it and to keep that restraint just was really tough for them. They felt I really rejected them and not gotten close. It was a very poignant moment and really kind of sad.

In addition to the isolation and constant need for vigilance, all of the various forms of male–female relationships involving male professionals and non-professional staff women where the men are either peers or senior to female professionals spill over onto the female professional's work life. On the one hand, she may be, in effect, treated as if she is in the same group as the students, secretaries, and daughters and thus receive similar treatment, not the professional interaction that she deserves and to which she is entitled. On the other hand, within the female professional's mental framework, a split is formed as a result of these factors. She may identify with these women from other groups as a woman, and at the same time she may distance herself from them as a professional. Chances are that the latter tendency will win out overall and the female professional will learn modes of disregard for the non-professional female support staff and clients. The difference for a female than for a male in adopting these postures is that the female professional will have to take another step first, which is to dissociate herself from the others as a female. That is, she will need to renounce her identity as a woman, which will induce another round of trying to assimilate. This, of course, takes a toll in the end and becomes part of the process of demoralization.

Even while women are entering professions in greater proportions, the basic attitudes about them doing so have not changed or have become more fiercely negative. This is perhaps to be expected as women continue to break barriers and excel, in spite of the odds against them and in spite of the stumbling blocks thrown in their way.

GENDER COMPOUNDS

In contrast with the fairly normal operating procedure of constant low-level harassment and even the sustained case of stalking that was described in the Gender Basics portion of this chapter, now consider that Emily walks into an openly hostile environment in her first job. In her first week on the job, she is virtually isolated: no one will so much as say hello and goodbye to her, and she meets with fairly extreme behavior almost every day. Emily is haunted by the image of a friend of hers who related her stories of her first days on the job. One story in particular keeps ringing through Emily's mind:

It was my first day at work in my first job. I held out the shiny new key to my office as I walked down the hall, with a stack of papers and books under my arm. I was very proud of myself, and knew it. I put the key in the lock with some ceremony and opened the door. It took me a moment to recognize what I found. My desk and the floor surrounding it were piled high with blood-soiled Tampax.

At the end of her first week, Emily was greeted with a dildo placed on her desk before she arrived. Emily did not know how to get rid of it, or if she should show it to anyone first. Fingerprinting it crossed her mind. In the end, she rejected the idea as ridiculous, got a paper towel from the bathroom, picked it up with that, and threw it in the garbage. She didn't tell anyone about it at all, not even her friends.

Such crude forms of hostility are not uncommon in the professional world. The men perpetrating these acts of harassment are professors, doctors, lawyers, and other professionals. They are people with years and years of advanced degree education in many cases. When the issue is gender, the professional realm is no more safe from open battle than any other work environment.

Emily found herself looking over her colleagues' faces and wondering which one did it. She sadly concluded that it could have been almost any one of them or a group of them together. Everyday thereafter, Emily hesitated before entering her office, even if she had just left it for a few moments. The image of the dildo on her desk did fade with time, but she found it hard to sit at her desk and work without feeling soiled for several weeks. Combined with the chilly treatment she was receiving from her colleagues and the consequent shoddy attention that her work was receiving, Emily felt more than tentative and isolated in her job, and even in her profession as a whole.

Emily had initially hoped that, as time went by and people got used to her and if she performed well in her job, the cruelty would subside and she would find at least a couple of allies. Although colleagues did begin to become accustomed to her presence to the extent that they would acknowledge her presence, Emily's situation did not improve substantially. Emily began to feel cheated and more and more confused. She could not fathom why she had been hired. She was clearly in a double-bind. In staying, she would not be racking up the credentials necessary to apply elsewhere, so it was only becoming increasingly difficult for her to transfer out. On the other hand, if she tried to remain, not only did it not seem that the situation had the potential to improve but Emily's morale was also definitely declining markedly. Her confidence in herself was eroding as the weeks went by, and her ability to cope with the hostile situation was about to evaporate.

Agitation was also settling into Emily's psyche because she knew that if she doesn't emerge from a first job strong and with impressive work, her future career will be an uphill battle with diminishing prospects. She already knows that to make a move now, she'll need to take a cut in pay and in status. Emily can only hope at this point to transfer to a lesser job in the same area of specialization.

GENDER ACTION

One person cannot singlehandedly change the ambiance of an entire work environment. But one can make small changes in a poor environment and can minimize the harm that such a work situation can have on one's own psyche and self-perception as a professional and as a person. The typical internal degradation that results from, at the very least, unpleasant work environments can be prevented. Of course, the clearly illegal behavior that Emily confronted in the Gender Compounds section would need additional attention as a purely legal matter, and she would need to consult legal counsel in order to ascertain how to proceed in that case.

There are two principal components of a program to help Emily create more acceptable working conditions for herself in the more ordinary case of poor work ambiance. The first concerns her self-reflective attitudes and thoughts. Emily needs to learn to accomplish the task of separating her own view of herself from that of her colleagues, and thus to respond to remarks and behaviors in a way that preserves her authentic response. This requires training and will by no means come overnight. The difficulty and time required are attested to in the following woman's reflection:

I turned 25 at that job. I'd been on the job about six months, and I realized it was this big, big turning point for me. I decided, I'm not going to smile anymore unless I feel like it. Like if someone's making a stupid sexual remark and just so it's not uncomfortable, you smile through it. I decided not to do that anymore. I just decided I wasn't going to let that happen anymore. So I felt this great freedom, which actually took me 15 years to integrate. It was just an idea, a new concept that has taken me my true adulthood to develop and really start doing because I continued to smile even when I didn't feel like it.

The second component of the program concerns creating a community among the women at work at all ranks, professional and non-professional. In order to do this effectively, one must first view one's own self as a woman. For most women, what in a different culture would be an integral part of the maturation and individuation process is no simple task and will only be achieved over time, in stages, in discrete levels of recognition. Each woman can begin by observing her own behavior, perhaps keeping a chart if this is useful in keeping an accurate tally. She needs to discover whether she herself speaks and regards her female and male colleagues differentially. She also can keep track of what her behavioral differences are in interacting with female professionals and the non-professional female support staff. Once she has some grasp of any discrepancies at each level, the woman can begin to learn new habits of interaction that will undermine and transform her behavior. Beginning to accomplish these tasks will more than likely increase her own career aspirations and expectations.

As a further step, one should make it routine to share one's own work experiences and professional goals with female colleagues and to listen with respect to theirs. This sharing includes, but should not be limited to, discussing any incidents or problems stemming from gender bias. It should also be second nature to welcome new women as colleagues, thereby breaking down the system of female rivalry and creating a community of female camaraderie. Although the benefits of accomplishing a flow of professional female interaction will be far reaching and lasting, doing so will require consistent effort for an initial period. This is due to the fact that in this situation not only one's own attitudes and behavior are at issue but also breaking down the ingrained and biased disposition of a group. Moreover, such groups are composed generally of ambitious, hard-working women under multiple stresses who often feel that other women are a distraction and perhaps detrimental to meeting their own professional goals. It has been proven time after time that, in fact, nothing could be further from the truth and that female-to-female professional interaction enhances every aspect of one's self-respect and accomplishment on the job.

17 FIRST JOBS

GENDER BASICS

Upon graduating and obtaining her first job, Emily's frame of mind was that a new life was opening up to her. She had a sense that all of the work she had done in school, the agonizing over career choice, program applications, and job interviews were all finally paying off. She was about to launch the career and adult life that she had chosen for herself and planned for. Whatever her experience in graduate school, chances are that, unless it was extremely negative, Emily has largely put it behind her and has only the highest expectations for her future.

The first round of disillusionment on the job might be somewhat subtle. Emily may have had the impression from the interview and negotiation process that the fact that she is a woman was even a benefit for the job. One often hears this type of comment in the course of the interviewing process, as Emily did repeatedly. She was told that because there are so few women working in her field that she will be an asset, that she will bring a new perspective to her work that is currently lacking. Emily may wonder whether she has or wants a different perspective concerning her professional work simply because she is a woman or whether she wants to be hired because she is a woman, possibly *the* woman entrant for the year, but at least she will feel that there is a benefit she is accruing because of her sex that her mother's generation would never have experienced. Yet, in the end, Emily will come to conclude that, in fact, the reality of her colleagues' attitudes runs to the contrary. A literature professor expressed her experience with this type of consideration as follows:

I think that again like a lot of other women what you find out is that they want someone like you, but maybe not quite as much like you as you actually are. They want somebody who is going to stir things up a little bit, and want somebody who's going to teach feminist criticism, and want somebody who is going to bring this sort of new life into the department, but really they want you to do that and leave all of them alone. And you can't make trouble and leave people alone at the same time.

It is also quite likely that a second and more concrete round of disillusionment with the work situation will result because Emily, like most professional women just starting out in their early years on the job, expects equality at work. A law professor remarked,

Law graduates today are really expecting equality. So I'm sure it's difficult for a lot of our law students when they go into the world and find out it's really sexist.

Emily probably believes that a more-or-less operational merit system is in place and that she will be appreciated or not based on her professional performance. Although she anticipates perhaps some minor inappropriate remarks from senior members at her workplace, she does not expect to find the sort of gender bias that might actually hamper her career in any significant manner.

It is important to understand that this is the frame of mind with which most young female professionals enter their careers. This is an attitude that blossomed in the expansive years of the 1980s. It was not true to the facts then, nor is it now. Throughout the '80s, the constant message in the media was that the problems of women and work have been eradicated, and this was believed to be all the more true of women working in professional fields. The young professionals of the '80s and '90s could walk an equal path with their male peers, in part thanks to the work their mothers had done to accomplish equal access to education and jobs. And surely, in many advanced degree programs, admission is virtually equal at this point, or it will be some time in the readily foreseeable future. Yet, as is reported in the Sadkers' 1994 study, *Failing at Fairness*, although forty percent of the Yale Law School graduating class of 1991 was female, for example, seven times as many male graduates as female in the class were recruited to clerk for a federal appellate court.

Clearly, this frame of mind of the young professional and her expectations are in fact harmful. They are like blinders that prevent her from acknowledging patterns of behavior in the workplace as biased. And, thus, yet again, she is sent on a path of internalization and personalization, not to mention isolation, that could be prevented by a more realistic assessment of the gendered environment of her profession.

Thus, when Emily sees, which she will very early in her first job, her male peers being assigned more interesting work and being treated with greater professional respect than she is, Emily is going to take it personally. One lawyer observed the patterns at her first job:

The work, as it was distributed, was distributed discrimi-
natorily. I definitely got more work that was just writing briefs.
I say "just." I was very good at it and I liked it very much, and
it was an important job, but still on the hierarchy the way the
firm perceives it, it's just writing briefs. So I would get much
more work that was in-the-office work, not seeing clients. I
would get much less work that would require any court appear-
ance. The men who were my peers, older and younger, would
get their own cases to take to court.

When Emily is thus treated as not yet competent to have a
hand at comparable work to what her male peers are handling,
she begins to feel that the inequitable flow of work is justified.
She begins to doubt her own competence as a result of not
being given the same sort of responsibility as most of her peers.
Emily may not notice that her female peers are being accorded
the same treatment that she is. She may not have any female
peers at all.

In some jobs, women are often singled out and given different sorts of assignments because, in certain instances, being
female is seen as pertinent to the job. One woman explained
her predicament thus:

I always played with boys; I didn't like the more female
games. I think I've always had a lot of masculine qualities.
And I never got pushed around; I was always a leader. So
I had those fantasies fulfilled. I was never a wimpy girl, until
I got into my professional life. And then I was the wimpy
young bimbo. Even though I wasn't a bimbo. And they knew
I was smart, but I still fulfilled that purpose of being the cute
girl.

Another woman described how her boss tried to make use
of the fact that she was a woman for the firm's benefit:

They saw me and part of my role was that I was attractive to the client, and that was a real bonus. And they would flirt with me, and I was always thrilled by it. I liked their flirting with me. But I hated having my boss indicate that that was part of my value. I mean I always saw that as a personal attraction that happened to exist that I was never going to act on. And neither were they. It was totally just for fun and for fantasy. But then my boss would say things like, "Well go down and, you know, make his dick hard." That's how he would try to suggest that that was part of my job. And I did not feel comfortable confronting my boss on those occasional comments. It would burn me up.

Because of her belief system upon starting her job, Emily also may not notice that as a matter of course, quite apart from their relative abilities, her male peers are accepted more readily as colleagues of the senior members and that it is considered a necessary part of their work experience that they begin as quickly as possible to assume responsible work assignments. The junior males are accorded professional respect, and their opinions and ideas are weighed heavily. Hers may not be, and she will tend to take this as a sign that her ideas are not that interesting or substantial. A geneticist expressed her experience thus:

They think that men are saying something more important. For example, we have big meetings and if I express a scientific opinion about something we're working on, people will— my division chief for example—turn to my mentor to get confirmation of what I said. Anything that I say, people go for a second opinion from someone more senior. A man who is quite junior to me, whenever he opens his mouth, nobody questions what he says or looks for confirmation. In fact, he opens his mouth and expresses opinions in my field, which he's not in. He'll open his mouth on such a matter, and my division chief

*will just say, "Oh" and incorporate what he said as fact. When
I open my mouth about something in my own field, she'll go
for confirmation.*

Women in their first job experience particularly are considered and treated as if they are subordinate to other males
as well, not only their colleagues. For example, female doctors are treated as subordinate by their patients, female lawyers by their male clients, female professors by their male students, and so forth. One telling mark of this is the ease with
which clients, patients, and students call their female lawyer,
doctor, or professor by her first name, whereas the first name
of a comparable male would probably choke in their throats.

Generally, a woman in a position of authority vis-a-vis a man,
especially a young woman, will be greeted with skepticism. The
male will question her judgments, scrutinize her training, and
doubt her abilities. In this culture in which degrees, status, and
specialized knowledge are revered, the woman who has obtained them is held at arm's length and questioned, whereas
her male peers are respected, heeded, and paid attention to.
One young humanities professor describes her experience with
students thus:

*I'm really more of an informal type of person, but I learned
very quickly that a female up at the front of the classroom cannot afford to be casual because then she looks soft. My students
already assume that my course will be an easy A that they won't
learn anything in. They patronize me and assume that they
know better. I'm short and I'm young and I'm female, and that
about sums it up for them.*

*I've learned how to control some of this. I wear suits. I make
sure they call me "Professor." And I don't stand for nonsense
in my class. I keep the discussion orderly and don't let the men
interrupt at all, not me and not the other students. I grade fairly,
but not leniently. I just stay on the alert, always.*

Another way in which women start out their professional careers at a relative disadvantage to their male peers involves the choice of a specialty. At some time between the end of the degree program and the first few years on the job, depending upon the profession, one must choose an area of specialization. And there remains a tracking system that tacitly channels the women into those fields that have been designated as appropriate for women. Not coincidentally, these fields are lower in status and in pay. Thus, for example, in medicine, pediatrics has been a specialty that women have gone into in substantially higher numbers than others, such as neurosurgery. In law, family and civil rights law are areas more open to women than, say, antitrust. Art history and education are fields that have more women than chemistry or political science. Biology has more than mathematics or electrical engineering.

In general, there is a lack of seriousness accorded to the professional woman early in her career. Not even the people who would benefit from her performance, who would benefit from encouraging her to excel and strive to achieve greater accomplishment in her field generally take her seriously. Even those directly in charge of hiring do not yet have it in their mental framework that young professional women are perhaps more dedicated, serious, and capable than their male peers, not because of innate factors but just because they have had to fight harder every step of the way.

The following is a detailed account given by a young doctor in her first job, when she joined a medical practice and had to contend with inappropriate behavior from her boss. This woman faced obstacles that most people would not even dream of being able to surmount. The fact that she attended a prestigious college and medical school is testimony to her brilliance, her tenacity, and her endurance. She is quoted here extensively not only because her story portrays in vivid detail the continuous harassment that young professional women encounter but also because she was so candid in her thought processes that they become palpable for the reader. That this strong and confident woman not only endured but to an extent participated in her harassment reveals the power of authority, of sexism in our culture, and of the demoralization process itself. The following passage shows, step by step, how coercion on the job operates and how effective it can be.

The first night I ever remember thinking there was something going on was a Saturday night, and I was home dying my hair and it had to stay on for 45 minutes. The phone rings, and I have this dye in my hair. My hair is dripping, and I had this towel on. So I go to the phone, and it's him. So I said, "Oh, hi. How are you?" He says to me, "Well, hi. I'm glad you're home." And I said, "Yeah, I'm home." So he says, "So what's a girl like you doing home on a Saturday night?" And, I said, "Oh, I was just washing my hair." And he said, "I just called to see how you were doing." And I said, "Oh, I'm fine," and I left it at that.

And then he said, "So, aren't you going out tonight or anything?" And I said, "No, not really." So I said, "Well, what about you?" and he said, "Well, yeah, I had some plans. I was going out later." And I said, "Oh, that's nice." And he said, "Yeah, I have a date." So, jokingly, I said, "Oh, well I hope it's with your wife," but I was just joking. And he said, "Well, no, actually it's not." Then I said, "Oh, I'm sorry. I didn't mean to pry. I was just joking." And then he said, "Well, actually my wife and I are getting a divorce." And I said, "Oh, I really didn't know that. I'm sorry." And he was like, "No, no, I'm happy about it." And he starts telling me about the situation.

Anyway, so then he starts asking me about what my story was. And he said, "Well, aren't you seeing anyone?" I told him just in a nutshell. I said, "I was going out with somebody for four and a half years, but it didn't work out. And that was it. And I haven't been seeing anyone since." So that was the conversation.

But then after that he started calling me more often. He was calling me all the time. So, then, at one point, he left this message on my answering machine. He said, "This is Dr. X calling. I wanted to speak to you about some things. Can you please give me a call at home?" He always wanted me to call him at home. So I got home later, and then he called a second time. He said, "This is Dr. X again, and I just wanted to talk to you about some things." And then he says, "I'm always calling you. How come you never call me?" I just thought, that's odd. So I called him back and I said, "I'm sorry. I wasn't home. I'm sorry I didn't call you back earlier." And he said, "Oh, well, where were you?" I said, "I was out." Then he said, "How come you never call me?" And I said, "What do you mean?" He said, "I'm always calling you." And I said, "Well, if I have a particular question, I'll let you know." If he wanted to talk about business, we could talk about business, but if I don't have any questions, why would I call?

It was weird. So I was a little concerned, and I said to my girlfriends, "This guy is calling me all the time. Do you think there is something going on here?" And they said, "Well, I don't know. What does he ask about when he calls?" So I told them, and then they said, "Well, maybe he has got something in mind, but, no, he'd have to be crazy. I doubt it."

I was out one night, and when I get home, there were all these messages from X on the machine. He wanted to say how good he felt about me in the practice; he called the first time to say that. And then he said, "Well, give me a call when you get home." So then he called back later, maybe at twelve or one, and he's like, "Oh, you're still not home." What's with this guy? So I didn't call him back because I got home so late. So the next day he calls me; he pages me, he starts calling me on my beeper now. Like it wasn't enough to just call me at night. He starts calling me during the day on my beeper. And he said, "What happened? I was worried about you. You weren't home." And I said, "Well, I was out on a date, if you must know." And he's

like, "Oh, yeah? Who's this guy now? Who's this guy you're
seeing?" And I said, "Just someone I met." But he wanted to
know the details. And I said, "It was just some guy." And he
said, "Well, I hope we can be friends, that we can talk about
these things."

I was starting to get a little uncomfortable. And after that he
started calling me more often. He started calling me during the
day on my beeper, and these other two girls that I work with
said, "Something is fishy. This guy has some other agenda.
You've got to watch it." And I said, "Well, what am I going to
do?" I had already blown off two other jobs to take this one.
And at that point, he wasn't really overt about it. He was kind
of being subtle about it and I felt, well maybe he liked me a
little, but I didn't think it would go anywhere. You know, I
thought, "Nah, he has got to have more sense than that."

So, anyway, one night after a meeting, he said, "Have you
had dinner? Let's go to dinner." I said, "No, I can't, thanks."
And he said, "Oh, come on. You have to eat anyway. We'll get
something quick." So, we went. We're eating and talking, and
he's telling me what a bright future we have and all this stuff.
Then he says, "Can I ask you something?" And so I said, "Well,
what?" And then he said, "Well, forget it. Never mind."

Later on, he says again, "Well, can I ask you something?"
So I said, "Well, what is it?" and he dropped it. Then a few
minutes later, he said, "You know, I was thinking maybe some
weekend we can go away someplace." I said, "What do you
mean?" He said, "You know, I was thinking maybe we could
go to the Caribbean or something." I said, "What do you mean?"
And he said, "Forget it." He said, "I'm sorry I ever mentioned
it. I was just thinking out loud." And I said, "Well, I don't think
that would be a good idea because we are working together and
I don't think . . ." He's like, "Oh, no. I didn't mean anything by
it. I just thought it would be nice and I want us to be good
friends." Like he tried to cover it up. And then I just thought to
myself, I'm going to have to put this guy on ice because this is

not good. If he is thinking what I think he is thinking, that can't work.

So we finished, and I drove him to his car, and then I got this feeling that when he was sitting there that he wanted to kiss me. Like he was sort of lingering in the car. I was saying, "Well, good night. Thank you for dinner." And he was just still sitting there. So I got very uncomfortable and I said, "Well, thank you, I had a great time." And he said, "Well, now we really have to go out." And I said, "What do you mean?" And he said, "Well, this was just a casual restaurant. I want to take you someplace very nice." He was just sitting there and staring at me. So I just felt so uncomfortable, I just reached out my hand and I said, "Okay, well, good night." I shook his hand, and he finally left. And I just thought to myself, I'm in deep shit here. So I go home, and of course, he's called me already.

This man was out of control. From that day on, that's when he started up everything and after that he started calling me incessantly, two, three times a day. So I just thought to myself, I'm not handling this properly. I have to let him know that this can't happen. So then he called, and he wanted to set up this dinner. We were supposed to go out to dinner to celebrate. So I said, "I really don't think this is a good idea because I have to work for you, and I just think it's nice that we are friendly and we get along well but I really don't think it should go any further than that." So he was like, "Oh, don't take it the wrong way. I'm sorry if I did anything to offend you, but I promised you we'd go out to a nice restaurant; that's all I had in mind. If you don't want to go, I understand but I really would feel very hurt if you didn't go with me." And I said, "Well, I just don't want to give you the wrong impression. We already went out once." He said, "But that wasn't planned. It wasn't a fancy place. I want to take you to this one place." He was going on and on and on about this special restaurant; he always goes there, it's a Japanese restaurant. They fly in fresh fish from Japan every Wednesday, and he wants to go on Wednesday.

And they have this and this. So he's going on and on and on. So I said to myself, "Okay, I'll go." I talked to my girlfriends and everything. They said, "Okay, you have to just lay it on the line and tell this guy just cut everything out."

So I prepared this whole speech I was going to give him even though he hadn't really—I mean the thing about the Caribbean was kind of blatant—but he hadn't really said exactly that he wanted to sleep with me or anything. Then he retracted it. So, I wanted to just clear the air. So we go out and he's all dressed up and acting like this is a first date kind of thing. So we go to this place and we have dinner and it's great. And we're talking about other things. So after the restaurant, he wants to go for drinks somewhere. So we go to midtown, to the Hyatt Hotel. And we're talking there and I said, "Look," I said to him, "You know, it seems like you've got something on your mind other than just being my boss. And I really don't think it's a good idea. I really think that we have to keep this strictly business because it just can't work out, this kind of thing. You know, I have to work for you. This is going to be an ongoing thing, hopefully. I'm going to be working for you for three years. Then, if things work out, it will lead to a partnership. We're talking about a long-term commitment here. And I really want this job. I really feel it's important to me and I feel that if something like this would happen, it really would jeopardize things. It would jeopardize the job and my position." And I said, "I really want this to work. So I just don't want to do anything that is going to jeopardize my job."

And he's like, "Oh, no no no. Nothing could be further from what I want. You know, I want everything to work. I want this to be primarily a business relationship. I want this to work out well. I want us to get along together. I want the practice to grow. I think you'll be great for the practice." And then he said, "You know, and whatever else happens between us, I just hope that we are good friends." And he was like skirting the issue. He wasn't really addressing what I had just said.

So I said, "Well, it just seems that you have some other agenda." And so then, finally, he was like hemming and hawing, and he said, "Well, to be honest," he starts telling me about how since his wife left, he's been lonely, and well he just feels that he and I get along so well, we have a lot in common. I'm intelligent, and he can talk to me about things. He said that when he was with his wife he felt that she wasn't his intellectual peer. Because she was a nurse and he just felt that he couldn't talk to her about a lot of things because she didn't understand. But he feels with me that we were intellectually equal and he likes the way my mind operates, the way I think, you know, all this crap.

Then he said, "I would be honored if you would go out with me." I said, "Well, what do you mean?" And then he said, "I would like to see you on more than just a professional basis." And I said, "Well, that's what I'm saying can't happen." And I said, "Really, this can't work and I really don't want it to happen." Then I went to Plan B, I thought, "Well, I had given him the whole speech and it went in one ear and out the other." So then I said, "The other factor is you're a lot older than I am. You're 52 years old and I'm 29." I said, "This is not what I'm looking for. I'm looking to meet someone. I'm looking to settle down, looking to get married. I'm looking to have children a couple of years down the road. You know, I haven't done any of these things. You have your whole life behind you." I said, "You've already been married twice. You have four kids. You have a whole family. You're looking toward taking it easy, relaxing. A couple of years down the road you want to retire." I said, "I'm just starting my whole life." I said, "We're in totally different ballparks here and you know, you're not what I'm looking for in a man."

And he's like, "Well, you know, I don't want to rule any of that out." He wasn't hearing me. Like he starts saying, "Well, you know, see what happens. But I'm not ruling out any of that. It could happen." In other words, he could have more kids.

*Then I went to Plan C. I said, "Look. The other thing is, you
know, I'm not attracted to you. You know, I like you, you're a
very nice person, you're intelligent, but you're really not my
type. I'm just not attracted to you, I don't feel anything for you
physically." I mean, how much more can you say to someone?
So, we left it like that and he just said that he was very upset
and he was very disappointed and he hoped I would think about
it, have an open mind. So I shook his hand again, and he went
home. The next day, it was like I had said nothing. He was at
it again, and basically, from that point in April, for the next six
weeks, that man was calling me two, three times a day. All the
time. He was calling me at work, a couple of times, at home.
He would call me constantly. And he was badgering me, always
badgering me about getting together, doing this, doing that. And
I just kept putting him off and saying, no, this can't work, and
reiterating what I had said that it's not a good idea; it has got
to stop. I work for you; it just can't work.*

*He wasn't just trying to do this because he was my boss and
he was trying to take advantage of me. I'm sure that wasn't the
foremost thing in his mind, but it was still in his mind. It had to
be in his mind somewhere. Because he took the day I signed
the contract to really start in with all this stuff. Because he knew
I was committed; I was going to be there working everyday with
him. It was just crazy. Anyway, he kept calling me, keeping me
on the phone for hours at night when I was trying to study for
the medical board exams.*

*This was going on for six weeks, this wasn't one or two days,
but six weeks of someone calling three, four times a day, telling me how wonderful I am, how beautiful I am, all these things,
right. And then I thought to myself, "Well, maybe this guy really
feels this way about me." And after awhile of him going on and
on like this for so long, I started to think, "Well, I don't know
what to do because I keep telling him no, no, no, and he keeps
pushing it. Either way I have to work with the guy." I just felt
like after a while I started buying into this whole thing. Here's*

this guy telling me I'm everything and given that he knows, I assume he knows, the risks involved in this whole situation, he knows how bad this whole thing is, and he knows what a terrible outcome it could have. If he's going to risk all of that and after all these contract negotiations and lawyers and paying all this money to get me to come work for him, he would risk all of that because he wants me so much, he must really want me so much. He started to really convince me of the fact that he really wanted me this much.

So he meets me and he's all decked out in this great suit, and he whisks me off to Manhattan, and he takes me to Windows on the World. I had already had dinner, so we went and had drinks up there. So we're sitting there, and there's this unbelievable view of everything, so he starts talking and telling me his whole life story, and about his first marriage, and second marriage and this and that and his future and all these things. And he's saying he hopes that it will work out between the two of us, and he wants to take me to the Caribbean, and he wants to rent a yacht, and take me on a private yacht to the Caribbean. Like he's got all these plans and schemes and everything.

And I'm saying to him, "Listen, I'm working for you. This can't work." You know, I keep saying this in a million different ways, and he just says, "Oh, we can make it work. If you are willing to go along with it, we can make it work." And I said, "Well, what is it that you want from me?" And he says that he wants to make love to me and he wants us to have a relationship. And I said, "Well, where do you think this is going to go?" And he said that he hopes that it will be a long time. And I said, "Well, like what? You know, I want to have children and marriage and all of this." And he said, "Well, I can't promise you that because I haven't decided about that because I already have four kids and I hadn't really thought about being a father again. I mean we'd have to discuss this further." He's thought this out, all this stuff.

And I guess he just started to have an effect on me after all this. So anyway, we were leaving, we had some drinks, and so we get in the elevator up on the top floor of the World Trade Center. And we're the only ones in this elevator, and all of a sudden he just grabs me and kisses me. You know, like one of those "sweep you off your feet" kind of kisses. So that was the first time he had ever kissed me or anything. I guess at that point I just said to myself, "Well, I'm not going to able to convince him that this isn't going to work." And I was starting to go along with all this also. I knew that it was a bad idea, but it just didn't seem like there was going to be a way out of this. I just really couldn't see a way out of it because I felt like no matter how many times I'd said no, he was coming back with another angle and he was trying some other way. It's not like he tried once and I said no and he stopped, or even twice or three times. This went on for six weeks basically, and everytime I said no, he just kept trying harder and harder and harder.

So it just didn't seem like it was possible not to; it seemed like the only two choices were to go along with it or to look for another job because it didn't seem that he was going to back down. No matter what I said, no matter how nasty I was, and there were times that I got really nasty with him and I just said, "Leave me alone! Stop calling me! Get a life!" I meant all these things I said, and that just didn't do it. It just seemed like I had those two choices basically because he wasn't going to not pursue this. I guess at that point I just started to convince myself. I didn't want a new job; I had just got this one. I had found an apartment, applied for hospital privileges; I had my malpractice insurance. Everything was all lined up. And a large amount of money had already been doled out in lawyers' fees, fees for hospitals, in the malpractice insurance, and housing. I just felt like, "Well, what the hell. Let me just go along with this," at that point.

I just felt like there wasn't a way that I was going to convince him that this wasn't going to work out. And he just kept up; he kept it up and up. And he wasn't being mean, he was being very nice, he was being incredibly nice and Mr. Charming, Prince Charming, telling me all these wonderful things about myself and this and that and the other, and just basically romancing me to death. If he were not my boss, I probably wouldn't have done anything with him because of his age, and I wasn't really physically attracted to him. So it wouldn't have even gone to that point. This guy just tried so incredibly hard, and he was so charming and romantic about it that I actually started buying into it and thinking maybe he does love me, maybe he does think I'm all these wonderful things. And I guess I just did it, you know. Like there was a certain point where I said to myself, "Well, I'm not going to talk him out of it, and I don't want to lose the job, so I guess I'll just have to go along with this." And he's not such a terrible person, I mean he's a nice person, he's sweet, he's romantic, he's wonderful, he's intelligent, he's everything. So it's not like he's a 350-pound cigar-smoking ogre. So I did it and I guess part of it also was my own vulnerability because I hadn't been with anyone in such a long time, and I was lonely.

So, I think I was with him a couple, I think it was four times total that this happened, and one time he took me away. It was the weekend before I had my boards, and I had been studying and I was a nervous wreck over this test because basically if I didn't pass this test it was a disaster because I needed to be board eligible. To have your hospital privileges you have to be board certified in a certain number of years, and if you don't pass it the first time you have to wait a whole year to take the test again. So this was a very important test and not to mention that you have to pay $500 to take the test. And I had just spent $1,500 or $2,000 to take the course to pass the test. And I was a nervous wreck. So the weekend before the test, I told him, "Look, I can't see you. I have to study. Leave me alone, I have to study. It's important for you too that I do well on this test."

So he calls me up, I think it was Friday night and says, "You know, I have to see you. I have to see you." I said, "Listen, let me study." My test is on Tuesday. And he says, "Well, you know, I had a fight with my wife, my ex." And I said, "Well, I'll talk to you but I can't see you; I have to study." And he said, "I have to talk to you. I have to see you. You're the only one I can talk to. You're the only one I can confide in. You're the only one who knows about these things." He was basically saying, "I have no friends. You are my only friend." So then I said, "Well, okay. Maybe we'll have dinner or something." And he's like, "No. No, let's go away somewhere." I said, "What do you mean, go away somewhere?" He said, "Well, let's go away. Let's go to Rye." He wants to go up there because it's quiet, and it's a nice long drive. So, I said, "Listen. But I have to study." And he's like, "Oh, bring your books. You'll study." Right.

I think I had to work Saturday during the day so he comes and gets me Saturday evening and we go up there. And I don't open a book the whole weekend, forget it. And I'm a nervous wreck. I had a suitcase full of books because I thought he'd see that I had really wanted to study, and I put all my books out. Forget it, I never opened a book. And I don't know, so that was just a washout. I mean we had a nice time and everything but I was worse of a nervous wreck when I got back the next day. So anyway, I took my test and I got that over with.

And then later, he was starting to get worried, and he got scared and started to panic because he realized that people might find out that he and I were having an affair. People might sense it in the office. I said, "Well, what do you think I have been saying all along since day one?" And he said, "Well, I hadn't really thought of it like that, but now that I've started thinking about it more and realized that you're right, it's not a good idea." So he's basically ditching me and cutting me loose after all of this. After he got what he wanted, he basically threw everything back in my face and said, "You're absolutely right. This is not going to work. And you're too young for me, I'm too old, I'm this, I'm that." And that he's got this other woman, and we'll still be friends. Well, I just couldn't believe it.

After this, at this point, our relationship became very strained. I was very, very nasty to him, and I basically had no respect whatsoever for him. And I was so angry at him for what he had done that I was just a bitch to him. Whatever he had to say, I had something to say about it. I couldn't take any criticism from him. I'm supposed to be working for these guys, right; they're supposed to show me how they want things done. But I couldn't take any criticism from him. I just couldn't. I couldn't bear it. After what he had done I didn't want to hear anything from him. He'd try to tell me, "You should do such and such . . . you should do this that way." I'd say, "Why?" I wouldn't say, "Yes, sir." I'd say "Why?" He'd say, "Well because I've been doing this for 25 years and I think that this is a better way to do it." And I'd say, "Yeah, well, in 25 years things have changed and there are a lot of new techniques." I was just undercutting him every way. I mean, basically he couldn't say a word to me; we just could not get along at all at that point. I just couldn't forgive him, and I wanted to hurt him. I wanted to hurt him and get back at him for what he had done to me because I just felt like he was using me.

Finally, there was a meeting with the three partners and me. They sat me down, all of them were there, and they had a secretary taking shorthand, and they tape-recorded the meeting. They made a couple of preliminary remarks. Then they started on the real agenda, which was me. The senior partner said, "Medically, I think you are a good doctor. Patients love you. I have never had a problem with anything you've done medically." Which is true—they've never criticized me about any medical decision I ever made. He said, "But you're so difficult. You're so god-damn difficult." And then he says to me, "You're such a ball breaker." And I said, "I really think that's a sexist remark." He's like, "That's not a sexist remark for God's sake." And he just went off, screaming at me, calling me everything.

*All on tape. He went on and on. And I couldn't take it any-
more. I just couldn't stand it. Then X pipes in and starts saying
to me how I'm this and I'm that. I'm difficult. I said, "Listen. I
can't stand this." I said, "I can't listen to this anymore." And I
said, "You guys have undercut me, you've done this, you've done
that."*

*And all three of them had done stuff behind my back, gone
to people. And I pointed at the three and I said, "You undercut
me in every way." I said, "You went to Dr. So and So and you
said such and such about me. And you called the director of
my residency program and bad mouthed me. And X bad
mouthed me in the male locker room." And the other two said,
"What? What are you talking about?" And they didn't know,
so I told them the whole story. And I said, "The three of you
have done everything to undercut me and do everything to make
me miserable. So no wonder I'm so belligerent and I have to
protect myself."*

*I said, "It's like the three of you are always on my case about
everything." I said, "If I come late to the office, I get a memo
about that. If I do this, I get a memo about it. I have a whole
file full of fricken memos that you guys have written me." I said,
"I can't stand it. I feel always on the defensive." And then he
starts telling me how I'm nasty and this and this. I couldn't take
anymore. I just felt like I had to start crying, because I'm very
emotional. So I got up and excused myself; I went to the bathroom, and I just lost it. I started crying, and I just wanted to
flee. I just wanted to leave there and just forget I had ever met
these people. I was so miserable. And it didn't matter, my career
didn't matter, nothing mattered, I just hated them so much. I
wanted to just get out of there. They were making me so unhappy.*

*I said, "In medical school, I got where I am by being tough,
and working hard, and being aggressive. And I'm not going to
let you guys walk all over me. I just can't let it happen." I said,
"I give you an inch; you take a mile. Everything that I have
conceded and gone along with the game plan to be a team*

player, every time I've done that, you've taken advantage of me." And I said to them, "You know, when I started working here, I really wanted this to work. I had the best of intentions. This was my first real job as a doctor in private practice. I was so enthusiastic about it. I was excited about the whole package, the whole idea of everything working out. If you say I'm not a team player it's because I've really gotten disillusioned with the team that I'm on. You have broken so many promises along the way. A lot of things that you promised me never came through."

And I just said, "I can't let you do this to me. I'm not happy here. You're obviously so unhappy with me. If you want to fire me that's fine, but just give me some notice because I have a 72-year-old mother whom I'm helping support. I just want notice. If you're going to fire me I want to know." They were always threatening to fire me. I said, "Give me some notice so I can look around for a new job because I have a mother to support. And that's all I ask of you." So I made my speech.

So then the senior partner says, "Oh, this is good. This is cathartic." He said, "I'm glad you got this all out of your system. And maybe this is good. Maybe we can work with this. Maybe we can try to make things work." He was waiting for me to say no. He had something already written. The secretary types it up, gives it to me, and basically it's a whole new policy of the Board of Directors that they knew I can't accept. It makes me their slave more than I already am. I said, "Well if that's how you feel, then it's not going to work out, and why don't you just fire me?" And he said, "Because I don't want to fire you." I said, "What do you mean you don't want to fire me? If you're so unhappy, if I'm so miserable. If I'm insubordinate, if I'm everything you say I am, then why don't you fire me?"

And he said, "Because I don't want to hear about it ten years later." I said, "What do you mean?" He said, "I don't want you to come back and say we forced you out of your job. I don't want you to pull some Anita Hill situation." I said, "What are you talking about?" And he said, "And that's why I don't even come in the room alone with you." I said, "What?" He said, "I don't want you to accuse me of sexually harassing you." And I said, "What are you talking about?" I knew he didn't know about the whole thing between me and X. And he said, "That's why I wrote the new policy now because I don't want you to accuse me of ever sexually harassing you. And I said, "But you never did anything that would be construed as sexual harassment. Why would you think that?" And he said,"Well you're so irrational, you could say anything."

Meanwhile, this is the middle of my office hours, and I have a waiting room full of my patients who are waiting to see me. And he's screaming at the top of his lungs. And I was so humiliated. It's not what he was saying although what he was saying also was bothering me, but the fact that he was saying it within earshot of everyone. And I just was so humiliated, I was saying, "Be quiet." He just goes off and starts screaming. And I just said, "Just stop. Stop this." And he just kept screaming. Kept carrying on; he was impossible. I started crying again. I couldn't help it; I just lost it. And he's like, "Oh here she goes again with the tears. I can't talk to you if you're going to cry like this. I can't deal with you. I can't." And he storms out. And meanwhile, the whole staff is listening and I couldn't leave. I was so humiliated, I couldn't go out of the office. Because I didn't want all these people to see me. I couldn't look anyone in the face.

So I just sat there. The office manager came, and she said, "All these patients are waiting." I said, "Rosemary, if there was a trap door here, I would crawl out and just disappear. I would just leave." I said, "There hasn't been a time in my life where I couldn't care less what happens to me. I don't care what happens to my career. I don't care about anything anymore. I am so miserable and so unhappy here that I just don't care. I hate this place. I really like the patients. I wish I could just take care of the patients and do my job and not have to deal with these guys." You know, like in nine months you really develop an attachment to patients and there were patients whom I started seeing when I first started there in July who are now due to have their babies this month. And I knew I was going to leave them, and I couldn't tell anybody. And it just broke my heart. And these people whom I would see every week, and they expected me to deliver their baby.

But I was so humiliated I couldn't even go out of the office. I sat in that room, and the senior member went and saw the patients. I couldn't face them. He went and saw the patients. I waited till all the office staff left. And I just sat there till everyone left, and then I just left. When he was screaming at me like that, I physically got nauseous. Not what he was saying—if we were alone in the room and he was saying stuff like that to me, I would have just blown it off and you know, "Fuck you. You're an asshole." And that's it. But because he was doing this in front of all those patients and staff, he publicly humiliated me. I was getting nauseous, like I was just feeling so horrible. These are patients who look up to me and respect me, or some patients who were new patients who don't even know me, and what are they going to think about me now? And I couldn't face anyone.

So I just left that night and I went home, and I called in sick the next three days. I couldn't face anyone. I just literally could not go into the office. I wasn't sick, but I just couldn't face anyone. I just stayed at home. And they kept calling me during the day to make sure I was home and everything. I was home; I just moped around for three days. I just felt horrible. But it was in that time that I decided I had to leave and that was it. And then I left the next week. The next Monday I left basically. I said I didn't want any trouble. I want to cooperate. And I said this to them, "I want this to be as amicable as possible." In other words, my fear was that they are going to go behind my back and try to bad mouth me to the people at the hospitals. And they were going to try to undermine me in whatever endeavors I may pursue in the future.

So my lawyer drafted up a proposal saying we agreed to mutually terminate the contract and we would mutually agree to cooperate in future endeavors, patient matters, and this and that. And they would agree not to say derogatory or denigrating things to members of staff of the hospital, or in the future when I apply for privileges at hospitals, they wouldn't try anything. Because in the past they have gone to people at various hospitals and said bad things about me. And I was offering that if they agreed to leave me alone and not bad mouth me and not try to prevent me from going on further, I would agree that I wasn't going to press any charges or bring up anything relating to X, or make any complaints, whatever. I don't want to use this against him. I just want to drop it, and walk away, and just forget the whole thing ever happened, and pretend I never met him or any of these people again.

But they're refusing to sign the release. They just said to my lawyer they don't feel they have to sign anything. Even though my contract says that if it is terminated for any reason, it has to be done in writing. So far they haven't given me any written thing that says I'm terminated or that I left. In other words, they could say I walked out of the office Monday afternoon and abandoned my patients. They could say anything because nothing's written down. So, it's very important for me that we sign something that says we mutually agreed to terminate because it looks better. But if they don't want to do that, then they have to say that they terminated me. They're afraid to say that because then they'd have to prove they terminated me for cause. And they don't have real cause.

GENDER LESSONS

Most women go along with far too much. They put up with far too much. That's characteristic of the inequality that operates in this culture. We all know that women work much harder than men for the same kind of reward.

Not only do women work harder and more but they do so to achieve fewer and smaller benefits or professional standing. This occurs mostly because women fling headlong onto a vicious treadmill when they enter a professional career. On the one hand, those in positions of authority have at best an ambivalent response to hiring women and working with them (even when women are in positions of authority) and thus have not modified their sexist behavior. In some cases this behavior has increased, and so too has the concomitant hostility. On the other hand, young women are perhaps even less equipped than their mothers and grandmothers to recognize their working conditions as political, as part of a pattern of discrimination, of bias against their succeeding professionally. These two factors create a situation in which the dropout rate for women is significantly higher than it is for men. Yet, other explanations for this dropout rate are employed that sidestep the facts of women being discouraged, not encouraged, and not accorded fair working conditions or opportunities. Thus, the vicious cycle continues and is handed down to another generation.

Not uncommonly, graduates from B.A. programs emerge full of energy and enthusiasm for graduate and professional training and go on to good first professional jobs, only to retreat from the myth of the supermom a few years down the road by staying home with children. There is, of course, nothing wrong with choosing to stay at home with one's children, given a relatively neutral choice set from which that one is selected. But that is not what typically happens. Because the husband's work is valued more highly than the woman's, whether he earns more or not, and because the current social structure makes it all but impossible to carry on the demands of what amounts to much beyond full-time hours of work for a young professional woman, and starting a family, with or without significant help with child care, the woman often resolves to stay at home while her children are young, to re-enter at a later date. Not only is re-entry not that simple in most cases, but staying at home with children, however delightful they are is not easy on one's psyche either, given the current climate. The 1980s myth of the super-mom working woman has given way to young women who find it noble to have a career and drop it for the sake of sole responsibility for home, hearth, and children. This trend might otherwise be described as a rationale for succumbing to personalization and internalization of the poor working conditions for professional women.

In addition, first jobs provide a strong lesson in the effects of tacit collusion. What is, in effect, collusion often feels to the woman more like a smoothing of her path, an attempt not to ruffle feathers over trifles in the name of her career goals. Because women are still made to feel like outsiders in the professions, they must constantly make choices about how to respond to the charged atmosphere in which they work. Coping strategies often involve, again, the distancing from other women and quiet assimilation into the male work environment, which includes accepting biased behavior as the norm. In the long run, this choice rarely serves the woman.

GENDER COMPOUNDS

Suppose that Emily joins a law firm and is generally treated well and given challenging assignments. However, one client that she is assigned to exhibits sexist attitudes and makes constant remarks about Emily's age, cuteness, and adorableness. In addition, he has made it clear indirectly that he is generally skeptical of her competence as a lawyer. Emily has noticed this client's behavior and has attempted to smooth over the belittling remarks with smiles and a businesslike demeanor; she has even attempted to modify her bodily movements so as to keep herself contained and unfeminine. She has not mentioned this client's behavior to anyone and does not view it as much beyond somewhat uncomfortable and fleeting. This is one client among several and she loses no sleep over it, knows that she is nevertheless doing a good job for the client, and assumes that it is appreciated.

One day, however, she comes to work to find a memo on her desk from a partner stating that this client has been reassigned to another lawyer in the firm and that the next time she is having difficulty with a case, she should consult one of the partners immediately. Emily pursues this cryptic memo with the partner who wrote it. Emily determines in conversation that there was in fact no substantive allegations concerning the work that she did for this case. She finds that the partners have no problem pulling her off a case, in effect, simply because a client feels uncomfortable working with a woman. This example provides a lesson in the ease with which women are undercut professionally due to background cultural assumptions even when it is not necessarily in the best interests of the institutions for which they work. Although Emily knows that she should not take this personally, the situation nevertheless leads to classic feelings of self-doubt.

GENDER ACTION

Going into a first job with a clear head and realistic expectations would go a long way to, at least, preventing the emotional turmoil that many young professional women experience today. Part and parcel of undoing the vicious cycle effect in place is informing oneself what the choices are in difficult situations that involve bias and then building a support network to deal with them.

The first job is the time, if one has not already done so, to adopt a professional comportment and not to succumb to stereotypical female behavior in the face of flirtations. In other words, one should make an effort to maintain one's own part in keeping business interaction just that, direct and straightforward. Such a demeanor will enhance colleagues' professional responses and can also lead to an improvement in one's self-image as professional. The young professional woman should continue to strive to create a professional persona that feels comfortable. And she must try out different strategies for interaction with male clients, patients, students, and colleagues that are both effective and comfortable. Similarly, one must seek ways of interacting with superiors in a productive, professional manner. Not allowing oneself to be ostracized or to be made to feel out of place is key, even if it means feeling overly assertive in the moment.

In short, one must begin to learn to own the authority one has earned and begin to break the holds of collusion with the *status quo*. Feeling at home in one's profession—owning the right to practice what one trained, prepared, and obtained a job for—is powerful and invaluable.

18 ADVANCEMENT

GENDER BASICS

In terms of professional advancement, there are three parallel tracks that need to be examined: the glass ceiling, the state of mind of those in the position to make promotion decisions about others, and women's response to the rate of their own advancement.

The federal Department of Labor Glass Ceiling Commission ended its three-year study in 1995, concluding that the glass ceiling is very real and omnipresent nationwide. The study found, for example, that women remain consistently underrepresented at the highest levels of corporate America. Women in professional occupations, of course, know this fact. They remark repeatedly,

Women are trapped, and there is a glass ceiling.

Even the progress to this ceiling is arduous. As one woman described the path,

It's only after being out of school for about four years that you start going up the hierarchical ladder. And then at each step it gets harder; as you get to a higher stage it gets harder.

In many professions, women feel the crunch of gender bias long before they are up for a promotion, but in some it is not until this point that it becomes evident that women in fact are receiving differential treatment in the profession. In many of its subspecialties, law is one such profession, as a law professor attests:

The fact is that it still is more difficult for women to please the mostly men who are making the decisions. . . . It's harder for a woman than a man to become a partner. It's much more difficult than for a man.

And, again, another woman's voice joins this chorus:

So by the time you get up near the top, there's a weeding out, not necessarily on merit at all. But there's a weeding out that more men are likely to make it than women, given equal qualities.

The glass ceiling has been discussed at length in the media and is well documented. If one looks across professions, the proportions of women uniformly and steadily decrease from somewhere between sixty and seventy percent at the entry level to, at best, the roughly ten percent mark for the top-level positions.

Consider the common experience shared by a professor concerning her own stalled promotion process:

Encountering this academic sex discrimination has forced me to reconsider my whole career. I've always assumed that one is rewarded for doing good work. And I've done many difficult things in my life, and I've made many difficult choices about which way my life was going to go. I feel I've really accomplished a lot in my work. When I entered as a professor at this institution, it was by invitation, and everyone was enthusiastic and optimistic about my coming to the department.

I feel I was instrumental in turning the department around into a lively, rigorous department. And I am very well liked there. I just assumed that because I had worked so hard, because I had never said no, always performed all of the tasks that were required of me and others that were not even required of me, and all of this extra work that was put on me knowing that I was up for promotion, I assumed that it was just fair play. I had kept my end of the bargain, and now it was time for the payoff. And the payoff never came. The way my treatment was conducted was a very degrading and humiliating experience. Had I had even more insight into the situation, I probably would have handled it quite differently. I would have thought it through at the time it was happening.

If I had it to do over again, I would have the guidance of an attorney who would have followed me through the process as it was happening because there were so many kinds of illegal and gender-biased moves that were being made against me. It was very difficult to determine what kinds of positioning one could have taken in that scenario if one knew that this was essentially set up to railroad me. It was a railroad job, and I could have used professional counseling on this. So at least if I wasn't going to be hired, I wouldn't have gone through as much emotional turmoil as I actually experienced.

The position I was up for was created, and it was created because of the enthusiasm and enrollment and energy that the program that essentially I had put together singlehandedly was generating. And in creating this position, of course, a national search had to be conducted. And I felt that that was the only honorable thing to do anyway. In conducting this national search, they set no final date as to when the applications had to be due. So it was an open-ended search. They came up with five finalists, and it was posted on the department door as to when those finalists would be coming to give lectures. There were four white men and myself. I get into school on Friday ready to give my lecture, and I notice that now two more names were added to the list. It was clear to the administration at that point that I was considered a very strong candidate and that they had to do something about the strength of my candidacy. So they upped the ante, and they upped it with two more white male candidates. So it was one white woman and six white men.

The atmosphere in the department was that the job was essentially mine. And people were talking about why the administration was making things this difficult. Initially when all the men's names were up on the door, people were making jokes. But my candidacy turned out to be a mere ploy. They needed a woman up there on the list, for affirmative actions reasons, to satisfy the guidelines. They had no interest in actually hiring a woman. They had no interest in hiring the person who built the program, and they had no interest in hiring the person who had the experience. I wasn't even candidate number two.

In discussing the situation with people on the search committee, and people who were privy to the inside information of the decision making, it was clear that I had the most number of votes. Everyone on the search committee voted for me; the students were behind me one hundred percent. The faculty were all behind me. If it had been an election, I would have won by a landslide. So how can one explain my not getting the position? It was explained that the decision involved political maneuvering from the higher levels in the administration.

I could have stayed on in the position I was in, but their choices and their treatment were so callous and misogynist there was no way I would stay on in a half-time position with no future, no benefits, just to prop up the system. Essentially that's what they expected me to do. I don't think that they expected me to leave. I think they expected me to stay for a number of reasons. One, I had become such a fixture there, I had been there for six years and they knew how much I liked the job, and they thought I probably would not have been able to leave. Two, the economic situation was very disastrous at that time in terms of trying to find another job. And since the search went on through June, the chances of my being hired someplace else for the following year were probably zero.

In my conversations with the chair, he made several comments, that he hopes that I will stay even if I don't get the position and that he would try very hard to keep a half-time position for me. I think that pretty much he was offering me this bait. The person they did hire has no experience in administration, no theoretical background. He's been accused of sexual harassment in other institutions. He's a good old boy; he's one of the guys. It wasn't a fair search. It wasn't based on anything rational. The decision was arbitrary based on in-house politics. Even in 1992, to come up with six white men and one white woman as the candidates is disgusting.

I quit. I wrote a very brief letter of resignation. Once it was all over, I had to change my life. In re-evaluating the situation, it's very clear to me how quickly people forget, and how politics stop at one person's checkbook, and that it's essentially as if nothing ever happened. People are anxiously holding on to what they have, and all of their political discourse evaporated into the air. I find it very disturbing that not even a letter went on record expressing disappointment that I wasn't hired. There was talk of lots of different action, a student strike, a faculty protest. None of it happened. Everyone in the end just protected their own positions. I understand that people need the money, but where and when and how does acknowledgment of this kind of situation take place if everyone just protects their own interest? I just find it appalling.

Once it was all over, I knew that no longer was I going to be manipulated by a situation. If I am hired to do something, then

I'm going to do what the job description says. I'm going to create options for myself so that I have a larger bank to choose from. The situation put me in a difficult position. Do I stay in there and say, "Yes. It's okay to treat me as second-class citizen; I need the money"? Is that okay? It's not okay. And I think if you don't draw the line somewhere and say that this has gone too far, then it will come around. If an unjust institution or process doesn't get you at one place, it will certainly sting you at another.

This happens all the time. Women go in, they do the job, they do it very well for three years, and then they're fired.

On the whole, the mechanisms by which promotions are made render any bias involved invisible to those making the decisions. Because underlying attitudes that color and shape people's beliefs are implicit, they are almost always unavailable to their owners. Instead, the people making promotion decisions come up with different explanations, usually couched in terms of merit, for why they have decided to promote one person over another. As one woman observed,

I think it happens very subtly. It happens mostly without ever being discussed. People get together in terms of making promotion decisions, and there's a lot of cloning that's going on. So people choose the person they're most comfortable with, and that person's usually a man. And if it's not a man, it's usually a woman with male attitudes like I used to be. Which is less threatening.

Often pervasive and sweeping patterns of gender bias, such as no or few women being promoted past a certain, often junior, level, are also explained in terms of the bad luck of not finding qualified female candidates. It is the rare person today who will say directly that he just does not want to promote a woman, regardless of her credentials. That is, there is unlikely to be more than a small set of people nationwide who are willing to recognize their sexist attitudes and their role in their promotion decisions. One reason for this is that it is now illegal to do so. As one lawyer observed about the law partners with whom she participated in promotion decisions,

I really think that they didn't call it sexism to themselves. They called it one of these things that happens sometimes to everybody. And that's because they didn't understand the systemic nature of sexism. So it was a little thing that happens to everybody.

A recent twist to our collective thinking, which bolsters the perception that those in positions of authority are not biased when they do not promote women, is that, in fact, women are readily promoted. An ideology is prevalent in the current professional climate, that holds that a woman will be promoted over a man even if she is less qualified than the man. The fact that the numbers do not support such a belief does not stop it from being circulated as truth.

In fields in which there have been traditionally virtually no women past the entry levels, and now there is, say, five percent, the number of women is likely to feel large and overwhelming. One woman expresses a similar sentiment in her department:

There's this idea that "Oh, it's so easy for women to do stuff now. Because all you have to do is be a woman and it's like you got the prerequisite, you know. That they're looking for women to do stuff. The good traditional men out there aren't getting work because they're being edged out by women." I don't see too many departments being run by women. There are 60 people here and there are 14 women. I don't think that that's means we're taking over. If you've got even half, it seems overwhelming.

In a profession such as law in which more than half entering classes are women in certain cases, it would make sense to begin to see similar proportions at the higher levels, such as partners in the smaller firms. This is not happening, and part of the reason is that if the proportion of women at higher ranks merely increases from its traditionally very low levels it feels like a stampede. One lawyer chuckled as she envisioned law firms with fifty percent of their partners female:

At the point at which women are going to be half of the partners in a major firm, men would go crazy.

In part because of this prevailing attitude that, if anything, we have a system of reverse discrimination in the professions, in many cases, women are shocked when they hit the wall. Even when a woman is well aware of the glass ceiling in other professions and even in her own, she will nevertheless be taken by surprise if it is applied to her. It is natural to feel entitled to the professional rewards that one deserves and that one sees one's colleagues receiving on a regular basis. It is natural for women to expect advancement almost as much as men do. Yet, a major flaw to their expectations is culturally pervasive. This is the background assumption that the male model is central and basic. Clearly, the male model of professional advancement has little to do with the actual facts of women's promotion trajectories.

Women's disassociation from other women is a factor that abets the vision problem that permits women to remain blind to the potential and likely impact of the glass ceiling on their own careers. Many women do not recognize the professional barriers for what they are and personalize their lack of progress on the professional ladder. Consequently, many opt out of their careers altogether. Interestingly, one of the most common responses to discovering that the glass ceiling exists in one's own profession is to embrace the ultimate stereotypical female action: to start a family. Others switch careers, often only to find similar barriers to entry to the top ranks. And again, some women try to make peace with the ceiling without losing sight of it. One woman remarked,

There definitely is this ceiling. I do have a sense that if I were male it would be different, that I would do it differently. I would do it more, I would do it bigger, I would do it somehow in some other way. I very definitely have been constrained as a female.

GENDER LESSONS

Advancement is an issue that starkly exhibits the deleterious effects of going along and remaining blind to the real factors involved in gender bias. The glass ceiling is self-perpetuating in part because women continue to act individually in professions, hoping that if they just do it all well and more, they'll be the one to pass through the barriers unrestricted.

Women's own awareness and response to the glass ceiling are an exercise in maintaining the status quo. Keeping themselves underinformed of the situation and personalizing it are two of the mechanisms by which the system of not promoting women to the higher levels in professional occupations is sustained. Were women to begin *to enter* the professional world armed with sufficient knowledge concerning not only the glass ceiling but also the tools for sustaining that knowledge, and, along with it, a belief in their own capabilities and training, the more the blockades will crumble. When women accept their lack of professional progress or opt out of the field, the more the existing system is permitted to be justified. Moreover, those in positions of authority who are making promotion awards are currently left with their rationales intact. When challenged, there is always a way to render decisions appropriate. As one woman relayed,

I think that I expected to be able to make some changes, but I don't think that I articulated that too much, even to myself. So it seemed natural for me. I saw these patterns of discrimination in the flow of work. It seemed natural I would call it the way it was, and things would be cured. So every time I tried to do that people would say, "Oh no, that's not what's happening." Both for me and for other women. They would always say, "That's not what's happening." They would be painting the picture; they would be telling the story. So when I said this is happening, well it wasn't happening because they said it wasn't happening. I knew it was happening, but they didn't. Did they not think it was happening, or did they want to paint the picture their way anyway?

In this instance, it was merely one woman's voice against an established practice. In addition to commencing professional occupations with knowledge of gender bias and the glass ceiling, here again is an instance of the value of creating a community of women from which to draw strength. Promotion decisions can be challenged and corrected, but rarely is this successful when the critique is coming from a lone voice.

GENDER COMPOUNDS

Suppose that Emily is a lesbian. This sexual orientation virtually brings her career advancement to a halt when it is discovered. Whereas before she came out she was advancing even slower than the other women because she was perceived as different in a vague sort of way, although no one knew anything definite about her personal life, now she will not be so much as considered for a higher-ranking position. One woman expressed her situation after revealing her sexual orientation:

I was clearly held back for being a certain kind of woman. I couldn't trot out my kids like the men could when they are up for promotion. And I'm the one who gives them juice and feeds them breakfast in the morning. But because I'm a certain kind of woman, I've been held back from promotions that my work has more than merited.

Sexual orientation, of course, has nothing whatever to do with Emily's performance on the job. Yet, she is now clearly not only a woman but a woman who can be perceived in our homophobic culture as different, radically different, from other women. Emily's personal choices are the grounds on which her co-workers implicitly base their feelings of discomfort in working with her and their difficulty in viewing her work as valuable. Gender plus sexual preference have too often provided the excuse for not promoting women, and this combination is far more potent than gender alone.

GENDER ACTION

I have a very strong sense of being stunted. Like having an iron on my head. A heavy flat thing that's the ceiling, as they call it. There's a ceiling for me, and I would have to do incredibly dramatic things to break through it. Within that amount of space that I perceive for myself, I think I've found a way to live and work that feels good and that feels strong. I've been able to work professionally on a level I feel comfortable with and feel good about and with people that I feel good about.

This woman is working within the space allotted to her under the glass ceiling. In order to set out to break through it, women need to start taking out professional *insurance*. They need to approach their careers as small businesses, or as construction projects, and set out a plan replete with the stages to complete it. The first stage would be to ascertain what completion would entail, that is, to set clear goals.

Having done this, a woman can discern what the steps are that a man would need to do to achieve that goal. This could be considered the basic plot, which would be in need of revision when the player is a woman. Incorporated into this plot should be awareness of not only the obstacles in place that make it difficult for women to follow this basic plot but also the extra work and other duties that will be required of women on the path to the goals.

The third phase would involve a plan to continuously broaden support and increase one's options. The place to start is within one's own self. A woman must be her own best supporter. She must believe in her talents and stand behind her work. She owes it to herself to clarify and separate bias from an objective evaluation of her work. She then also ought to constantly broaden her professional contacts with others inside and outside her own place of work. And it would be invaluable to build a community of women, professionals in her field and others on whom she can rely for constructive criticism and support.

In other words, women in professional occupations can benefit from approaching their careers as well as the bias they confront clearly, directly, and in a businesslike way. One way to be able to accomplish this is through awareness of the factors involved. Information about the obstacles helps one to pull the situations out of the personal sphere and into the mainstream as part of a failing social trend.

PART VII
DISCLOSURE

The Hollywood movie, *Disclosure*, portrayed a contemporary American woman, Meredith Johnson, who had made it to the top of her profession. Johnson is well endowed physically and wears what is considered typically sexy clothing, including her office attire. And, she is incompetent at her job. In her rival's words,

She doesn't know the difference between software and a cashmere sweater.

In achieving her professional standing, she is chosen over the hero of the movie, Tom Sanders, a man who deserved the promotion. She got the job not through merit but because of her abuse of her sexuality. Once in power, she immediately proceeds to engage in behavior that in the movie is called sexual harassment of Sanders. He is portrayed as a happily married, honest, hard-working, intelligent, wonderful family man but one with a past reputation as a womanizer.

There are so many confused messages and morals in *Disclosure* that it is difficult to isolate and analyze them. The effort is worth it, however, since the movie boldly captures much of contemporary thinking about and fear of professional women, particularly those who make it to the highest ranks in their field.

First, a clear theme concerning affirmative action runs through the movie. Because of the cultural climate, the faulty reasoning proceeds, there is a demand to place women and minorities in high-ranking positions. Even unqualified women attain high rank, at the expense of qualified white men and at the expense of the firm or institutions who will thereby, virtually of necessity, have inferior leadership as a result. This is, in other words, the cry of reverse discrimination. In the movie the credentials that won Johnson her job comprised her sex, the drive to hire a woman, and her sexuality, which titillated the company's owner and associates. And Sanders, who was passed over for the position, actually deserved it, strictly on merit.

The second theme that rings out loud and clear in the movie and one that is pertinent to this section is that it is authority itself that enables and perhaps encourages persons to commit sexual harassment. It is proposed that the sex of the offenders as male is based merely on the circumstantial evidence that it is in fact men who are currently the holders of authority in most cases but that this is not actually part of an accurate characterization of the crime. Under this conception, the sex of the aggressor is irrelevant, both women and men equally could be the perpetrators of sexual harassment, sexual assault, and, by extension, sex discrimination.

Third, the movie having rendered sex irrelevant on the theoretical plane, ironically, gender and, in particular, female sexuality are the definitional features of Johnson. This portrait of the professional woman encompasses every negative stereotype and contradiction in currency. She is sexy and provocative; she is tough and masculinized in her aggression and at the same time her aggression is supposed to represent the dark side of female sexuality; she is an overachiever and underintelligent; she is clearly not qualified for the job; she is manipulative, opportunistic, and is consuming of males; and she wants to overpower them sexually and otherwise. In effect, she is castrating. She is beautiful, bad, and bubbleheaded.

A subsidiary theme emerges about the suppression of femininity in order to achieve professional success. The overwhelmingly female Johnson is, after all, ousted in the end for poor performance. She is replaced not by Sanders but by a middle-aged, hard-working, serious, kind, and generous woman whose clothing and comportment signal assimilation to the male model. At the same time, the movie goes out of its way to stress that, in her past, this successor has also fulfilled her natural female function: she is the mother of a son who has now reached adulthood. Thus, Johnson's successor leaves no questions open: she is a team player who has been accepted as one of the boys, she doesn't complain when she is passed over by the 33-year-old inexperienced Johnson, and her womanhood has not only been fulfilled but it has also been packed away as part of the past and out of sight on the job.

Thus, a professional woman must be female, but it shouldn't show. She needs to have exercised her femininity through child bearing and raising, but it cannot affect her on the job. She must work harder for less financial and other recompense than her male peers, she must be an obedient team player, and she must endure sexual harassment and sex discrimination with a smile, all to be told that she is a pawn in an affirmative action scheme that robs deserving white males of their professional rights.

Unlike the fantastical portrait of professional women in *Disclosure* as seen in the character of Johnson, most real high-achieving professional women live out the inverse of the female lead's description. Many are fiercely unsure of themselves in spite of the gains that they have made by struggling through years of hard labor above and beyond what was asked of them and surpassing by far what men of their rank were required to do to achieve the same measure of success. Many are ambivalent about their success and status. Many know that their positions are precarious and that they do not in fact have the same authority that a man in their position would. Many question their own sexuality simply because of their professional success, and they question their own values as a result of not fulfilling the paradigmatic female life. The self-doubt, the level of hostility, and lack of respect commanded by such women from their peers and subordinates are overwhelming. It is a marked and significant contrast to the image constructed in Hollywood of professional life for females.

19 WOMEN AT THE TOP

GENDER BASICS

Here is the breakdown of tenured women and men in mathematics of the top colleges and universities: 3 women, 274 men. That's nice. Of these three women there's a qualification for each. At Harvard, the person who's tenured is somebody in a program that they call "the practice of mathematics." It's the education part of the Harvard mathematics department, which is not the research department. And it's not the thing that earns Harvard this position on the list. So to count her is in many ways really begging the issue. So it should be two. It's no accident.

Now of the two, somebody at Berkeley and somebody at Michigan . . . both were what were called "affirmative action" appointments. Meaning that there were extra lines that were given to the department just for women.

Here are some other numbers from the mathematical association. Honors and service: speakers and special session, women 8%. Invited addresses, women 8%. Trustees and council mem-

bers, women 10%. Members of editorial boards on journals, that's
a big job but it's a prestigious one, well 1991, women 8%.
Pretty bad, I would say.

Now, compare this situation with what might be considered
more feminized fields in the humanities. According to a 1995
survey by the American Philosophical Association, only nine
percent of all full professors in philosophy are women, as compared with the already low national average across fields. In
the top ten philosophy departments in the country, only seven
percent of the tenured professors are women. According to *The
Digest of Education Statistics* in 1991, only twelve percent of
full professors are women nationwide.

A study by the *National Law Journal* in 1988 revealed that
women comprised less than ten percent of law partners in firms
nationwide. This finding was reconfirmed by Mona Harrington
in her book, *Women Lawyers*, in 1993. And, to cite one more
statistic, according to the study found in *The American Woman*
(1992–93), only one in eight of the corporate board members
of Fortune 500 companies are women. So, plus or minus a small
amount, ten percent appears to be the magic number for
women allowed to pass beyond the glass ceiling. As is discovered below, often this small population is permitted passage
in body only, and the women's ranks at or near the top do not
carry the customary standing that goes along with that level.

In other words, by the time Emily makes it to the top rung
of her profession, her peers consist of a sea of men. Although
she will continue to confront forms of sex discrimination for
the rest of her working years, as the numbers cited above indicate, many of the gender issues Emily will confront in the years
to come at this level are complex and largely psychological.

Interaction with her professional peers is often strained. On
a regular basis, Emily has the feeling that she is being held at
arm's distance. She does not experience the free flow or casual
exchange of work-related discussion that she observes among

her colleagues. The collaborative work that Emily does with peers is usually of the sort in which each does his or her own work individually and then splices it together at the end, rather than the genuine collaborations that she witnesses in operation frequently when these same people work together with other men. In meetings and other group discussions and decision-making events, Emily continues to have the feeling that her voice does not count for nearly as much as the others, that her presence is merely tolerated, and that she is taking up a space that could better be filled by someone else. She often feels virtually invisible.

The men and women who work under Emily exhibit much greater ambivalence toward her than toward her male peers and also other women in the field. On the one hand, her accomplishments and authority command respect, and yet, most do not actually respect her. Emily finds that she is confronted with fear in the eyes of the men who work under her, and she is disdained by many of the women.

Although Emily's self-consciousness concerning her professional demeanor has lessened over the years since her first days on the job, it has not disappeared. There are many aspects of her professional self that she finds troubling and others that an objective observer might find contradictory. For example, in order to achieve her standing, Emily needed to be assertive. Yet, assertiveness is a trait that is still frowned upon in a variety of subtle ways in women. Assertive women are often treated as anomalies and freaks. This attitude in turn creates anxiety in the successful woman. She will, more often than not, learn different and more convoluted manners of behavior at work. Emily is no exception. She employs a pattern of speech that makes it appear that what she is saying is tentative and hesitant. Because her words alone convey the opposite, her speech patterns communicate a mixed message. In this way, Emily and many women in a similar position unconsciously attempt to comply with the standards of their gender.

At this point in her career, clothing is a relative non-issue for Emily. This does not mean that she is free to choose how to dress, but rather the opposite: in most professions at the highest levels, conformity is a necessity. And in virtually all cases, this spells conformity with the male dress code as closely as possible. Ironically but understandably, it is often the women who have achieved high rank in the most male dominated of fields who break the dress codes; for example, by wearing their hair long and free. Often, however, these departures from the required norms in an attempt to reinforce one's shaky sense of one's femininity result merely in diminished respect from colleagues, employees, clients, and students.

Moreover, because professional success is identified with a male paradigm, women who have achieved the highest standing in their profession often question their own sexuality and are predominantly male identified. This leads to many problems at work, not only for the woman herself but also for the women who are her juniors.

Emily is ambivalent about her rise to the top as well. She continues to entertain the lurking suspicion that she has had every step of the way that it was perhaps an unjustified promotion. She has this feeling despite the actual facts of her career, her hard work, her dedication and sacrifice, and above all, her excellent performance on the job on a continuous basis. Emily also has mixed feelings about being at the top. She, like many women, is exhilarated at the same time that she is uncomfortable with the authority that her rank brings. Unlike many men in a similar position whose already strong sense of self-worth would only experience an explosion of self-confidence and command, Emily is in many respects cowed by her status. Under the surface she is intimidated by the force and authority required to get the job done. Not that she is not a powerful and strong person, but that boldly exhibiting these traits is something that she has subtly been steered away from since birth. Emily is fully capable of carrying out her job and of providing clear leadership. Yet, the greater her status, the greater the conflict that rises within her about what is appropriate, in spite of her not believing consciously in the societal stereotypes of women. It is a virtually inevitable feeling of discomfort that arises under the surface in many successful professional women. It would take more than superwoman nerves of steel to completely wipe out a lifetime of training in appropriate female comportment and ability.

Complementing this complex of self-definitional questions that arise anew for Emily each time that she is promoted is a continuation of the disassociation that she has felt from other women. At this point in her career, however, the disassociation not only affects herself but also has a profound impact on the women who work under her. Instead of actively encouraging other women to achieve in her field, Emily actually discourages them and diminishes their chances for success by employing the same stereotypes and negative attitudes about women's professional potential that are in currency. Thus, as a consequence, Emily is more likely to encourage young men than women, simply because they appear to her to be brighter, more competent, more eager, and more assertive.

Another factor that prevents Emily from promoting women is that, in marked contrast with the clout that her position affords, Emily has a continued feeling of vulnerability and precariousness. In part, this feeling arises from her continuous observation of what her actual power and authority are relative to that of her male peers. She is also treated as less by employees, peers, students, and clients now that she's at the top. She is loathed, feared, and resented, and on some level she is very aware of others' perceptions.

Thus, Emily feels that, by some fluke, she is the one woman who was allowed to rise through the cracks in the ceiling. The flip side of her guilt concerning her privileged status is fear— fear that if she lets another woman through, she will be ousted. As one woman summed up her own situation:

So I had all those things that came with my status, and what I thought is if I tried to make this department any bigger and hire more women, we would have problems. If it becomes too big, then I'm going to make my position here shaky. Really, it was just an awful bind to be in, that when the department was small, they were very nice. . . . And as a member of the executive committee, I always felt this depends on keeping things small.

When women are made to feel more uncomfortable the higher their rank, they will thus keep themselves and the set of women working in their area as small and contained as possible in order to get the job done with a minimum amount of friction. Those women who have achieved high standing who try to make some changes or who try to help women who are junior to them are often quickly frustrated. One lawyer recounted her situation thus:

(As partner) there were other things that played into my situation. For example, at the partners' meetings when I started to use non-sexist pronouns people would titter, you know, laugh as I would say "Congressperson." I'd be reporting on testimony I gave to Congress and say something about a Congressperson, people would titter. As I became more aggressive in talking the language I'd wanted to talk, I began feeling like I wasn't supposed to do that. I was starting to rock their boat, and they didn't want that. They had me there as a partner to not rock the boat, and now I was rocking the boat. So I began to feel less accepted, although to this day I'm very much accepted. But they didn't want me to rock their boat and they did not want me to be a feminist.

At the same time I was starting to come to the aid of other women who were not given very good work. And every time I tried to make any point of anything I would get the response, "Well this person isn't really good at this." So everything would be torn apart so that you couldn't see a pattern. In other words, they'd try to sweep it under the rug or take the picture away. You know, I'd build the picture, but they'd wipe the picture away, so that they'd never admit there was any picture or pattern.

I felt totally powerless. . . . I didn't try to become a partner for this, but why was I even here if I couldn't help other people. I was really a token. I never understood before that I was a token because I worked hard and my work was good. But I finally realized I was a token because I could not do anything for anyone. And as soon as I tried to exercise the power I thought I had, I found out I didn't have any power. I wasn't there to be a feminist.

I was furious. I was very angry. I felt totally compromised, and I felt if I stayed there, I'd be totally compromised for life. . . . Their pretty partner, their lovely lady partner. That's what I was.

GENDER LESSONS

The theme of the unnatural woman is strong at the top ranks of professions. On the part of male colleagues, students, and clients, this theme is used, in part, as an intimidation tactic. As part of the internal view that women harbor of themselves, it is a reflection of their feeling of being out of place and misassigned. They feel that they are not good enough for the job, that they got to their position by mistake, fraud, or sexuality. And to complete the circle of no-win reasoning, they are not good enough as women because of their rank and job.

At this stage, women make many compensations in an attempt to alleviate some of their feelings of uneasiness with their professional standing. They adopt a masculine work style, using the existing male models as their own. In the words of a psychotherapist reflecting on her colleagues,

The women therapists who have made it big are quite ste-reotyped. They are more masculine. They take on mannerisms, the way they speak.

This is not to support the current notion that there are distinctly female and male modes of operation, going beyond what is socially conditioned. Rather, what is pertinent to the male work model is that it is designed for a simpler, more one-dimensional life than that to which most women's actual lives conform. This model that high-ranking professional women try to squeeze themselves into is in fact unsuited for the realities of women's lives, which encompass much more than men's do. Women must perform more jobs, they shoulder more responsibilities, and they maintain and are required to maintain more facets to their personalities. The assimilation, this identification with the aggressor, often solidifies and feels justified at this stage.

The no-win, contradictory situation that women at the top find for themselves is complex, and the women themselves are caught up in the daily living of it. Therefore, becoming conscious of the details of their situation is a slow and often arduous process. For example, many women wait to have families until the ultimate promotion has been achieved. What they find at the top, however, is not that their situation feels substantially more secure there than it did at lower ranks. Often they find that they are not in the strong positions they thought they would be. Even when their rank, such as tenure, cannot be easily revoked, they can readily be harassed due to their choice to start a family. They can be given poor assignments; be professionally shunned; not be invited to collaborate and speak at conferences; not receive other promotions, recognitions, and honors; and be harassed in many many more ways, subtle and otherwise.

The process of coming to recognize that there is gender bias in their profession and that it has been directed at them is harder for the woman at the top of her profession and the ramifications more forceful than at earlier points in a woman's career. Consider the words of one law partner, who endured years of biased incidents that went by unseen by her until she experienced first hand not only a blatant but also a chronic episode of devastating sexual harassment:

I finally understood. And it was very hard to understand because I was part of the system, I was promoted by the system, I was pampered by the system, and to the end even despite these awful stories of great humiliation, I was still accepted by them as their woman partner. As their exceptional woman partner. ·

An important lesson to learn from women at the top of their professions is that if they wait until they achieve this level of professional standing before coming to grips, and even recognizing, gender bias in their field, then greater professional and personal consequences and devastation can result than at earlier stages. There is more at stake and the shock is greater. The feeling that one's entire professional life, one's whole adult life in many cases, has been a fraud can be powerful and overwhelming, often leading to rash behavior that harms only the woman herself.

GENDER COMPOUNDS

Emily, because she feels she is in a position of authority, decides that it is time to acknowledge instances of sexual harassment and sex discrimination for what they are and to try to make some changes in her department. Emily has been preparing for this action for a long time. She had begun to take mental notes about the gender bias in her field some years back and has spent a fair amount of time reflecting on the patterns of bias she has observed. She even has taken the time to categorize them in an informal way into those that are salient and those that are subsidiary.

Emily has also laid the groundwork in other ways. She has been diligent about creating support networks for herself and other women with whom she works. She is on good terms with the non-professional support staff. She is also secure in herself. She trusts in her professional accomplishments and in her abilities. She knows that she has earned her status, and she loves her work. Emily has also done her best to forge good working relationships with her male peers, employees, and students. Thus, in all, she feels that at this moment, she is in as good a position as anyone could be to attempt to raise the level of awareness concerning gender bias at work. She proceeds with caution and circumspection. She has a good sense of how many of the women feel and has heard many of their experiences related first and second hand.

When she is ready to make a move, she first approaches the department head. She makes an appointment with him for an informal chat and is surprised to find herself shaking as she enters his office and hears her voice quaver with her first words. She has the sensation of being a young graduate student meeting with her mentor to present her own work for the very first time. Emily nevertheless forges ahead with a statement that she has prepared in outline form. She wanted to make sure to present herself in a non-aggressive and calm fashion even though the issues are highly emotional and of great importance to her.

After covering what she thinks are the most basic levels of bias, skipping over for the time being the more subtle and more difficult to understand forms that she has witnessed and experienced, Emily pauses to gauge the response. She is pleasantly surprised to find that the department head encourages her to speak and that he has the comportment of concern. Thus, Emily continues on until the two of them have spent two hours discussing the various forms of bias that Emily has catalogued in the department and statistically in the field as a whole. Emily leaves feeling that she may have accomplished something and that there is the promise of a chance to heighten awareness department-wide with the assistance of the department head.

Emily is unfortunately unprepared for the reality of the situation, for the crudeness with which gender bias is still handled. Although her situation does not unfold as badly as many do, Emily returns to work the next day to find a chill in the hall as she walks down it to her office. Emily had no sooner vacated her seat in the department head's office than he was on the telephone calling an immediate meeting of everyone of senior rank in the department. Everyone, that is except for Emily. In that meeting he repeated, probably with a degree of embellishment, everything that Emily said, portraying her as irate and out of control. At this meeting, the executives also called on the advice of a lawyer as how to best handle the situation and save themselves from costly and potentially devastating litigation. In short, the stakes were raised in a matter of minutes from a friendly dialogue into a full-scale legal battle.

Because quickly very few people—women and men alike—were talking to her, it took Emily some time to piece together what had happened. Although eventually, the affair was smoothed over, in part by intervention from people outside the department and in part as a result of some backpedaling on both the part of Emily and her colleagues, Emily herself was shaken by the event. She was unprepared for the strong reaction that she received in the end to what she felt were mild comments. Emily was also wholly unprepared for the display of just how precarious her standing at work is. She could not be demoted or fired as a result of such an incident, but the ambiance, although perhaps poor before, deteriorated to such a base level that she was astounded. The incident and its aftermath certainly wreaked havoc for some time on her ability to function and perform well on the job. Her concentration and enthusiasm waned, and she began to question her own self-worth in the field.

Although the outcome of voicing concerns about gender bias at work can be more productive than in Emily's experience, it can also be far worse and more destructive to the woman's career. It is the latter possibility that stops many from seriously entertaining the idea of action, however small. As one woman described her reluctance,

I realized that anybody who tells the world about the terrible things is terribly vulnerable. Terribly vulnerable. If you go out the next day and say, "This whole firm is sexist," they'll find reasons why I was a terrible lawyer. Anybody is vulnerable for criticizing the establishment. And I realized that it might have been a little bit better for me not to get myself out on a limb that I could be out on. Because people's reputations can be killed easily. People who tell on the establishment, whistle blowers, are so vulnerable.

Certainly, one is vulnerable when acting alone. Had Emily been part of a group of like-minded people in her profession, the outcome may have been entirely different. Gender bias is so highly sensitive an issue in the current climate that singular action rarely can benefit the woman who steps forward alone. In contrast, it has been shown repeatedly that voicing specific concerns together with a plan for remediation, and acting in a group can be productive and effect lasting change.

GENDER ACTION

Women who have attained the highest rank that their professions afford have both more and less freedom than at any other point in their careers. They have less because the pressure for high-quality performance is at its greatest now. The woman at the top feels all eyes on her, as if waiting for her to flop or crash. Many such women feel intensified pressure, as if they are the sole role model. They often sense that they can either forge open the gates for other women or shut them forever, depending upon their performance. They feel that to make a mistake, to underperform, would be devastating both personally and politically. And this is, of course notwithstanding the fact that the expectations of these women are greater than for their male colleagues in comparable positions.

At the same time, being at the highest rank can be an excellent time for the successful professional woman to stop and reflect on the past choices that she has made in regard to her profession and her professional persona. It is a moment at which she has a degree of freedom to make modifications that might suit her better than the existing models tendered in the field. It is thus a good time to return to Part II, "*The Nutcracker Suite*," and review the exercises provided there. With the wisdom and experience that her professional life has afforded, the woman's psyche is likely to have been monkeyed with and skewed beyond recognition. The exercises in the beginning of the book were designed to highlight areas in need of concentration and development. For many professional women, it is time to re-evaluate choices that have been made both tacitly and explicitly along the way.

Women can now look closely at all the aspects of their professional standing, from the small to the large and from the simple to the most complex—from how they dress in the morning to their manner of execution of their work; and how they interact with clients, students, employees, peers, and women and men. If they are still, for example, apologizing for their successes in a variety of ways, they can make a commitment now to learning how to accept, adopt, and accommodate to their authority and command of their field. Professional women can at this point take a long, serious look at how they have resisted or redefined stereotypical behavior and then decide where they feel they would like to make modifications.

PART VIII
VERTIGO

The Hitchcock movie classic, *Vertigo*, embodies themes that explain much of our cultural difficulty with breaking old patterns of gender bias and replacing them with a new status quo of human interaction. The principal female characters, Madge and Judy/Madeleine, along with the response of the male lead, John, to them, exhibit the range of circumscribed female choice. Madge, a longtime, sincere, hard-working, successful, practical, and caring friend to John, is not only not romantically attractive to John but she is also barely visible to him at all except as a reflection of his own needs.

Judy is more complicated. In her appearance in the first half of the movie she plays the image of the fictitious Madeleine, with whom John falls obsessively in love. The Madeleine role is pure, idealized, stereotypical, feminine romance. She is beautiful and largely silent and exists to live out the lives of her foremothers. She cannot break the old patterns, not even being aware of them. Judy, as herself, is a lesson in the process of female collusion. Tearing up her letter telling John the truth about her deception as Madeleine, she opts to go along with

John's plot to recreate the Madeleine image through her, come what may, in the hope of retaining John's love and approval.

Neither John nor Judy allow Judy to retain her integrity. She is stripped of every aspect of herself, even of physical details which are perceived as significant only with respect to women. In a telling exchange during the reconstruction of Madeleine, the degree of both John and Judy's individual desperation is evident:

> *John: Judy, the color of your hair.*
> *Judy: No!*
> *John: It can't matter to you.*

Judy lives on as a reflection of an idea in John's mind of the image of Madeleine to which he clings. In this way, both Judy and John approximate to a standard of gendered behavior. John does so unconsciously and Judy consciously. She is a collaborator in her own personal demise. What makes this perfect cooperation possible is Judy's belief that she has more to lose than to gain by breaking away. She has this belief because of her identification with the aggressor, with the goals, norms, and operations of the male stereotype, which she accepts as central. Culturally we do, in fact, like Judy/Madeleine, stand at the precipice of the present/future and shiver with vertigo at the possibilities. Instead of taking that step forward to at least ascertain what the choices are, collectively we too often stand in line to accept yesterday's mold of behavior.

20   THE FUTURE

It is time to try to envision what the choice, in fact, is. The question being posed here is, if today's gendered pattern formations were broken, what would come in their place? What would women and men need to give up, and what would women and men gain?

Let's revisit Emily's life experiences under a different social organization. Chances are that Emily would have grown up in a household in which the home maintenance and child rearing were split between the parents fairly equally. Or if one parent had taken on the greater proportion of home and child care, it would be just as likely to be her father as her mother. In this situation, it would be a job that is as freely chosen as other jobs in the world are. In either case, Emily would have access to both male and female roles models in her own home and in those of her friends, which were just as likely to contain a nurturing father as a nurturing mother and just as likely to contain a professionally or financially successful mother as a professionally or financially successful father. Thus, children's future options in terms of their imaginations and aspirations would be expanded, rather than crippled at the outset as they are today.

Similarly, the expectations of Emily and of her brother would be comparable. Emily would be no more or less expected to be mommy's helper than her brother. In fact, the expression, "mommy's helper" would lose its current content. Emily would be encouraged to excel in school and in sports just as much as her brother would be; the different expectations would result from actual differences in the children's capabilities and interests, not from their sex.

Not that girls and boys would wear identical clothing, but girls would no longer be encouraged to strive for frailty and dependency in the myriad ways that they are now. Not that eating disorders would disappear, but a boy would be equally likely to have one as a girl and, chances are, their incidence would dramatically decrease. Girls and boys both would seek physical strength, academic mastery, and emotional depth, and in similar ways.

Girls and boys both would leave high school with similar levels of self-confidence and future aspirations and would retain or modify them through their college years in similar patterns. Majors in college would not be sex segregated, and whether or not a student maintained a high profile through speaking up and doing consistently good college work would depend again on personality and ability, not on sex. Teachers from preschool through professors in college would be just as likely to be female as male, as would be doctors, dentists, garbage collectors, fire fighters, homemakers, bankers, college presidents, corporate partners, high-profile litigators, and politicians, including the President of the United States.

Thus, again, in terms of role models and of girls and women conceiving of their options, there would be no inherent restrictions based on a long tradition on gender bias. Pay scales would be equal for men and women, whatever the profession. Promotion, tenure, partnership, and all such milestones would be awarded, perhaps not solely on merit but at least independent from the sex of the candidate.

What would all of this mean on a *personal* level? How would it affect Emily on a day-to-day, minute-to-minute basis? She would not wake up in the morning already concerned about her attire, worrying about avoiding not only street harassment but also the comments she'll be greeted with in her office from peers, clients, students, bosses, and mentors. She would not need to take up space at the back of her mind with a constant query about how to blend in and be one of the boys for fear of the fact that she is female is too evident. She would not be continually battling with herself over the fact that she's working harder and producing more or superior quality work to her male peers for less, if any recognition. She would be valued and rewarded as the person, worker, and colleague whom she is, on a par with females and males alike. Differentiation would not be based on sex or expectations based on gender stereotypes. And, of extreme importance, she would not be expected to, nor would she consider, performing a double shift, one at work and the other at home, as if each were invisible and done as if by magic. In short, Emily would be as able to carry on a professional life just as easily as the next person, male or female, free from the myriad worries and extra loads that have been described throughout the course of this book.

It appears to be all gain for Emily in the future. Is there anything that she must give up? Definitely there is. Emily would need to cede her reign over the home and children that she has perhaps reluctantly become accustomed to holding. She could no longer be the child expert, knowing what is best for her children. She could no longer be the manager of the household and merely attempt to delegate jobs as she sees fit. Yes, she is likely to be the one to conceive, bear, and nurse the children. She, in fact, is likely to know them best through their early year or two. However, she must find ways to engage her partner or other adults who will be raising the children with her at every stage. She must give up her exclusive rights as mother. In fact, the very concept of mother as we know it must erode. Many women will readily give this up; others will hold to it beyond all else.

Most women in the middle ground—if women and men are to be on an equal footing, if women are to be able to genuinely pursue professional careers on a par with men—must share with men the command over the children and the home. In reality, with one's newborn in one's arms, sucking on one's own breast for his or her very life, this is a difficult step to take. And this step does not necessarily grow easier as the child weans away from its dependence; rather the "motherly" reflexes can tend to snowball.

Therefore, it is right at the beginning that all adults concerned must find ways to *share* in the process without depriving the baby of its birth-given right to access to its biological mother to the greatest extent possible. It, after all, has just spent more or less nine months literally inside its mother's body and knows her rhythms, smells, voice, and habits intimately. The baby *was* its mother and needs to feel the skin of its mother, to suck her milk, to hear her, and feel comforted by her warmth. All of this is crucial. Yet, it is not, it cannot be, the extent of the infant's life after birth. Its other parent, over time, must come to be as intimate with the baby as its birth mother. They must become as concerned, as knowledgeable, and as capable concerning this life they have participated one way or another in creating.

Men also must cede certain aspects of their lives and will make gains in others. Professionally, they will cease being in the vast majority in most fields. They will cease to automatically hold the top-ranking positions by virtue of their sex. By the same token, they will cease to be the one responsible in a heterosexual family unit for producing the bulk of the income to support the household. They will no longer necessarily be the one with greater earning power. This release of financial pressure, on balance, could be seen as a relief more than a source of grief.

Men will be freer to enjoy their children, to play with them, to care for them, to partake of the developmental stages of their intellectual, emotional, and physical growth. Instead of fleeing from their home and family life that is under the dominion of a frustrated and probably exasperated woman, through equal participation, the home will be a mutually shared and created environment in which both adults feel equally responsible, comfortable, and capable. Chances are, their marriage or other form of domestic partnership will be more satisfying as well by virtue of these changes.

Since the end state of this thought experiment is net gain all around, what stops us from getting from here to there? Inertia, overburdened frenetic America lives in which every person feels under too much pressure with too little time, no clear vision of the goal, and a lack of understanding of the requisite tools to get there. People look to the top of the system for change, to the law and government. Yet, all real change must come about not by large, legislative strokes, but through a modification of detail. Although rights on paper are, in some cases, better than none at all, without the backup of follow-through by the population at large, change remains at the level of superficial talk.

Every time we say yes unreflectively to some small, old habit, we are perpetuating the remains of a poor social contract. In contrast, each time a woman gets out of bed and dresses as she pleases, not the way others expect her to according to the contorting dreams from Madison Avenue; every time she speaks clearly and directly rather than deferentially; every time a father swoops down and gives his kids a warm bear hug; every time a man pauses to consider his emotions; every time a woman pauses to consider how she really wants to respond to a question; every time a boy is encouraged to cry and express how he feels in words when sad and a girl is encouraged to play roughly or climb a tree, the *status quo* is budging into a new format. The cliché that it is up to each and every one of us is a truism. Cultural patterns consist of small habits repeated reflexively.

We must each go through the tedium of pausing over every step in the walk. We must suffer through not knowing what precisely to do in every instance and fumbling around for answers. A period of time is required for trying out new patterns and failing at some before we come closer to the goal. And we must each wade through not knowing exactly what the goal is in every instance. We must deal with the guilt of wanting to opt out on many occasions and just rely on the familiar. We must also work hard to resist this tendency, rather than learning to live with the guilt. Women must be careful not to become bias police in their households, and men must resist the desire to be told what to do at home. Yet, we cannot shy away from sometimes being the one to point out problem areas and suggest modifications. We must all be free to admit when we need help in understanding the next steps, and we must work together to find them. This is not a utopian and unattainable vision of a gender-free world, but rather an outline of what the gritty, minute-to-minute existence might be like in the transitional phase. Not only is this possible but some are already living this out with local success.

It is hard work to change how we operate with respect to the minutia of daily life, but with each breaking of an unconscious action, we can breathe a little easier, as the weight of inertia slowly lifts off our chests. How many of us have suffered through the breaking of a chemical addiction, such as cigarette smoking? It is a slow, painful process, but every minute of it is well worth it. What is wonderful about the groups one can join for help in completing such a process is that they lift one out of a horror in isolation and place one in a social context with companions in the struggle against a harmful dependence. So too, with our weaning away from our gender-biased norms. It must be a *social*, shared process if it is to be successful. This sort of change cannot be accomplished by a few elite decision makers, but by the culture at large. For this to happen we must all understand clearly how to do it and what the personal benefits are.

Considering that we are currently living in the midst of a society in which dissatisfaction is the norm, change in some form is inevitable. Living through a transformation is surely a wobbly experience, as if going through a second adolescence on a cultural level, but even it could be an exhilarating, transitional period, the other end of which would result in greater satisfaction across the boards. And the vertigo will surely subside as we move from the need for recognition and resistance to bias to being free-standing individuals, undifferentiated professionally by sex, that is, to women and men alike feeling free to take up and move about in professional space.

Summary of Gender
Framework, Themes,
Trends, Rituals, Actions,
and Exercises

GENDER FRAMEWORK

GF 1.   Household labor and child care are a female province, and it remains unspoken and unpraised.

GF 2.   Men spend their days out of the home, at work, and this is often discussed and highly valued.

GF 3.   Females, and not males, attend to their physical appearance in great detail.

GF 4.   Girls need to be careful, do things smaller, quieter, and be "mommy's helpers."

GF 5.   The world's active population is largely male.

GF 6.   Boys are entitled to take up space of all kinds; girls must defer.

GF 7.   Boys and girls are divided and in conflict.

GF 8.   Boys are loud and active; girls are channeled toward quiet, neat, and attentive behavior.

GF 9.   Intellectual and public achievement are a largely male province.

GF 10. The war between the sexes is a backdrop to everyday life and the girls are supposed to lose.

GF 11. Sports are for boys; girls need to take care of themselves and not get hurt.

GF 12. Peer harassment, as an everyday occurrence, is a piece of the backdrop of life.

GF 13. The female role is subsidiary in sexual/romantic attachments with males.

GF 14. Sexuality informs most other behavior and attitudes.

GF 15. Safety is an educational issue.

THEMES

T 1. Girls checking each other out as a method of dominance, submission, exclusion, *and*, most important, disassociation or disdain of other females, together with dissatisfaction with oneself

T 2. Tacit female collusion in the system that is biased against them

T 3. Internalization

T 4. Personalization

T 5. Invisibility

T 6. Ambivalence

T 7. Physical appearance above all else

T 8. Masking one's intelligence to bolster boys'

T 9. Self-consciousness about appearance to the exclusion of all else

T10. Disassociation from females

TRENDS

Trend 1. Lowered self-expectations

Trend 2. Lowered self-confidence

Trend 3. Opting out of sports, science, math, and computers

Trend 4. Self-restricting choices for the present and the future

Trend 5. Classroom gender bias that can result in lower grades and job profiles for women students

RITUALS

Ritual 1. Celebration of entry into kindergarten
Ritual 2. Celebrate the onset and process of menstruation.
Ritual 3. Celebrate girls' academic achievement.
Ritual 4. Celebrate girls' emergence into young adulthood, responsibility, self-determination, and career planning at the end of high school. Start early in their senior year; don't wait until graduation.

GENDER ACTIONS

GA 1. *Language*: Teach children correct English that is unhampered by gender bias. Modify the use of generics to use feminine and masculine in equal proportions or the feminine solely. Change noun phrases to be gender neutral.

GA 2. *Home and child maintenance*: Create a housework schedule that is equitable. Have all adults in the household create multifaceted relationships with the children.

GA 3. Select or modify classroom materials including songs and games so that they are gender balanced.

GA 4. Encourage respect and play among girls and boys in school.

GA 5. Secure equal inclusion of girls and boys in all subjects and sports.

GA 6. Include women's achievement in the actual curriculum.

GA 7. Create play time with kids that debunks gender stereotypes.

GA 8. Begin parent–child discussions of sex and sexuality, at least by the time it becomes a subject among peers.

GA 9. Begin parent–child discussions of gender roles.

GA 10. Involve girls in sports as a matter of course.

GA 11. Involve girls in science, mathematics, and computers.

GA12. Enhance the classroom environment so that girls participate freely.

GA 13. Give girls permission and encouragement to take risks.

GA 14. Assist the growth of self-confidence and self-determination through gentle encouragement of entitlement to make choices.

GA 15. Create intervention and awareness programs in school for students, teachers, and staff.

GA 16. Develop school policies and procedures for gender bias.

GA 17. Continue to question and modify the core college curriculum.

GA 18. Monitor faculty hiring and tenure sufficiently in order to recruit more women.

GA 19. Secure campus safety for all students, staff, and faculty.

GA 20. Have professors make a greater effort to obtain awards, grants, and research positions for their female students.

GA 21. Increase students' recognition of gender bias in their courses.

GA 22. Develop the habit of discussion of gender bias on campus with other females.

GENDER EXERCISES

EXERCISE 1

1. Imagine yourself as a female toddler learning constantly about all the things people do when they are older than you are, the places they go, the ideas they have, and so on. You hear little about yourself and your own age

group. Take your time and try to grasp what your thoughts and desires would be in this situation before proceeding to the next step.

2. Now, imagine a similar situation in which *sex* is substituted for age, so that you are a girl learning largely about what boys can do. Think through the implications of this on a young female mind.

EXERCISE 2

Girls and women often incorporate other people's desires into their own concept of the world. In order to address this tendency, try the following three steps:

1. For two weeks, whenever you are confronted with a choice, pause, count to five, and ask yourself, what do I want? Give yourself enough time to thoroughly consider a serious answer to this question, no matter how small the decision seems.

2. At the end of the two weeks, examine the results. Try to recognize how successful you were in choosing what you actually want rather than what someone else wants you to want or what you think you're supposed to want. Try to determine what sorts of decisions were most difficult to make independently and continue working on making conscious deliberate choices in those areas.

3. If there is a toddler in your life, allow her the space to make as many decisions for herself as is feasible. Try to expand the realm of choices open to her. In this way, she'll develop the mental habit early of allowing herself to discover what she wants in a situation.

EXERCISE 3: THE TEN-SECOND BARBIE MAKEOVER

Another move that especially parents, but teachers as well can make at this point is to take emblems of stereotypic female gender identity and turn them around. Barbie, for example. Why does she have to be considered a bimbo? Granted, her appearance does not promote a healthy attitude about oneself in girls. In many ways, for the time being, Barbie is a fact of life for many of our nation's girls. Thus, why not put her to work?

Using Barbie as a tool of change is not difficult. Create games which include Barbie playing sports, and winning, for example. Build a Barbie-sized baseball diamond in the dirt and have her play hard. Play an imaginary game with Barbies in which Barbie is a scientist or a mathematician or an expert in mining and minerals. Why not? Play games with Barbie in which she engages in assertive, self-determined behavior and words.

Do not let her frilly attire or heel-ready feet affect what she says or does; make it irrelevant. If Barbie must play bride to Ken's groom, then have her do the asking and make sure she gets an agreement with Ken about mutual respect and independence, have them split the housework, and have Barbie enjoy at least as satisfying a career as Ken's. Just because Barbie has been manufactured and marketed to fit and encourage a certain mindset doesn't mean we need to keep her stuck there for good.

EXERCISE 4

1. Imagine yourself as encapsulated in a box that fits snugly around your body, but that can be expanded. Now, spread your arms sideway, front and back, upward, and diagonally to enlarge your imaginary box. Then push the box out in all directions with your legs. Move your body outward in any way you can in order to create the largest box possible. Stand back, and compare your initial box size with the one you ended up with.

2. For the next two weeks, take note of your "box size," and try to enlarge it comfortably. Notice your size in particular when you are seated in conversation. Find positions that take up maximum box size. For example, shift from

a legs-crossed, hands-folded position to putting your feet square on the floor, legs parallel, with your arms comfortably open.

3. Try steps (1) and (2) in tandem with a girl, and encourage each other to expand your "boxes."

EXERCISE 5

Girls and women often start off questions and remarks in the classroom with disclaimers that discount their own credibility, such as: "I may be way off base here, but . . ." This occurs even when they have a good knowledge of the subject being discussed. In order to combat this self-defeating tendency, try this three-part approach.

1. Make a simple chart in a small notebook that you can carry around with you easily. Mark down the number of times in a day that you speak tentatively and unsurely and in what situations this occurs. Do this for one week.
2. At the end of the week, go over your chart. Try to find out if your disclaimers are clustered in specific sorts of situations. Examine whether the patterns you've discovered are the result of really feeling shaky with the subject or situation. For the next two weeks, practice more direct ways of getting your point across.
3. After these two weeks, carry the notebook around once again and take note of when and where you are still using disclaimers. Discover if there have been any changes in your pattern, and determine how to sustain the progress.

EXERCISE 6

Try this three-step method for approaching problems of gender bias:

1. Awareness: Learn to be aware of the obstacles that stand in the way of girls' and women's self-respect and access to opportunities.
2. Clarification: Look deeper into the situation in order to recognize the forces at play and the way in which we've been taught to think about girls and women and their role in society.
3. Action: Know when and how to respond to these larger issues and specific events.

References

The American Association of University Women Report: How Schools Shortchange Girls (1992). Washington, DC: American Association of University Women.

American Philosophical Association (1995). *Proceedings and Addresses,* Vol. 68, No. 5.

The Digest of Education Statistics (1991). Washington, DC: Center for Education Statistics.

Glass Ceiling Commission (1995). *A Solid Investment: Making Full Use of the Nation's Human Capital.* Washington, DC: Labor Department.

Harrington, M. (1993). *Women Lawyers: Rewriting the Rules.* New York: Plume Books.

National Law Journal (1988). New York: NY Law Publishing Company.

Sadker, M., and Sadker, D. (1994). *Failing at Fairness: How America's Schools Cheat Girls.* New York: Charles Scribner's Sons.

SUGGESTED READING

Apter, T. (1993). *Working Women Don't Have Wives*. New York: St. Martin's Press.

Bell, D. (1987). *And We Are Not Saved*. New York: Basic Books.

—— (1994). *Confronting Authority*. Boston: Beacon Press.

Bergmann, B. (1986). *The Economic Emergence of Women*. New York: Basic Books.

Berry, M. F. (1993). *The Politics of Parenthood*. New York: Viking Press.

Brant, C., and Too, Y. eds. (1994). *Rethinking Sexual Harassment*. London: Pluto Press.

Caplan, P. (1993). *Lifting a Ton of Feathers*. Toronto: University of Toronto Press.

Chamberlain, M. ed. (1991). *Women in Academe*. New York: Russell Sage Foundation.

Chernin, K. (1986). *The Hungry Self: Women, Eating and Identity*. New York: Perennial Library.

Dick and Jane as Victims: Sex Stereotyping In Children's Readers. (*1972*). Princeton: Women on Words and Images.

Evans, S., and Nelson, B. (1989). *Wage Justice*. Chicago: University of Chicago Press.

Fausto-Sterling, A. (1985). *Myths of Gender*. New York: Basic Books.

Findler, B. ed. (1995). *Listen Up: Voices from the Next Feminist Generation.* Seattle: Seal Press.

Group For The Advancement Of Psychotherapy. (1975). *The Educated Woman.* New York: Scribner's Sons.

Hayden, D. (1984). *Redesigning the American Dream.* New York: Norton.

Hostile Hallways: The American Association of University Women Survey on Sexual Harassment in America's Schools. (1993). Washington, DC: American Association of University Women.

Jamieson, K. H. (1995). *Beyond the Double Bind: Women and Leadership.* New York: Oxford University Press.

Jeruchim, J., and Shapiro, P. (1992). *Women, Mentors, and Success.* New York: Fawcett Columbine.

Katz, M., and Vieland, V. (1993). *Get Smart: Everything You Need to Know (But Won't Learn in Class) about Sexual Harassment and Sex Discrimination.* 2nd ed. New York: Feminist Press at CUNY.

Mahony, R. (1995). *Kidding Ourselves: Breadwinning, Babies, and Bargaining Power.* New York: Basic Books.

Morrison, A., et al. (1992). *Breaking the Glass Ceiling.* New York: Addison-Wesley.

Orenstein, P. (1994). *Schoolgirls: Young Women, Self-Esteem, and the Confidence Gap.* New York: Doubleday.

Petrocelli, W., and Repa, B. (1992). *Sexual Harassment on the Job.* Berkeley: Nolo Press.

Pipher, M. (1995). *Reviving Ophelia: Saving the Selves of Adolescent Girls.* New York: Balantine Books.

Pogrebin, L. C. (1980). *Growing Up Free.* New York: Bantam Books.

Rich, A. (1979). *On Lies, Secrets, and Silence.* New York: W.W. Norton.

—— (1981). *Of Woman Born.* New York: Bantam Books.

Ries, P., and Stone, A. (1993). *The American Woman 1992–93: A Status Report.* New York: W.W. Norton.

Sanday, P. R. (1990). *Fraternity Gang Rape.* New York: NYU Press.

Schwartz, F. (1992). *Breaking with Tradition.* New York: Warner Books.

Scully, D. (1980). *Men Who Control Women's Health: The Miseducation of Obstetricians and Gynecologists.* Boston: Houghton Mifflin.

Sidel, R. (1994). *Battling Bias*. New York: Viking Press.

Simeone, A. (1986). *Academic Women*. South Hadley, MA: Bergin & Garvey Press.

Thorne, B. (1993). *Gender Play: Girls and Boys in School*. New Brunswick, NJ: Rutgers University Press.

Wall, E. (1992). *Sexual Harassment*. Buffalo, NY: Prometheus Books.

Walsh, E. (1995). *Divided Lives: The Public and Private Struggles of Three Accomplished Women*. New York: Simon and Schuster.

INDEX

Advanced studies. *See* Graduate school
Advancement, 288–299
actions recommended in, 298–299
basics of, 288–296
denial of, 11
gender role lessons in, 296–297
gender role social compounds in, 297–298
lesbianism and, 139
Advertising, gender bias and, 62, 63
Advisor. *See* Mentor/advisor
Affirmative action
job discrimination and, 302
professional achievement and, 305
Ambivalence, sexual abuse, preschool age, 50

American Philosophical Association, 306
Athletics
childrearing and, 26–27
elementary school experience, 56–57, 61–62
mentor/advisor relationship, 201

Body image. *See also* Clothing; Physical appearance
elementary school experience, 57
junior high school experience, 69–70
Books
elementary school experience, 55
preschool experience, 43, 52–53
Bureau of Labor Statistics, 22

Career. *See also* Employment
 advancement, 288–299. *See
 also* Advancement
 childbearing and, 135–148
 first jobs, 260–287. *See also*
 First jobs
 gender bias and, 237–238
 graduate degrees, dossiers,
 and interviews, 185–192
 graduate school experience,
 117–134
 marriage and, 114–116
 professional ambiance, 239–
 259. *See also*
 Professional ambiance
 Red Shoes example, 113–116
Childbearing, 135–148
 actions recommended in,
 147–148
 basics of, 135–143
 gender bias and, 123
 gender role lessons in, 144–
 145
 gender role social
 compounds in, 145–147
Child care arrangements,
 employment and, 142
Childrearing
 actions recommended in, 34–
 38
 basics of, 29–32
 future trends, 323–326
 gender bias and, 25–27
 gender role lessons in, 32–33
 gender role social
 compounds in, 33–34
 rituals in, 65–66
Civil Rights Act of 1964, 22

Clothing. *See also* Physical
 appearance
 preschool experience, 40
 professional achievement
 and, 308
College, applications to, 82–83
College experience, 89–111
 actions recommended in,
 107–111
 basics of, 89–99
 gender role lessons in, 99–
 101
 gender role social
 compounds in, 101–107
Culture
 denial of bias and, 9, 10
 elementary school
 experience, 62–63
 false accusations, 13
 gender and, 22
 language and, 170
 sexual abuse, preschool age,
 gender role social
 compounds, 44–47
Curie, Marie, 57
Curriculum. *See* Education

Disney movies, 62
Division of labor, graduate
 school experience, actions
 recommended, 132–134
Divorce, career and, 146–147

Education
 college experience, 89–111
 gender bias and, 27, 60–61,
 71–72, 82, 94–95, 99,
 165–166

recommended action
  college, 108–111
  high school, 86–87
  junior high school, 76
  role models and, 57, 60
  women and, 10
Education Amendments of
  1972, 22
Elementary school experience,
  55–67
  actions recommended in, 65–
    67
  basics of, 55–59
  gender role lessons in, 59–
    61
  gender role social
    compounds in, 61–64
Employment. *See also* Career
  childbearing and, 137–148
  opportunity and, 11
  women's movement and, 9

False accusations, sexual
  harassment, 13–14
Family dynamics
  future trends, 321–323
  preschool age, 44
Feminism, negative association
  of, 10, 16
First jobs, 260–287
  actions recommended in,
    286–287
  basics of, 260–283
  gender role lessons in, 283–
    285
  gender role social
    compounds in, 285–
    286

Games
  elementary school
    experience, 58–59
  preschool experience, 41–42
Gaslight effect
  described, 1–2
  results of, 2–3
Gender, defined, 22
Gender bias
  advancement, 288–299
  career and, 237–238
  childbearing and, 123
  childrearing and, 25–27. *See
    also* Childrearing
  defined, 22–23
  denial of, culture, 9, 10
  experience of, 15–16
  forms of, 8
  marriage and, 121–122
  men and, 14
  mentor/advisor relationship,
    200, 206–207, 213–
    215
  professional ambiance, 241–
    242
  against professional women,
    6, 7
  science labs, 177
  siblings and, 30
  women and, 8–9
Gender role
  elementary school
    experience, 55–67
  lessons in
    advancement, 296–297
    childbearing experience,
      144–145
    childrearing, 32–33

Gender role
  lessons in (*continued*)
    elementary school
      experience, 59–61
    first jobs, 283–285
    graduate degrees, dossiers,
      and interviews, 190
    graduate school admission
      and funding, 155
    graduate school course
      work and qualifying
      exams, 168–170
    graduate school
      experience, 128–130
    high school experience, 84
    junior high school
      experience, 73–74
    mentor/advisor
      female, 232–233
      male, 216–217
    preschool, 43–44
    professional ambiance,
      253–255
  lessons in, professional
    achievement, 311–313
  social compounds in
    advancement, 297–298
    childbearing experience,
      145–147
    childrearing, 33–34
    college experience, 101–
      107
    elementary school
      experience, 61–64
    first jobs, 285–286
    graduate degrees, dossiers,
      and interviews, 190–
      191

graduate school admission
    and funding, 156–157
  graduate school course
    work and qualifying
    exams, 170
  graduate school
    experience, 131
  graduate school theses and
    dissertations, 182–183
  high school experience,
    84–86
  junior high school
    experience, 74–75
  mentor/advisor
    female, 233–234
    male, 217–220
  preschool experience, 33–
    34
  professional achievement,
    313–316
  professional ambiance,
    255–257
  wage levels and, 37
Gender stereotyping
  elementary school
    experience, 66–67
  graduate school experience,
    118–119
  preschool experience, 39–54
  recommended action, junior
    high school, 76–77
Glass ceiling
  denial of, 10
  existence of, 288
Graduate degrees, dossiers, and
    interviews, 185–192
  actions recommended in,
    191–192

basics of, 185–189
gender role lessons in, 190
gender role social
compounds, 190–191
Graduate school admission and
funding, 151–158
actions recommended in,
157–158
basics of, 151–155
gender role lessons in, 155
gender role social
compounds in, 156–157
Graduate school course work
and qualifying exams,
159–173
actions recommended in,
171–173
basics of, 159–168
gender role lessons in, 168–
170
gender role social
compounds in, 170
Graduate school experience,
117–134
actions recommended in,
131–134
basics of, 117–128
gender role lessons in, 128–130
gender role social
compounds in, 131
mentor/advisor
female, 225–235
male, 195–224
Graduate school theses and
dissertations, 174–184
actions recommended in,
183–184
basics of, 174–178

gender role lessons in, 178–182
gender role social
compounds in, 182–183

Harrington, Mona, 242, 306
High school experience, 79–88
actions recommended in, 86–88
basics of, 79–84
gender role lessons in, 84
gender role social
compounds in, 84–86
Hill, Anita, 7, 9, 281
Household labor, childrearing,
actions recommended in,
36–37, 38

Incest, excuses for, 14
Internalization
consequences of, 12–13
gender bias and, 8, 12
sexual abuse, preschool age,
48–49
Interviews, graduate degrees,
dossiers, and interviews,
185–192
Invisibility
gender bias and, 8
preschool age, 49–50

Job discrimination
affirmative action and, 302
excuses for, 14
first jobs, 260–287
Junior high school experience,
68–78
actions recommended in, 75–
78
basics of, 68–73

Junior high school experience
    (*continued*)
    gender role lessons in, 73–74
    gender role social
        compounds in, 74–75

Language
    childrearing, actions
        recommended in, 35–
        36, 37–38
    college experience, 95
    culture and, 170
    elementary school
        experience, 59
    preschool experience, 42, 52
Law schools, women in, 10
Legal profession
    gender bias, 242–243
    women in, 306
Lesbianism, advancement and,
    139, 298

Male mentor/advisor. *See*
    Mentor/advisor
Mamet, David, 13
Marriage
    career and, 114–116
    gender bias and, 121–122
    graduate school experience,
        119–121
    profession and, 122
Media, gender role,
    childrearing, 34
Medical school
    sex discrimination in, 175,
        179–180
    women in, 10
Men
    childbearing decision, 135–136

    gender bias and, 14
    mentor/advisor relationship,
        198
Mentor/advisor
    college experience, 97–98, 100
    female, 225–235
        actions recommended in,
            234–235
        basics of, 225–232
        gender role lessons in,
            232–233
        gender role social
            compounds in, 233–
            234
    male, 195–224
        actions recommended in,
            220–224
        basics of, 195–216
        gender role lessons in,
            216–217
        gender role social
            compounds, 217–220
    role of, 193–194
Movies, gender bias and, 62–63

Non-professional women,
    treatment of, 251–252

Parents, childrearing, actions
    recommended in, 36
Paternity leave, male attitudes
    toward, 136
Peer groups, preschool
    experience, 39–54
Personalization
    consequences of, 12–13
    gender bias and, 8, 12
    sexual abuse, preschool age,
        48–49

Physical appearance. *See also* Clothing
  elementary school experience, 56, 64
  graduate school experience, 124–125
  high school experience, 79
  junior high school experience, 69
  professional achievement and, 308
Power relations
  college experience, 96
  high school experience, 84
  sexual harassment and, 302
Preschool experience, 39–54
  actions recommended in, 52–54
  basics of, 39–43
  gender role lessons in, 43–44
  gender role social compounds in, 44–52
Profession, marriage and, 122
Professional, defined, 22
Professional achievement, 305–320
  actions recommended in, 316–317
  basics of, 305–311
  gender role lessons in, 311–313
  gender role social compounds in, 313–316
Professional ambiance, 239–259
  actions recommended in, 257–259
  basics of, 239–252
  gender role lessons in, 253–255
  gender role social compounds in, 255–257
Professionalization, graduate degrees, dossiers, and interviews, 190
Professional women
  advantages of, 5–6
  fantasy as men, 16–17
  gender bias against, 6, 7
Promotion. *See* Advancement
Puberty, effects of, 70

Rape
  college experience, 92–93
  excuses for, 14
  graduate school experience, 162
Religion, gender role, childrearing, 33–34

Sadker, D., 242, 262
Sadker, M., 242, 262
Science labs, gender bias in, 177
Sex
  college experience, 91–92
  defined, 22
  elementary school experience, 59
  femininity and, 302–303
  graduate school experience, 127–128
  high school experience, 80–81
  junior high school experience, 68, 70–71
  mentor/advisor relationship, 202–203, 218–219

Sex discrimination
advancement, 288–299
defined, 22–23
medical school, 175, 179–180
Sexual abuse, preschool age,
gender role social
compounds, 44–47
Sexual harassment
college experience, 96–97,
102–107
defined, 22–23
elementary school
experience, 58–59
experience of, 15–16
false accusations, 13–14
first jobs, 267–283
graduate school experience,
162–165
graduate school theses and
dissertations, 178
high school experience, 81–
82, 85
mentor/advisor relationship,
208
power relations and, 302
professional achievement,
313
professional ambiance, 239,
240, 244–251, 256
professional women, 7
results of accusations of,
209–210
Sexual orientation. *See*
Lesbianism
Siblings, gender bias and, 30

Social relations
college experience, 89, 90–
91, 97
graduate school experience,
125–127
high school experience, 79, 80
junior high school
experience, 68–69
Socioeconomic class, preschool
age, gender role social
compounds, 51
Songs
junior high school
experience, 72–73
preschool experience, actions
recommended in, 53
Sports. *See* Athletics

Teachers, preschool
experience, 42–43
Television, gender role,
childrearing, 34
Terminology, definitions, 22–23
Thomas, Clarence, 7, 9
Travel, mentor/advisor
relationship, 207

Wage levels, gender roles and, 37
Women
educational role models and,
57, 60
gender bias and, 8–9
non-professional, treatment
of, 251–252
Women's movement, history of, 9

About the
Author

Montana Katz, Ph.D., is co-author of the award-winning book *Get Smart: What You Should Know (But Won't Learn in Class) about Sexual Harassment and Sex Discrimination,* the author of articles about gender issues, and lectures nationwide on gender equity. She has taught at Columbia University, the University of California at Berkeley, and Vassar College.

"This is an essential guide for professional women to enhance our own strategies, mentor more effectively, and raise competent daughters. The story is told in the daily details of a girl growing into a woman and will help readers see how external bias can negatively affect the construction of an internal model of the self as effective and entitled. Now that women have entered nontraditional professions, we must learn how to support each other as we work to change the ambiance of the system."

—Nancy Kaltreider
Professor, Clinical Psychiatry
Director, Program for Woman
University of California, San Francisco

"*The Gender Bias Prevention Book* shows how we learn damaging gender lessons and offers gender actions that can help teachers, therapists, counselors, and parents change this world for women and girls. Montana Katz shows the impact of sexist assumptions, abuse, harassment, and discrimination even on the white, upper middle-class professional women who are falsely assumed to have 'made it' in a man's world. Read this book—you will hear the undercurrent of sexism that gives the lie to this notion that the playing field is level. Read it to also help you change your own life and your work with women and girls."

—Leslie R. Wolfe
President, Center for Women Policy Studies

"Montana Katz describes powerful shaping gender biases, some overt, others camouflaged in habit, from birth through professional advancement. Drawn from a wealth of information from studies and interviews, the author presents a lively and vivid composite tale of an American professional woman through each phase of her life. Katz presents practical, simple steps to recognize and dissolve gender stereotypic definitions and limitations. "

—David Krueger
author of *Success and Fear of Success in Women: a Developmental and Psychodynamic Perspective*